The Comedies of Terence

T.P. Wiseman on Frederick W. Clayton:

"He was a man in love with literature, and with the English and Latin languages. What he did was read texts (and teach them, of course); his memory was simply full of them, and he could hear echoes and spot allusions that no-one else had suspected. His translations of Terence's plays, with no attempt at scholarly apparatus, are done in brilliantly deft rhyming couplets with the fluency and elegance you'd expect from someone who had most of the English poets in his head."

Matthew Leigh, in his Introduction:

"The version of Terence presented in this volume renders the Latin comedian in elegant rhyming couplets. Professor Clayton thus achieves two significant ends: first he brings home the fact that Terence, like all the ancient comedians, was indeed a poet; second, he does so in a verse form which has typified English translations and adaptations of ancient comedy. . . "

Frederick W. Clayton (1913–1999) was Professor of Classics at the University College of the South-West, later the University of Exeter, from 1948 to 1975.

Matthew Leigh first became interested in Terence while serving as Lecturer in Classics and Ancient History at the University of Exeter. He is currently Fellow and Tutor in Classics at St Anne's College, Oxford. He is author of *Lucan: Spectacle and Engagement* (Oxford, 1997) and *Comedy and the Rise of Rome* (Oxford, 2004).

The Comedies of Terence

translated by
Frederick W. Clayton

introduced by
Matthew Leigh

UNIVERSITY
of
EXETER
PRESS

Cover illustration: based on a woodcut from an edition of Terence
published at Lyon in 1493 (the scene is from *The Brothers*).

First published in 2006 by
University of Exeter Press
Reed Hall, Streatham Drive
Exeter EX4 4QR
UK
www.exeterpress.co.uk

The publishers acknowledge the generous support of the Exeter University
Foundation.

British Library Cataloguing in Publication Data
A catalogue record for this book is available from the British Library.

Paperback ISBN 0 85989 763 X
Hardback ISBN 0 85989 757 5

Typeset in Sabon by XL Publishing Services, Tiverton
Printed and bound in Great Britain by Antony Rowe Ltd, Chippenham

Contents

Acknowledgements

Frederick W. Clayton's translations of the plays of Terence were unearthed from amongst the papers he left at his death by Thorsten Fögen, who is to be thanked for first drawing them to the attention of University of Exeter Press. Publication would not, however, have been possible had it not been for Vicky Stevens, honorary research fellow of the Department of Classics and Ancient History at the University of Exeter, who prepared the manuscript with meticulous care. Thanks are also due to Matthew Leigh, who, without prior knowledge of the translator, took on the job of providing an appropriate introduction; to Peter Wiseman for his discreet, generous support throughout; and to Simon Baker of University of Exeter Press who, despite setbacks, has stayed with the project.

M. T.-C.,
Zürich,
March 2005.

Introduction

by Matthew Leigh

(1) Terence and Comedy

P. Terentius Afer died young and died a martyr to his art. Maidens stolen by pirates, merchants ruined by shipwreck are essential features of the comic form in which the poet found fame; for all their stylization, they also reflect a painfully hazardous reality. This, however, was not enough to deter the poet from setting sail, for he had set his heart on a most particular cargo, and one on which the future development of his art must depend. When the homecoming ship went down, and with it the collection of manuscripts of the Greek comedian Menander which Terence was resolved to bring to Rome, the poet went with it. In a touching alternative version, Terence sends the manuscripts on ahead, hears of the shipwreck and their loss, and falls into a profound and finally fatal depression.

Such was the lamentable end of the great comedian. Yet by the time of his death he had already achieved much, and the works which he left behind mark a crucial juncture both in the transmission of Greek culture to Rome and in the development of the Western comic tradition. For all Menander's tremendous ancient fame, he was to survive antiquity only in the form of fragments cited by grammarians and anthologists; whole plays resurfaced only in the twentieth century with the discovery and publication of papyri hiding for two millennia in the sands of Egypt. For the Renaissance and the centuries which followed, the comic mode which his works helped define is represented instead by the Roman comedians Plautus and Terence. The works presented in this volume have thus as much to offer the student of Shakespeare, of Molière, of Machiavelli and Goldoni as they do the specialist classicist.

(2) Life of Terence

The ancient evidence for the life and career of Terence is intriguing. By no means everything preserved by ancient biographers is to be trusted but the poet's name would appear to confirm the statement that he was a slave raised in the household of the distinguished Roman aristocrat Terentius Lucanus and later freed: the poet takes the *nomen* of his former master and supplements it with the *cognomen* Afer. The Roman *cognomen* often identified a distinctive characteristic of its bearer—Paetus would suggest that the gentleman had a squint, Calvus that he was a slaphead, Rufus that he was a ginger—and in this instance Afer refers to his birth in the city of Carthage. Nothing more is known of Terence's origins or his enslavement; Carthage itself was a vibrant trading community and there is no reason to assume on the basis of his birth that the poet was Punic.

A further crucial source for the career of Terence is provided by the production notices transmitted either in the ancient manuscripts or by the late commentator Donatus. These relate information such as the festival at which the play was first performed; the magistrates who commissioned the work and the consuls in whose year it was seen; the name of the actor whose troupe staged the work and of the flute-player who accompanied them; and the author of the Greek original whose work the Latin comedy adapts. The literary vendettas against rivals and critics, the narratives of dramatic triumph and disaster which are so striking a feature of the prologues which Terence appends to each of his plays further supplement this picture.

The extant works of Terence all date from the years 166–160 BC. Four were first performed at what were known as the Megalesian Games, one at the Roman Games and one at the funeral games for the great politician and general L. Aemilius Paullus. It is further evident from the production notice for *The Mother-in-Law* that a given play could be put on at one festival, then revived repeatedly at others in subsequent years. Similar evidence for revival and reperformance is to be found in the prologue to the *Casina* of Plautus.

Ancient sources date the first festive performance of Latin drama based on the classic works of the Athenian stage to 240 BC. The earliest recorded dramatist, Livius Andronicus, composed both tragedies and comedies as well as translating the Homeric *Odyssey* into Latin verse. The same versatility characterizes his successors Naevius and Ennius. The years between these first beginnings and the emergence of Terence witnessed a parallel process which is essential to the understanding of the poet's place in Roman culture: the gradual expansion of the Roman festive calendar runs together with and is a product of the expansion of Rome from a provincial power to the dominant force in the Mediterranean world. The Megalesian Games, for instance, were instituted in 204 BC in celebration of the symbolic coming to Rome from Asia Minor of the goddess Cybele in the form of the stone of Pessinus. In order to achieve this end, the Romans engaged diplomatically with the Attalid kingdom of Pergamum and almost certainly made much of the fact that Pergama was one of the ancient names for Troy, itself home to Rome's mythical founder Aeneas. Rome could thus claim for itself an ethnic identity appropriate to its expanding horizons and its new spheres of influence. But the process operated in two directions at once. With the Great Mother came her retinue of eunuch priests; their annual procession through the city of Rome exposed to the population a strikingly alien presence at its heart. The dedication of the temple of the Great Mother on the Palatine in 191 BC was marked by the first performance of the *Pseudolus* of Plautus and hence-forth the Megalesian Games incorporated days devoted to theatrical performance. Inasmuch as the vast majority of those performances were of works derived from the Greek, it became a permanent vehicle for the trans-formation of Roman culture.

The coming of the Great Mother to Rome coincided with the final years of the Second Punic War and in part expressed the city's growing conviction that the long invasion of Hannibal could finally be repelled and the power of Carthage broken. The achievement of this end in 201 BC is a crucial histor-ical juncture in the transformation of Rome. The other key date in this period must be 168 BC, the defeat of Perseus of Macedon by the Roman forces under L. Aemilius Paullus. The opening to the dramatic career of Terence thus falls soon after the establishment of Rome as the dominant force on the Greek mainland and closes with the funeral games organized in celebration of the life of Paullus. The 160s BC also witnessed a dramatic acceleration in the Hellenization of Roman culture. In part this is to be attributed to certain accidents of policy: the decision to take 1,000 Achaean leaders as hostages to Rome resulted, for instance, in the long detention in the city of the great historian Polybius. He describes at length the influence which his friendship had on the moral and intellectual development of the young Scipio Aemilianus, the son of Paullus adopted by the childless P. Cornelius Scipio and later responsible for the sack of Carthage. Polybius was also a keen huntsman and his narrative celebrates Scipio's pursuit of excellence in a sport which owed more to the Achaean traditions of the great Philopoemen than it did to traditional Roman training. This then is one self-consciously Greek pursuit. Polybius, however, records other less wholesome instances of the craze, and it was perhaps in reaction to the new dedication to courtesans, fine dining and drink that the 161 BC Lex Fannia sumptuary legislation was passed.

The great conquerors and their families were among the most dedicated consumers of the culture of the conquered world. Cicero's history of Roman oratory, the *Brutus*, points to some crucial contemporary figures: the adop-tive father of Scipio Aemilianus was himself physically too frail to emulate the deeds of his father Scipio Africanus, but he still wrote a most elegant history in Greek; the praetor of 169 BC who oversaw the performance of the *Thyestes* of Ennius at the Apolline Games, C. Sulpicius Gallus, was the most devoted to Greek letters of all the nobility; his contemporary Ti. Gracchus, twice consul and twice censor, delivered a speech to the Rhodians in Greek. Yet perhaps the most significant figure here is L. Aemilius Paullus, the conqueror of Macedon. He followed up his victory with a grand tour of all the great sites of Greece and organized Greek-style games at which all the states of the Greek world were invited to participate. He is also noted for the devotion which he showed to the education of the two sons whom later he gave up for adoption, Scipio Aemilianus and Q. Fabius Maximus Aemilianus; traditional Roman training was not jettisoned, but it was supplemented with various more cosmopolitan refinements. To this end the boys were trained in grammar, rhetoric and philosophy; were treated to books plundered from the extensive royal library at Macedon; and enjoyed the supervision of the Athenian philosopher Metrodorus.

The two sons on whom Paullus lavished such care reciprocated their father's devotion through their organization of his funeral games in 160 BC. It was here that the last play of Terence, *The Brothers*, was first staged, and readers have often noted the overlap between the play's interest in fatherhood, adoption and education and the more controversial aspects of Paullus' system. Since antiquity, moreover, readers have also puzzled over lines from the prologue to the play which appear to locate Terence in an aristocratic literary circle devoted to the very Greek letters which the figures dicussed in the previous paragraph embraced:

> And as for Envy's tale that famous men
> Assist our poet, and often aid his pen,
> What Envy thinks a mighty condemnation
> He thinks his highest praise, the approbation
> Of men you all approve, as does the nation;
> Men by whose aid in war, peace, work and play
> Each without pride had profit in his day.

When Terence complains of envy, he almost certainly refers to the insinuations of his aging rival Luscius of Lanuvium. The seriousness of this rivalry and the degree of enmity can easily be exaggerated—a well-publicized feud is always good for business and encourages a more profound commitment to the artist on the part of the consumer—but it appears that Luscius has employed a recent prologue in order to allege that Terence does not even write his own Latin but has a coterie of literary philhellenes lend him a hand. Terence does not rebut the claim; but nor does he expend too much energy denying it. Rather, he embraces it as a compliment. Who exactly is being referred to, he is much too discreet to say. Antiquity provides various theories, and Scipio Aemilianus and his close associate C. Laelius are prominent among the suspects; the grammarian Santra queries this on chronological grounds and names various others, amongst them C. Sulpicius Gallus. We will never know, but it would make sense for Terence to hint at his closeness to one or both of the organisers of the games.

(3) Terence and New Comedy

New Comedy is the title conventionally given to the comic mode which came to prominence at Athens in the final decades of the fourth and initial decades of the third century BC. The most famous practitioners of the form are Menander, Diphilus and Philemon, while important contributions were made by Alexis, Posidippus, Philippides and others. Of these authors only Menander exists in other than fragmentary form and, as was noted earlier, even he was only rescued from the sands of Egypt in the course of the last century.

Greek New Comedy presents a stark contrast to the late fifth-century and early fourth-century Old Comedy of Aristophanes, Eupolis and Cratinus. Where the latter is infinitely inventive, frequently fantastical—birds create their own state between the heavens and the earth; a hero rides to heaven on a giant dung beetle; private citizens conclude peace treaties in despite of the state—and overtly political, New Comedy restricts itself to domestic concerns and to a stylized realism. To some extent this may be the product of gradual evolution in the form, but the relatively exiguous remains of the intervening period frustrate clear judgement. On the one hand, the final plays of Aristophanes, especially the *Wealth*, already suggest a move towards New Comedy, and we are informed that the Middle Comedy writer Anaxandrides introduced the theme of rape of virgins which is so prominent and troubling a part of the work of Terence as much as of Menander. On the other, much of what writers like Eubulus and Antiphanes appear to present is not so much an intermediate stage in any smooth progression as a substantially independent form in which mythological burlesque plays a major role. More specific historical conditions may therefore favour a sudden shift in form, and prominent amongst these must be the Macedonian occupation of Athens. In such circumstances, Aristophanic mockery of named contemporary leaders might be deemed an undue risk; one late source claims that, while the fifth-century comic mask was designed to make the specific target of the humour evident, the stylization of the New Comic mask, and the restriction of the form to recurrent stock characters to each of whom a given mask and costume might conform, was prompted by anxiety lest the resident Macedonian overlord should see himself under attack.

Greek New Comedy is therefore typically located on a city street and in front of two or three domestic houses. The city is conventionally Athens but numerous other Greek cities can be named instead should the plot so demand. Where once Athens had perceived itself as *the* city and its comedy had concerned itself with specifically Athenian concerns, now a character in Menander's *Arbitration* can opine that there are a thousand cities of which, it is implied, Athens is only one. This new perspective, allied to the form's predominantly social as opposed to political concerns, in turn facilitates the reperformance of Menandrean comedy in civic theatres throughout the Greek world and eventually in Rome. Fathers irate and mild; ferocious wives and indulgent mothers; libidinous spendthrift sons and chastely silent daughters; boastful soldiers, doctors and chefs; cunning courtesans and wily slaves are all types which the audience may know from their daily lives or which they may at least feel that they know. For it is a typical mode of late fourth century Greek thought to construct the world by different character types, and one which, quite apart from comedy, might be illustrated by reference to Book 2 of the *Rhetoric* of Aristotle or the *Characters* of Theophrastus. Realism or, better, naturalism will therefore only ever offer a partially satisfactory account of the procedures of Menander and his peers. For much of the time, the experience is more like that which a modern reader may have when feeling that they know someone because they recall one of the elaborately stylized character types created by Dickens.

'All comedy ends with a wedding.' So Northrop Frye. This claim, I would argue, is truest of comedy in its purest form, that is in the tradition which links Menander, his Roman imitators and the comic dramatists of the sixteenth to eighteenth centuries. This, of course, does not require that every comedy should end with a wedding per se even if a wedding or the prospect of a wedding is central to the final scenes of Menander's *Bad-Tempered Man*, *Samian Woman* and many others of his plays. Rather, what Frye implies is that all comedy must necessarily end with an image of social and familial reconciliation the most characteristic example of which is precisely a wedding. The initial motor of any New Comedy, therefore, is the element of discord or conflict which it is the duty of the drama to resolve. This can take various forms. In the *Bad-Tempered Man* it is represented by the entrenched alienation of the misanthrope Knemon from the rest of humanity, and particularly that part of humanity represented by the frivolity of the pleasure-loving urban rich; for this alienation has particularly damaging implications for his own family, not least for his chastely virtuous daughter. The end of the play, therefore, is both to reconcile Knemon to at least a partial acceptance of society and to engineer a double marriage between his family and that of the wealthy landowner whose fields abut his. In the *Samian Woman*, again, the end to which the play drives is the marriage of Moschion to the daughter of his neighbour, but it is equally important to reconcile the two fathers Demeas and Nikeratos and to remove the unwarranted suspicions which have brought conflict between the former and his concubine Chrysis. None of this can be achieved until Moschion is able to admit that he is indeed the father of the child born to the daughter of Nikeratos but lately cared for by the concubine. In the *Arbitration*, by contrast, what must be secured is a marriage already made and then renounced on the part of the husband. Again the male is a rapist and the breach in his marriage is the product of his wife giving birth long before she could have done were the child conceived during the marriage. By revealing that this child is the product of a rape committed by none other than the future husband, the play reaffirms the marriage and rescues the child, now legitimate heir, from the exposure with which he was threatened at the start of the play.

The forms of social reconciliation at which Terentian comedy aims are true to the basic model set down by the genre. Where his comedy is perhaps most striking, however, is in his subtle resistance to blanket or simple-minded reconciliation: the comedy closes in essence as it must in order to be a comedy at all, but some small area of incompletion perforce remains. In *The Brothers*, for instance, Aeschinus will indeed marry the mother of his child; Ctesipho will have his cithern-player; but the elderly Micio will be obliged to contract a wedding for which he has no enthusiasm; and the eventual resignation of the sons to the authority of their natural father Demea coincides with one last broadside from him against his sadly diminished brother. *The Self-Tormentor* ends in almost as striking a manner. There is a certain parallelism in the double plot in that both sons are reconciled with their fathers and each contracts a citizen marriage. Yet where Clinia is reunited with the father who drove him away and secures his heart's desire in Antiphila, the marriage of Clitipho is almost a punishment imposed upon him for his ruinous affair with the courtesan Bacchis. True, he is at least able to reject the 'green eyes, red hair, spots, snub nose' of the daughter of Phanocrates and to nominate the daughter of Archonides in her stead; but both these women are ciphers, unmentioned hitherto; neither is this young boy's dream, just the vehicle for an uneasy reconciliation with dad. Yet perhaps the strangest version of the happy ending is that provided by *The Mother-in-Law*. In a drama which has turned repeatedly on the inability of either Pamphilus or his bride frankly to explain their troubles to his parents, and where irreparable rupture is finally avoided only by the revelation of a pre-marital rape even uglier than that on which the *Arbitration* turns, it is decided that the best solution is actually to perpetuate the deceit. Thus Pamphilus to the courtesan and the slave:

PAMPHILUS: Has my old man heard
Any part of this?
BACCHIS: Not a murmur.
PAMPHILUS: Then mum's the word.
This isn't a made-up comedy, where the right end
Is only reached by all parties being enlightened
On every point. With us all know, who ought.
Who needs no teaching shall remain untaught.

The comic character foreswears the forms of revelation and reconciliation which would turn his experiences into a comedy; the author confronts the form in which he writes and exposes all the moral darkness which endures.

(4) Terence and the *Comoedia Palliata*

The Latin version of Greek New Comedy developed in tandem with that of tragedy at Rome and involved a parallel process of translation and adaptation of Greek originals. Comic adaptation could, however, be more or less free and an important contribution to the mode represented by the twenty-one extant comedies of Terence's great predecessor, Plautus, is made by forms which antedate 240 BC and the new dominance of the Attic. Rome's neighbours, the Etruscans, themselves possessed a varied and vigorous theatrical culture and other forms already established in Italy included what is known as Atellane farce and a primitive form of mime. Plautus clearly relished the stock characters of Atellane farce in particular: the stock parasite of his comedies is a hybrid combination of the parasite of Greek tradition and the Atellane glutton known as *dossennus* or *manducus*; a stern father worsted by his slave identifies himself with the fathead *bucco*. Modern scholars often compare this aspect of Plautine comedy with the Italian *commedia dell'arte* which came to prominence around 1550.

There is perhaps no better way to appreciate the cultural significance of what Terence sets out to achieve in his comedies than to read him alongside Plautus. There is, of course, some continuity between the two authors in terms of technique of adaptation. Both, for instance, dispense with choral song the presence of which between each of the five acts of the Greek comedies is marked in the papyrus manuscripts of Menander, even if the songs themselves do not survive. This necessarily required a certain degree of rewriting, for a choral song as act-break can cover implicit time-lags; the Roman playwright is obliged to remove a character from the stage somewhat earlier than in the Greek original and to create a degree of intervening action absent in his model. The act-breaks marked in this edition are indeed traditional, but the tradition in question is clearly post-classical. Terence further claims in the prologue to *The Woman from Andros* that he has blended elements from two separate comedies by Menander—*The Woman from Andros* and *The Woman from Perinthos*—and suggests that this technique is one first employed by Ennius, Naevius and Plautus. In the *Eunuch*, likewise, he talks of blending Menander's *Eunuch* and *Flatterer*, while the *Brothers* blends elements from a Menandrean original of the same name with the *Synapothnescontes* of Diphilus, filtered through its earlier Latin adaptation as the *Commorientes* of Plautus. A more specifically Terentian technique, though one which he chooses not to highlight, concerns the prologue itself. In most Menandrean comedy it is the function of a divine prologue-speaker not only to acquaint the audience with the background to the plot but also to reassure them as to its future development; this detaches them from the panic and anxiety of the characters themselves and creates a fundamentally ironic comedy. Plautus in turn makes intermittent use of the same technique, either through gods such as the Lar of the *Pot of Gold* and the Arcturus of the *Rope* or through the unidentified but evidently human speaker in the *Prisoners* and the *Little Carthaginian*. Terence, by contrast, makes the background information emerge through the speech of the characters—obvious examples are the dialogue of Parmeno, Philotis and Syra in Act I of *The Mother-in-Law* or the monologue of Micio in Act I of *The Brothers*—and leaves the audience in suspense as to what will now follow. Minute analysis of the process of adaptation is therefore a prominent concern of modern Plautine and Terentian scholarship, most notably in Germany and Britain. One of the greatest works of classical scholarship, Fraenkel's *Elementi plautini in Plauto*, is devoted entirely to this problem. Subsequent papyrus finds, most notably a passage from the *Twice-Deceiver* of Menander which can be compared to the Plautine version of the same scene in the *Bacchis Sisters*, have substantially confirmed the validity of Fraenkel's theses.

Yet Terence is also strikingly different from Plautus. At first sight, it can seem as if much has simply been lost. In Plautus, for instance, there are lengthy passages known as *cantica* from the fact that a character breaks into song; almost none of this survives in Terence. Of those Plautine characters prone to song, perhaps the most remarkable is the wily slave, most memorably embodied in the eponymous hero of the *Pseudolus* or the Chrysalus of *The Bacchis Sisters*. These figures are magnificent in their machinations; they are loyal allies to the young master, constantly on the alert for ways to loot the savings of the father; they dress themselves in metaphor as philosophers, generals and heroes of myth; feverishly though they imagine beatings and crucifixions, they are insouciant in their confrontation of such threats when levelled by the boss. Later writers refer to the delight of the Menandrean slave in tricking his master, but there is nothing quite to match his Plautine counterpart in the plays which we possess; where Terence introduces a slave as trickster, for instance Syrus in *The Self-Tormentor*, there is a palpable return to the more restrained methods of the Attic model. Much the same may also be said for the comic metatheatricality which is one of the glories of the Plautine stage. Here characters—and again most prominently the slave hero—are insistently aware of their own status as theatrical creations; they leap back and forth across the invisible fourth wall separating stage and audience; to effect a deception they disguise themselves with costume borrowed from the props manager; they joke about the length of the play and make reference to the famous actors of the day. There is some impulse towards this in Menander and, as was seen earlier in the lines quoted from the final scene of *The Mother-in-Law*, it is not wholly absent in Terence. Yet the difference is so great that it cannot be claimed simply to be one of degree.

What then is at issue in the Terentian elimination of so much of what makes Plautine comedy both distinctive and, in fact, funny? The answer, I suspect, lies in the poet's particular cultural project. The title given by the

Latin grammarians to the genre in which both Plautus and Terence write is
comoedia palliata, and this means 'comedy in a pallium'. As such it refers to
the cloak which becomes the distinctive marker of the characters' Greek identity in the form. The construction of this title is also a pointer to what made
the Roman version of New Comedy potentially so different from its Greek
inspiration. On one level, the very characteristics which permitted the trans-
portation and reperformance of Menandrean comedy throughout the
Greek-speaking world also held for Rome. Cicero, for instance, can claim in
his speech *For Roscius of Ameria* that there is nothing to render the plot of
a play by the dramatist Caecilius inappropriate as an analogy for the vicis-
situdes of the family at the centre of the case; he could, he says, as easily refer
to a neighbour or fellow-tribesman of his own, but it would be odious to
drag that person's name into the case without asking first; comedy will do
just as well because it offers a carefully moulded image of Roman life. Yet,
on another level, that 'pallium' was the perpetual reminder of otherness and
exoticism, a reassuring guarantee that the events portrayed belonged somewhere else. The tension between these two attitudes seems already to be
present in the works of Naevius, one of the first writers in the form. For he
makes jokes about guests from Praeneste, a hill-town only a few miles from
Rome, and shows in one play what happens when two lusty young sons go
on a visit to Tarentum and find themselves entangled in the wiles of a pair
of local courtesans. The point about Tarentum was that it was a famously
wealthy and luxurious Greek city, but one founded by Spartan colonists on
the southern shores of the Italian mainland. For all that the play probably
made its youthful heroes Greek, the image of dissipation which it presented
must have seemed the more accessible for the relative proximity of the city
in which it was seen to take place.

What the fragments of Naevius suggest, the twenty-one extant plays of
Plautus exuberantly confirm. At the heart of Plautine comedy lies the play
of national identity: dramas set in Greece are littered with allusions to Roman
topography, while in the *Curculio* the props manager even appears on stage
and takes the audience on a guided tour of the forum; characters, though
Greek themselves, accuse their more luxurious peers of 'Greeking it up';
Romans and their institutions, much as they were to many horrified Greeks
witnessing the first interventions on the mainland, are 'barbarian'; the Latin
spoken by the characters pullulates with Greek calques and neologisms, and
any list of luxury items is bound to be full of many such terms. The entire
effect is resolutely and hilariously non-naturalistic. Terence, by contrast,
studiously avoids the introduction of jarring cultural references and employs
far fewer Graecisms than are to be found in Plautus. The cultural implications of this procedure are significant.

An intriguing light on what Terence endeavours to achieve is cast by
tributes to him from two of the most famous figures of the century after his

death. Reference has already been made to the *Brutus*, the great Cicero's history of Roman eloquence. Throughout this work various Roman orators are praised for their ability to speak Latin well. This, one might think, is no signal achievement in an orator. To Cicero, however, it was far from obvious that all native Latin speakers were competent in their own language. To those born and raised outside the metropolis, indeed, it might never be possible to be so; Cicero offers an intriguing catalogue of orators who attained distinction in Bologna or Ascoli Piceno but regrets that such figures miss the elegance which somehow attaches itself peculiarly to Latin as she is spoken in Rome. Others fail through an excessive appetite for archaisms or an undue readiness to coin neologisms where the current state of the language fails to offer the precise term. Cicero also quotes with some satisfaction the tribute paid to him by Julius Caesar—it is a mark of how much is at stake that the latter should take time out from the plunder of Gaul and plotting to overthrow the Roman Republic to write a treatise on the topic—as the greatest master of the Latin language. In this context it is therefore striking to find in the Suetonian *Life of Terence* verse tributes from both Cicero and Caesar to the quality of the comic poet's Latin. Cicero praises the refined language (*lecto sermone*) with which Terence translates Menander, and describes him as speaking agreeably and saying everything sweetly (*quiddam come loquens atque omnia dulcia dicens*). Caesar, meanwhile, hails him as half a Menander (*o dimidiate Menander*), dubs him a lover of pure language (*puri sermonis amator*) and regrets only that he did not have more force (*vis*).

Two claims may therefore be made with regard to this new linguistic purism. The first may at first sight seem somewhat paradoxical but is in fact inescapable. Terence becomes half a Menander by aiming to reproduce the naturalistic style of the Greek comedian, and the essence of theatrical naturalism is to induce the audience to forget that they are watching something staged and make them feel that they are observers of an event. Metatheatrical reminders that this is indeed a play deliberately undermine naturalism and must therefore be minimized if not entirely removed. Likewise a theatrical language which delights in its own artificiality and originality, and which jars back and forth from Latin to Greek, draws attention to itself *qua* language. The best way to emulate the Attic original is thus to speak as pure a Latin as possible and to eliminate the Greek.

The second claim is that Terence embodies an increasingly elitist aesthetic and one which can best be understood by reference to the development of theories of Latin oratorical prose in the century after his death. Let me offer an example. In the prologue to *Phormio*, Terence refers to the complaint of Luscius of Lanuvium that his plays are 'thin, trivial, light' (*tenui ... oratione et scriptura levi*). In the prologue to *The Self-Tormentor*, meanwhile, the prologue-speaker describes the 'static-dramatic art' (*statariam*) of the play, and begs indulgence for a work which is pure speech (*pura oratio*) and will therefore spare his aged legs. It is worth observing the overlap between this form of self-description and the ways in which Cicero, a hundred years on, talks about rhetoric. In the *Brutus*, for instance, he is confronted with the classic instance at Rome of a Stoic orator: P. Rutilius Rufus. Central to the Stoic philosophical creed is its critique of the passions, and the defining characteristic of Stoic rhetoric is therefore its refusal to indulge in any of the standard oratorical techniques designed to arouse the emotional sympathy of the jury: brandishing babies, bringing forward distressed parents, baring the defendant's honourable scars. From a true Stoic orator indeed one might expect no emotional gestures, not even an indignant stamp of the foot. All that was required, they held, was a simple statement of the truth. P. Rutilius Rufus put this belief system into practice in 92 BC when unjustly accused of provincial maladministration, and much good it did him. Yet, adds Cicero, he would not wish to see the city devoid of such speakers, and, just as on the stage there is a place not only for those who engage in swift and difficult movements but also for the static (*statarios*), so there should be room for orators whose only weapon is the unvarnished truth.

Along with the Stoic orators came a second group whose style of delivery had much in common with theirs, but who were motivated by more strictly stylistic doctrines. They dubbed themselves Atticists and idealized the unadorned if subtle speeches of the great Lysias and the highly intellectual prose of the historian Thucydides. Cicero repeatedly complains that the title Atticist is a misrepresentation of the range of Athenian oratorical achievement and even goes so far as to publish translations of paired speeches by Demosthenes and Aeschines in order to prove the point. Yet when, in his work the *Orator*, he sketches the ideal Roman Atticist, that figure emerges as one peculiarly similar to Terence. This, Cicero argues, is the appropriate mode for the orator whose lack of force (*vis*) leaves him unsuited to the grand style required in the greatest trials; the same somewhat pejorative term which Luscius allegedly used of Terence is then employed to describe the slightness of the Atticist (*tenuis*); the ideal Latin diction at which he will aim is pure and clear, free of archaism, neologism and excessive metaphor (*sermo purus et Latinus*). Cicero himself has employed this style where appropriate, and recommends it in cases turning on more complex issues of civil law and delivered before a single judge. This, I suspect, is the oratorical equivalent of literary elitism: the orator seeks a single, competent assessor of his words rather than entrusting himself to the verdict of the mob, just as the poet prefers the understanding of a learned coterie to the debased judgement of the mass. It is in these terms that I understand the prologue to *The Mother-in-Law*: at its première the play fell victim to the rival attractions of rope-walkers and boxers; at second staging the auditorium was invaded by the fight-fans looking forward to the gladiators on next and all ended in chaos; now the audience is asked to watch in silence and not allow a small clique make a monopoly of the muses' art. Whether that small clique is composed of traditionalist poets pushing Terence out or rather of refined spectators able to appreciate his gifts, the message is effectively the same: the Roman theatre must make room for something more refined, more demanding, more pure.

(5) Stage, Costume and Mask

The comedies of Menander were primarily written for the great civic dramatic festivals of Athens, and were staged in the same Theatre of Dionysus where the comedies of Aristophanes were performed. It is hard, however, not to feel that the impressively visual spectacle of a comedy like Aristophanes' *Birds* would have employed the very substantial scenic space on offer more effectively than the more intimate works of New Comedy. In Rome, by contrast, there was no permanent stone theatre within the city walls until the Theatre of Pompey was opened in 55 BC. Rather, both stage and seating were temporary structures erected for the period of the festival of which the theatrical games were a part, and that structure was not, by Athenian standards, at all large. The stage itself was relatively shallow. Characters would enter the stage and leave it either through the doors leading into the houses at the back of the stage or via the two exits to the side. The conventional destinations for those leaving to left or right are the country-side, the forum, the port or perhaps a family house located elsewhere in the city. Contrary to what is sometimes claimed on the basis of statements found in the Greek encyclopaedist Pollux and the Latin architectural writer Vitruvius, there seems to be no fixed relationship between the individual side-exits and specific destinations (e.g. left to the country, right to city or port), and the final criterion for their distribution will be pragmatic.

The essence of stock characterization is that you know the characters by having seen them before, and the place where you will have seen them is in the comic theatre. The characters of Terentian comedy therefore begin to tell the audience about themselves long before they ever speak or reveal their names. They do so by the visual signals projected by their costume, their wig and by their mask (the ancient evidence suggesting that masks were adopted only in the century after Terence is almost certainly false). The same Pollux who describes the Athenian exits to left and right also provides a remark-able list of forty-four masks pertaining not just to individual types—the old father, the son, the courtesan, the slave—but even to minute sub-divisions within these types. Similar if rather less detailed evidence for costume in Roman comedy is furnished by the late antique commentator on Terence, Donatus. The degree to which these lists reflects the precise types present in the plays we possess is disputed but the basic principle still holds: the slave wears a tawny wig; the old man's hair and costume is white; the courtesan's saffron-hued dress reveals her appetite for gold. Costume, wig and mask thus become part of a complex system of communication, and all the great comedians derive subtle effects from them. In the *Bad-tempered Man* of Menander, for instance, the young lover Sostratos is commended by the once-suspicious Gorgias for not having feigned his character and for having demonstrated readiness to embrace the farmer's toil. In fact, what Sostratos has done, and this at the suggestion of Gorgias himself, is temporarily to trade his luxurious city-slicker's gown for a yokel's goat-skin and a hoe in the hope that he will be seen by the father of his beloved and taken for the opposite of what he really is. He returns to the stage hobbled by unwonted exertion and without having contrived to be seen. He has, however, acquired a sun-tan in place of his urban pallor and it is this which eventually convinces Knemon that he must be all right. The implication is that the actor has changed a very colourless mask for something rather ruddier. With his bride safely back in town, Sostratos will surely once again don the gown proper to his type and do all that he can to lose that sun-tan, that ruddy mask, and all that they imply about actually having to work for his food. Contrary to what Gorgias wishes to believe, there is no other Sostratos lurking beneath his mask and gown; he is what he wears.

Both the Latin playwrights exploit similar issues of masking and identity. The *Prisoners* of Plautus turns on a cunning plot in which young master and slave, both now prisoners of war, contrive the former's escape by exchanging costume and mask. They thus enter the stage as each other; the oddity in all this, however, is that the young master is later described by one who has known him since long before his imprisonment as having reddish hair, i.e. as giving off the visual signals associated with a slave. At first entry, therefore, we have the young master in the mask, wig and costume of a slave, and a slave dressed to look like the young master but, at least as concerns his wig, still looking disconcertingly like a slave. All very appropriate to a play which poses the question 'Where do slaves come from?' and asks us whether there is any way to distinguish the rightly and the wrongfully enslaved.

Terence, according to Donatus, added a new stock figure to the comic repertoire in the form of the good courtesan (*bona meretrix*). The figures to whom he refers are the Thais of *The Eunuch* and the Bacchis of *The Mother-in-Law*. These women come dressed by Versace and they have all the accessories. In the case of Bacchis, one of these is a ring torn by Pamphilus from the finger of the girl he has just raped in the street on the way to see her (it is that grotesque). What therefore makes Bacchis a good courtesan is her late arrival on the stage in an attempt to reassure Pamphilus' bride that she has had no dealings with him since his marriage. This she does even though she knows that no other of her profession would do so and that marital discord is good for one in her line of business. When the bride recognizes the ring which Bacchis wears, the courtesan becomes the means by which the husband discovers that his wife is no slut but rather a victim, his victim to be precise. Bacchis again expresses her satisfaction at a resolution which *other courtesans* would not desire. A similar theme emerges in *The Eunuch*. The play turns on the desire of Thais to return to her true family in Sunium the beautiful young Pamphila whose many troubles began when she was snatched by pirates. This, however, is never simply altruistic, for Thais is alone in Athens and hopes to win the friendship and support of the family as a reward for her deed. Meanwhile, she also has to balance the books and that means jettisoning her regular lover Phaedria in favour of a couple of days with the boorish, dimwitted but distinctly lucrative soldier Thraso. Phaedria leaves as asked and Thais delivers a soliloquy admitting that nobody is dearer to her than Phaedria, and that she fears that he judges her according to the characters of other women (*ex aliarum ingeniis*). The issue, therefore, may be put as follows: can a courtesan truly possess an innate character different from that of her stock-type? can she transcend the mask? or are mask and character finally indivisible?

(6) Versification

The version of Terence presented in this volume renders the Latin comedian in elegant rhyming couplets. Professor Clayton thus achieves two significant ends: first, he brings home the fact that Terence, like all the ancient comedians, was indeed a poet; second, he does so in a verse form which has typified English translations and adaptations of ancient comedy from Udall's *Ralph Roister Doister* to Ranjit Bolt's contemporary translations of Aristophanes. There are, however, considerable differences between the effects which this versification achieves and those typical of the original, and it is perhaps appropriate here briefly to comment on the latter.

Clayton's couplets consist of lines of ten or eleven syllables, four of which are stressed; the final words of each pair of lines rhyme with one another. Latin metre is rather different. The guiding principle is that of quantity and each syllable is long or short either by nature or position. What is called a foot is a particular combination of long and short syllables, and different combinations have different names: short-long is an iamb, long-short a trochee, long-long a spondee, long-short-short a dactyl. The title given to a given metre therefore reflects the particular combination employed in each foot and the number of feet in a line: a line reading short-long short-long short-long short-long short-long short-long would, for instance, be an iambic senarius. So far so good. The real problem with comic metre, however, is that positive identification of a metrical foot is often less convincing than negative. It is, for instance, normal in ancient verse to regard one long syllable as equal in quantity to two shorts and even the metrically challenged can therefore appreciate that a foot scanning short-short-short would be as much an iamb as one scanning short-long. Yet the iambic senarius also makes room for feet which scan long-long or short-short-short-short. The one thing they cannot do is scan long-short because then, and only then, would they definitely be trochees and not iambs. Any of the above combinations is likewise admissible in the case of the trochaic foot except for short-long, when it would definitely be an iamb. Only in the final foot of each line is such resolution forbidden. It is perhaps no surprise that many medieval manuscripts of Terence simply write out his plays as prose; the copyists clearly had no idea how they might work as verse.

What is perhaps most crucial in comedy is variation between metres. Unaccompanied speech in Greek verse is delivered in the iambic trimeter and in Latin in the closely related iambic senarius. It is significant that Aristotle should regard the iambic trimeter as the verse closest to the rhythms of day-to-day prose; when Cicero says much the same of all comic metre in the *Orator*, he too must in essence be generalizing on the basis of the iambic senarius. Such verses take up just over half of all lines in Terence and far more in Menander. A quite different tone is therefore created when the poets move into one of a variety of longer verse lines which are not so much spoken as declaimed or recited to the tune of a pipe. This effect is often likened to operatic recitative. In Plautus it must contrast with those metrically baffling portions of the text, the *cantica*, where the characters actually burst into song. Terence permits himself only thirty such lines, but he does introduce various passages of recitative which are unusual for their incorporation of a variety of different metres at once. It is therefore the movement between these different metrical levels which is perhaps the most difficult aspect of comedy to replicate in translation. Those who are inspired by Professor Clayton's translation to read Terence in the original will not be disappointed.

(7) Reception

The *comoedia palliata* did not precisely die with Terence, but the years which followed were more remarkable for their exploration of alternative comic forms. Prominent amongst these, for instance, is the *comoedia togata*, an attempt to play out the typical situations of the *palliata* in an explicitly Roman or Italian setting. More fragments of the work of L. Afranius survive than of any other writer in this form, and he claims to have based much of his work on Menander and on Terence. Inasmuch as imitation is also perforce a mode of interpretation, it would be fascinating to see how Afranius thought that Terence's plays could be made to do what the poet appears most reluctant to claim for them, namely to comment on contemporary Rome.

The Roman dramatic festivals continued to thrive and what they offered must have been a vigorous mix of forms. New tragedies and comedies were written even if we do not possess them; the Atellane farce reintroduced by L. Pomponius Bononiensis made new the Plautine mode; different versions of mime thrived, from the highly literate to the cheerfully obscene. Yet there must always have been room for revivals of Plautus, Terence and the other writers of the *palliata*, and various references to Terence in particular make sense only if he was actually staged. At the same time, however, Terence had become and was to remain a staple of Roman literate education, admired for his Latin as much as his morals. When Cicero quotes from *The Brothers* in his speech in defence of Caelius, the familiarity with the play which he presupposes in his audience is as likely to stem from classroom reading as from actual performance. The Latin grammarians quote him profusely.

Evidence of various sorts attests to the popularity of Terence as a teaching text. One of these is the proliferation of commentaries on his work, the earliest of which, that of Probus, dates from the later first century AD. The only one of these to survive is that of the fourth-century AD Donatus but it contains substantial discussion of all the works save *The Self-Tormentor* and is a vital source of information, not least regarding Terence's response to the Greek models for his plays. The other crucial pointer to the popularity of Terence is simply the proliferation of manuscripts. One of these, the Bembinus, dates back to the fourth or fifth century AD and over 650 still survive from the start of the ninth century onwards. Some even contain line drawings illustrating staged performances of the plays.

A bizarre and fascinating example of the early reception of Terence is provided by the dramatic works of the tenth-century German nun Hrosvitha of Gandersheim. This is how Hrosvitha introduces her work:

> Many believers are to be found, and I cannot entirely acquit myself of this fault, who, thanks to the eloquence of their more cultivated speech, prefer the emptiness of gentile books to the utility of the sacred scriptures. There are also others who, though devoted to the sacred pages and spurning all other works of the gentiles, nevertheless read and reread the fictions of Terence and, while they take delight in the sweetness of his speech, are stained with knowledge of unspeakable things.

The nun's response is to compose six works which effectively reclaim the language, characters and situations of the comic tradition for Christianity. An example of this approach is the *Pafnutius*, a drama based on the tale in Rufinus' *History of the Monks* of the eponymous hermit's moral reclamation of the courtesan Thais. The attraction of this story, of course, is that Thais is also the name of the courtesan heroine of the *Eunuch* of Terence, and Hrosvitha plays off this model. In the pagan drama, the first encounter between the courtesan and her mistreated lover has him exclaim 'Oh Thais,

Thais!' Hrosvitha transports her hermit to the city, leads him to the house of his Thais, has him enter an inner sanctuary with her, and then utter the self-same 'Oh Thais, Thais!', but this time as the indignation of the Christian calling her to the true way. Thais is immediately converted, burns her jewels and gives her wealth away to the poor. The hermit then leads her to a nunnery where the abbess is instructed to keep her in a locked room to which access is to be had only though one tiny window by which food will be delivered. Thais trembles at the thought that there will be no en-suite facilities, but it is the spiritual foulness of her past life which she must confront, not the physical malodorousness of the present. Pafnutius finally returns to her as she dies and finds that she has had the moral strength to endure. Thais is thus united with 'the lover above' (*superno amatori*). All comedy, as they say, ends with a wedding. Even one as ghastly as this.

The tradition of Latin New Comedy was revived again by the Italian humanists of the fourteehth and fifteenth centuries, and original works are recorded for Petrarch, Vergerio, Ugolino and Piccolomini. It was, however, with the invention of printing that the Plautine and Terentian mode truly took off, first in Italy, then throughout Western Europe. The first printed editions of the Latin authors date from 1470 and 1472, and it was with the 1476 Florentine performance of *The Woman from Andros* that Terence returned to the stage for the first time since antiquity. The period in which Plautus and Terence most clearly defined the comic mode was the sixteenth to the eighteenth centuries, and it was to this topic, in particular as it related to the comedies of Shakespeare, that Professor Clayton devoted attention. The genuine complexity of work of this sort derives from the multiplication of direct and indirect traditions: one work may resemble a Plautine or Terentian original when in fact its author knows the work of the Latin comedians only indirectly through its Italian or French imitator, or as part of the common stock of endlessly recycled comic gags and routines, while another may represent a direct return to the classical model or a cunning grafting of elements from the classical model on to others provided by an intermediary imitation. The apparently direct recourse to the Plautine *Menaechmi* and *Amphitruo* in the *The Comedy of Errors* is perhaps unusual within the corpus of Shakespeare's comedies, but influence need never be so direct in order to be real.

The most convenient introductory guide to the reception of Roman comedy in this period is still that provided by G. E. Duckworth in his study *The Nature of Roman Comedy*. Duckworth and the works which he cites point not just to noted instances such as Molière's engagement with *The Brothers* in *L'École des Maris* or with *Phormio* in *Les Fourberies de Scapin*, but also to many others far more obscure. The German Scriptoralia series directed by E. Lefèvre is another excellent source of information on the reception of individual plays. Rather than reproduce all the material collected by

these scholars, I propose to consider one pioneering example. The earliest
English comedy to survive is Nicholas Udall's *Ralph Roister Doister*, c.1542.
The butt of the comedy is a native version of the Roman boastful soldier,
and he is as rich, vain and fat-headed as any to be encountered in the works
of Plautus and Terence. The principal beneficiary of his largesse is the aptly
named Matthew Merrygreek, and the two of them inter-act in a manner
which most closely recalls that of Pyrgopolynices and his parasite Artotrogus
in the Plautine *Boastful Soldier* and of Thraso and his Gnatho in *The Eunuch*.
As the play develops, however, it is the Terentian model which comes to
predominate, most notably in the mock-battle of Act V. iii–viii in which the
cowardly Roister Doister and his men are routed by Dame Christian
Custance, her nurse Margery Mumblecrust and the maids Tibet Talkapace
and Annot Alyface. The delight in coining absurd speaking names is
profoundly Plautine; the determination to lead from behind and readiness
to call retreat of Roister Doister are straight out of Terence. As significant
as these similarities, however, are the changes which Udall has wrought. For
the heroine of *The Eunuch* is the courtesan Thais and her affection for
Phaedria in no way precludes her taking in the soldier if he will help to pay
the rent. It is, by contrast, no accident that Udall names his heroine Dame
Christian Custance, or that her final happiness depends on her ability not
just to repel Roister Doister but also to convince her betrothed, Gawyn
Goodluck, of her loyalty and faith. The reconciliation scene over which the
duplicitous Merrygreek presides at the close of the drama has all the essential structure of that at the close of *The Eunuch*, but none of the cheery sexual
amorality which still makes some readers blush.

It is hard to imagine a modern staging of Terence. We are talking, after
all, of a writer three of whose six plays turn on sexual violence and one of
which features a lengthy account on the part of the rapist of precisely what
he has done. This aspect makes him tough enough to read together or to
teach, and to ask someone to engage academically with some issues may be
to tear open deep personal wounds of which we are as yet unaware.
Sometimes it is answer enough simply to close the book and walk away. Yet
others will be attracted to some of what is most repugnant in Terence
precisely because of his ability to tear away that veneer of all-too forgiving
civility in which the Roman gentleman, the self-styled *bonus vir*, dresses
himself, and reveal the cruelty underneath. That is what I find in the final
scenes of *The Mother-in-Law* and what makes it as brutal a happy ending
as one might see. So too, I suspect, Professor Clayton. For his version of the
play does not stop with Terence. Rather, he appends a 143-line epilogue
spoken in the persona of Terence and closing with the author's self-revela-
tion, yes as a comfort to the Roman ruling class, but finally as a slave, a freed
black slave, quietly loathing the oppressor whom he charms. In this remarkable piece, rape and the self-forgiving, self-congratulatory conceit of the

rapist are an extended symbol of the abuse of power: of men over women, rich over poor, white over black. Comedy, meanwhile, and all the devices which comedy finds in order to palliate rape and put it right, stand for the lies we tell the oppressor in order to allow him to admire himself.

One of the ways in which comedy puts rape right, as it does in *The Mother-in-Law*, is to furnish a recognition token by which the victim may be reunited with her rapist and allowed to be his bride. Amongst the most powerful lines in Clayton's epilogue are the following in which Terence reflects on how these tokens are gained, but also, implicitly, how in the real world they are not. The experience which the Roman poet attests is that of the Second World War, the defining moment in Clayton's life. A note in the margin attributes the air-raid shelter narrative to Lance-Corporal B. in Halstead, Essex, 1941:

> Playwrights use
> What fate or fashion gives, warts, moles, tattoos,
> Good or bad tokens. Charm-necklace, identity disk
> In war-time, might increase the rapist's risk
> With girls who had the wit to see and act
> In unenlightened days—or nights. Attic dark, out-blacked
> By black-out, could be on *his* side, however,
> That *omne animal* feeling *post coitum* clever,
> Finding it funny that he and she might meet
> Tomorrow morning in the village street,
> Unknowing, unknown. After all, in the air-raid shelter,
> The spice of the experience was, not seeing, he felt her
> More sensuously, so he said, and the cream of the joke was
> The girl would never know who the blacked-out bloke was.

What Lance-Corporal B. represents is comedy's guilty conscience: all the rapists who got away, the ones whose deeds the genre is too complaisant to encompass. Put simply, the reality of subjection. In other fields and times it is more likely to be Lance-Corporal B. who suffers and for General Z. that the sycophantic narrative is composed. Not far beneath the surface of these lines, I suspect, lies Clayton himself and his own pain. That is a story for others to tell. All I can testify is that in this epilogue Terence is disconcertingly, uncomfortably alive.

Publisher's note

The Epilogue to *The Mother-in-Law* referred to towards the end of the Introduction has been printed at the end of the book.

Select Bibliography

Text

Those wishing to read Terence in Latin are best advised to use the Oxford Classical Text of R. Kauer and W. M. Lindsay (Oxford, 1926). The two-volume Loeb Classical Library edition of Terence has recently been revised by J. Barsby and is also very helpful.

Commentaries

The following editions of the plays are recommended:

J. Barsby (ed.), *Terence. Eunuchus* (Cambridge, 1999).
A. J. Brothers (ed.), *Terence. The Self-Tormentor* (Warminster, 1988).
A. S. Gratwick (ed.), *Terence. The Brothers*, 2nd ed. (Warminster, 1999).
S. Ireland (ed.), *Terence. The Mother-in-Law* (Warminster, 1990).
R. H. Martin (ed.), *Terence: Phormio* (London, 1959).
—— (ed.), *Terence. Adelphoe* (Cambridge, 1976).
G. P. Shipp (ed.), *P. Terenti Afri Andria* (Oxford, 1960).

Studies of Terence and of Roman Comedy in General

W. Beare, *The Roman Stage*, 3rd ed. (London, 1964).
K. Büchner, *Das Theater des Terenz* (Heidelberg, 1974).
G. E. Duckworth, *The Nature of Roman Comedy* (Princeton, 1952).
W. G. Forehand, *Terence* (Boston, 1985).
E. Fraenkel, *Elementi plautini in Plauto*, tr. F. Munari (Florence, 1960).
S. M. Goldberg, *Understanding Terence* (Princeton, NJ, 1986).
——'Plautus on the Palatine', *Journal of Roman Studies* 88 (1998), 1–20.
A. S. Gratwick, 'Drama', in E. J. Kenney (ed.), *Cambridge History of Classical Literature*, vol. II (Cambridge, 1982), 77–137.
E. S. Gruen, *Culture and National Identity in Republican Rome* (Ithaca. NY, 1992).
D. Konstan, *Roman Comedy* (Ithaca, NY, 1983).
—— *Greek Comedy and Ideology* (Oxford, 1995).
M. Leigh, *Comedy and the Rise of Rome* (Oxford, 2004).
W. Ludwig, 'The Originality of Terence and his Greek Models', *Greek,*

Roman, and Byzantine Studies 9 (1968), 169–92.

G. Norwood, *The Art of Terence* (Oxford, 1923).

H. Parker, 'Plautus vs. Terence: Audience and Popularity Re-examined', *American Journal of Philology* 117 (1996): 585–617.

O. Rieth, *Die Kunst Menanders in den Adelphen des Terenz* (Hildesheim, 1964).

E. Segal, *Roman Laughter*, 2nd ed. (Oxford, 1987).

L. R. Taylor, 'The Opportunities for Dramatic Performances in the Time of Plautus and Terence', *Transactions of the American Philological Association* 68 (1937), 284–304.

T. B. L. Webster, *An Introduction to Menander* (Manchester, 1974).

D. Wiles, *The Masks of Menander* (Cambridge, 1991).

J. Wright, *Dancing in Chains. The Stylistic Unity of the Comoedia Palliata* (Rome, 1974).

A note on the editions of the Latin texts

It would appear that Professor Clayton used a Loeb or Teubner edition when preparing his translation. Some discrepancies will therefore be found if comparing the translation with the Oxford Classical Texts edition*, which has been used in preparing his typescripts for publication posthumously. The occasional departures from the text which are not authorised by these editions may usually be attributed to the requirements of the metre or rhyme scheme but sometimes involve a change of speaker.

Line numbers printed as part of the running heads refer to the line-numbering in the Oxford Classical Texts edition.

* *P. Terenti Afri Comoediae*, ed. Robert Kauer and Wallace M. Lindsay (Oxford, 1926), reprinted with additions by Otto Skutsch (1958).

The Woman from Andros

The Woman from Andros

PROLOGUE

Our poet, when he first took up his pen
Believed the task he'd undertaken then
Was getting his comedies generally approved.
But that belief he finds far, far removed
From fact. He wastes time writing prologues. Why?
Not to outline the plot, but in reply
To an old hack's[1] attacks, which are downright slanderous.
Listen what faults his malice finds. Menandros[2]
Wrote *The Girl from Perinthos* and *The Girl from Andros*.
Know one, and you know both—by plot similarities,
Though style and dialogue do show some disparities.
What features, now, of that first female fitted
The second, our poet—this is freely admitted—
Appropriated. That's the sin they seize on,
Adulteration. The pure ray of their reason

---

1 Luscius of Lanuvium.
2 Most famous poet of Greek New Comedy.

Blinds them. Blame our man, and you must blame Plautus,[3]
Ennius,[4] Naevius.[5] This is a fault they taught us.
Our poet would rather imitate their impurities
Than his opponents' rigidly right obscurities.
Let these be quiet, and quench their jealous jeering,
Or they'll be told their faults. Please grant fair hearing
To this new play. Don't judge it till you know it,
And then decide the prospects for our poet,
Whether his future plays, as some have been,
Shall be hissed off on sight, or be—first seen.

*Scene: a street in Athens, with the houses of Simo and Glycerium. The exit
on the right leads to the city centre, that on the left to the harbour.*

ACT I

(Enter Simo with Sosia and some slaves carrying provisions)

SIMO: *(to other slaves)*
Inside with that lot! Sharp! *(to Sosia)* You, Sosia, stay.
I have a few words—

SOSIA: Which you needn't say.
'See them well cooked'—I know my range, my purview,
So to speak.

SIMO: You're wrong.

SOSIA: How else can my art serve you?

SIMO: For what I have in mind, it's not your art,
But what I know you have—a loyal heart,
A still tongue in your head—that I require.

SOSIA: Sir, I'm all ears. Your wish is my desire.

SIMO: You know that, since I bought you as a child,
You've found me a fair master, tolerant, mild.
From slave I made you freedman, since as slave
You did free-hearted service. So I gave
The best reward I had.

SOSIA: I don't forget it.

SIMO: And I, for my part, Sosia, don't regret it.

3 Comic Roman poet. Twenty-one of his plays survive.
4 Author of the epic *Annales* as well as tragedies and comedies adapted from the
   Greek.
5 Author of the epic *Punic War* as well as tragedies and comedies adapted from the
   Greek.

SOSIA: I'm glad if anything I've done or do, sir,
Gives satisfaction and I do thank you, sir,
For your approval. But I take amiss
One thing a little. Reminding me like this
Sounds like reproach for benefits forgot.
I'd rather you just said in one word what
Your wish would be.

SIMO: I will. First, you must know
This wedding you think's fixed is—fiction.

SOSIA: Oh!
But what's the point of that, sir?

SIMO: You shall hear
The whole thing from the start. Then you'll be clear
About my son's past life, my present plan,
And your part in it. When he became a man
And had free rein—for, of course, one couldn't gauge
His character before, when tender age,
Timidity, teachers, all controlled him.

SOSIA: True.

SIMO: Well, now, you know the way that most lads do,
Go crazy on some hobby—keeping horses
Or hounds for hunting, or attending courses
On higher thought—well, he'd no special fad
But dabbled in them all. And I was glad.

SOSIA: Oh, I agree. The golden rule, I say,
Is 'Nothing in excess'.

SIMO: That was his way.
In every company bearing and forbearing,
Entirely at their disposal, always deferring
To their ideas. He never disagreed,
Opposed, or pushed himself into the lead.
That's the best way of making friends and winning
Ungrudged approval.

SOSIA: Yes. It's a good beginning.
In making friends agreement's the great virtue
These days. Sincerity makes them soon desert you.

SIMO: Well, now, a girl from Andros, three years back,
Came to live near us, driven here by lack
Of means, since her relatives wouldn't do their duty
By the poor creature. She was quite a beauty,
Still fresh and unspoiled then.

SOSIA: Oh, I smell danger
Approaching from the direction of that stranger.

SIMO: She lived a decent enough life at the beginning,
   The hard and thrifty way, weaving and spinning
   To make ends meet. Then easy money beckoned,
   At first one lover came, and then a second,
   And then a third. Well, we're all made to go
   Downhill, from hard to soft, as it were. And so
   She took their terms, set up in business. Then,
   As sometimes happens, some of the young men
   Who at that time were keeping her, took my son
   Along, to join, as it were, in the fun.
   At once I said to myself, 'He's caught. No doubt
   Whatever. He's had it.' I started looking out
   Each morning for the slaves of those young men
   Coming or going. I tackled them. 'Now then,
   My boy, if you don't mind telling,'—that's what I'd say—
   'Which of the young men's turn was it yesterday
   With Chrysis?' Chrysis was the wench's name.

SOSIA: I see, sir.

SIMO: Prompt enough the answers came—
   'Clinia', 'Phaedrus', 'Niceratus'—those three
   Were all her lovers at that time, you see.
   'But what about Pamphilus?' I then would add.
   'Just paid and ate his whack.' Well, was I glad.
   Daily I asked and all I could discover
   Assured me Pamphilus was not her lover.
   I felt he'd stood the test and proved already
   His sense and self-control. Whoever keeps steady
   When he's in contact every day and hour
   With characters of that kind must have the power
   To manage his life. Not only did I rejoice,
   The whole town sang his praises with one voice
   And said how lucky I was to have the sort
   Of son I had. In brief, this good report
   Was what made Chremes, without prompting, come
   And offer him, with a very handsome sum
   As dowry, his only daughter. 'Done!' I said.
   They were engaged. Today they were to wed.

SOSIA: Then what's the impediment?

SIMO: You shall be told.
   Within a week of our fixing it, lo and behold,
   Our neighbour Chrysis died.

SOSIA: Oh, I am glad!
   That Chrysis had me worried.

SIMO: Quite. My lad,
Being very much together with these young men
Who had been intimate with her just then,
Helped to arrange the funeral. He seemed moved,
Even to tears at times. And I approved.
If, with such slight acquaintance on his part,
I said, he takes her death so much to heart,
What if he'd loved her? What will he feel for me,
His father? I took all his acts, you see,
To be the courteous and kind behaviour
Of a nice, good-natured young man to a neighbour.
Well, briefly, just for his sake I went along
To the funeral, still suspecting nothing wrong.

SOSIA: Oh, sir, what is the trouble?

SIMO: You shall hear.
They carried her out. We walked behind the bier.
And then I spied, among the women there,
One girl, whose figure was—

SOSIA: Outstanding, sir?

SIMO: Yes, Sosia. And matched with a lovely face.
You never saw such modesty and grace.
And then I noticed she was more distressed,
And more refined and ladylike than the rest.
I went up to the maids, asked, 'Who's that?' 'Oh,'
They said, 'that's Chrysis' sister.' Like a blow
It hit me, like a flash. There, there's the source
Of all our tears and sympathy—of course!

SOSIA: Now I am worried where all this is leading!

SIMO: Meanwhile the funeral cortège was proceeding.
We followed it to the cemetery. The departed
Was placed on the funeral pyre, the wailing started.
And then—this sister I've just mentioned came,
Not noticing what she did, too near the flame
And was indeed in danger. Then, dismayed,
Beside himself, my son at last betrayed
His love so long concealed. Straight to her side
He flew, flung both his arms around her, cried,
'Glycerium dear, what are you trying to do?
Why do you want to kill yourself?' One knew
How long they'd been in love then, and how deep,
The way she fell back in his arms to weep
Where she felt most at home.

SOSIA: Well, well, what next?

SIMO: I went home, shocked and angry, really vexed,
Yet without grounds on which to accuse my son.
He might have answered, 'Why, what have I done?
What wrong, what harm? That girl was just about
To plunge into the fire. I plucked her out.
I saved her life.' A reasonable answer.

SOSIA: Yes, you're right there. You can't reproach a man, sir,
For saving lives. Or what are you going to do
To those who cause us loss or injury?

SIMO: True.
Next day comes Chremes crying, 'It's too bad!
I find that foreigner's living with your lad
As man and wife!' Well, I kept saying no,
But he insisted he was right, and so
He left me, making it clear he'd never wed
His daughter to my son.

SOSIA: And still you said
Nothing to Pamphilus?

SIMO: I'd still no grounds
To accuse him.

SOSIA: No?

SIMO: He'd say, 'Look. You've set bounds
To all this. Soon I'll have to take a wife
And live by someone else's rule of life.
Leave me alone till then.'

SOSIA: What grounds for accusing
Could you ever have, then?

SIMO: Ah, catch him refusing
To marry, making it clear that she's the reason—
That's flat defiance, something I can seize on.
Since I'm endeavouring, by a match that's fiction,
To get the facts, the true grounds for conviction,
Should he refuse. What's more, I want his man,
That no-good Davus, if he's got some plan,
To waste it while there's no match to be marred.
I know he'll do his damnedest, no holds barred—
More to thwart me than to oblige the lad.

SOSIA: But why, sir?

SIMO: Why? Because he's thoroughly bad,
Bad, heart and soul. And, trust me, if I find him
Doing anything to upset—but never mind him.
Assuming my arrangements don't miscarry
And Pamphilus doesn't, in fact, refuse to marry,

I've only got to do a bit of pleading
With Chremes, and I've no doubt of succeeding.
Your job is just to bluff with all your might
About this marriage, give Davus a good fright
And keep an eye on Pamphilus, see whether
Davus and he start putting heads together.

SOSIA: Right, sir, I'll see to it. No more to be said.
Going in, sir?

SIMO: Not just now. You go ahead. *(Exit Sosia)*
I'm sure my son is not prepared for a wife.
Davus, quite clearly, got the shock of his life
When I informed him just now of the match.
Talk of the devil!
(Enter Davus, talking to himself)

DAVUS: I knew there was some catch!
The old man's mildness always had me scared,
Wondering where it would lead to. When he heard
The match was scratched, he didn't take it ill
Or say a word to any of us.

SIMO: *(aside)*   He will,
And you'll be sorry I spoke.

DAVUS: That's just the thing
He wanted, though—to have us on a string,
Duped with false joys, all hope, no fear, then caught
Gaping, with no time left for careful thought
On how to mar his marriage. Very clever!

SIMO: *(aside)* What's the old scoundrel saying?

DAVUS: *(aside)*   Well, I never!
The master! Phew!

SIMO: Hey, Davus!

DAVUS: Yes, what?

SIMO: Hey!
Come here.

DAVUS: *(aside)*   What for?

SIMO: Well, what have you to say?

DAVUS: To what?

SIMO: To what? It's rumoured that my boy
Has got a mistress—

DAVUS: *(ironically)*   That's a tale to employ
The whole town's tongue, of course.

SIMO: Are you listening?

DAVUS: Rather!

SIMO: Well, I don't want to act the heavy father

By probing all that at the present stage.
The past's not my concern. At the proper age
I let him have his fling. Today's the start
Of a new life. That demands a change of heart,
And I demand, or, if the word's more fitting,
I beg you, Davus, kindly to permit him
To get back on his course.

DAVUS: You mean—?

SIMO: Just this.
Those love-sick lads are apt to take it amiss
When one provides a wife.

DAVUS: So I've heard said.

SIMO: And if a lad should let himself be led
By some old scoundrel, up to any trick,
He's apt to give a heart already sick
A good turn for the worse—you see?

DAVUS: God save us,
I don't see.

SIMO: Don't you?

DAVUS: No, sir. My name's Davus,
Not Oedipus.[6]

SIMO: You'd like to have the rest
Without a wrapping?

DAVUS: Yes, sir. Quite undressed.

SIMO: Right. If I find you playing games today
To mar this match or trying to display
Your talents in that field, I'll beat you first,
Then set you grinding grain until you burst.[7]
And this I promise you—if I ever find
I've let you win, I'll set myself to grind.
Have you got that? Or are you still not sure?

DAVUS: No, sir. I don't think that speech was obscure.
You went straight to the point. I couldn't miss.

SIMO: I'd sooner it was anything but this
You chose to cheat me in.

DAVUS: Oh, sir, how could you?
Saying a thing like that!

SIMO: Be funny, would you?
I'm telling you. I miss nothing. So take care.
And don't say later you weren't warned. Beware! *(Exit)*

6 Mythical ruler of Thebes who solved the riddle of the Sphinx.
7 Grinding grain is commonly regarded as the harshest form of servile labour.

DAVUS: Well, there's no time for tardiness and tarrying.
If I'm right, he means business with his marrying,
And, if I don't look out, that spells disaster
Either for yours truly or young master.
This really is a dilemma. Should I rather
Aid and abet the son or obey the father?
I fear for Pamphilus' life now, if I quit him.
But I fear the old man's threats as well. To outwit him
Will not be easy. He's spotted this liaison
And it's myself he's got his lynx-eyed gaze on,
In case I try some trick to mar the match.
I'm done if he finds me at it. In fact he'll catch
At any pretext anyway, good or ill,
If he's in the mood, to march me to the mill.
To make bad worse, this Andrian—wife or t'other,
I'm not sure which—is an expectant mother
By Pamphilus, and they've a little scheme
More like a lunatic's than a lover's dream.
It's so breath-taking—you really ought to hear it.
Whatever she produces, they're going to rear it.
Yes, and they're spinning yarns for all they're worth,
Maintaining she's an Athenian by birth.
There once was an old merchant of this town—
This is their story—and his ship went down
Off Andros, and he died. And then, they say,
This girl, an orphan and a castaway,
Was taken in by Chrysis' father. Well,
I ask you! That's the tale they're going to tell,
Though it all sounds most improbable to me.
Ah, Mysis coming from their house, I see.
But I must get down town to find the lad.
We don't want him caught napping by his dad.
*(Exit. Enter Mysis from Glycerium's house, talking to
someone inside at first)*

MYSIS: I heard, I heard. It's Lesbia I'm to fetch,
Of course, though she's a fuddled, muddled wretch,
Not fit to trust with any girl's first time.
What? Fetch her all the same? Oh, it's a crime!
Her boozing-friend, that's what she is. Let's hope
God gives a good birth here and leaves her scope
For practising her errors elsewhere rather.
(Enter Pamphilus)
But what's this? What a worried-looking young father!

Oh, dear, what can the matter be? I'll wait
And see what's up, what's put him in such a state.

PAMPHILUS: *(to himself)*
Is this fair, decent, human behaviour, this
The way to treat one's son?

MYSIS: *(aside)*   Now what's amiss?

PAMPHILUS: Did you ever see such an outrage in your life?
Doomed—now, today—no respite—to a wife!
He might have given me some hint, some word
What was in store.

MYSIS: *(aside)*   Oh, Lord, what have I heard?

PAMPHILUS: What can it mean? Did Chremes, who declined
To trust me with his daughter, change his mind
Because I wouldn't? Has he set his heart
On forcing Glycerium and myself apart?
If that's his game and if it works, I'm lost
Beyond all hope. Was ever man so crossed
In love, so damned unlucky? God in heaven,
Is there no escape? Must I be given
A wife by Chremes? Kicked around, snubbed, slighted,
Faced with fixed facts, rejected, re-invited—
And why? Unless my dark suspicion's right
That they've been bringing up some freak, some fright
They can't get rid of and I'm the mug.

MYSIS: *(aside)*   Oh, dear,
What I've just heard leaves me half-dead with fear.

PAMPHILUS: What can I say about my father? Oh,
To treat a matter of such moment so!
He met me in the market-place and said,
'Well, Pamphilus, today you're to be wed.
Go and get ready at once.' That was as good
As 'Go and get hanged at once.' And there I stood,
Completely dazed. Not one word could I speak,
Nor find one reason, even wrong, false, weak.
I was struck dumb. And what, you'd like to know,
Would I have done if I'd had warning? Oh,
I'd have done something, anything, so as not
To have to do this. Now I don't know what
To try or where to start. I'm stuck, I'm caught
In such conflicting feelings. I'm distraught.
Love, pity, panic at this match beset me,
And feelings for my father, who did let me
So tolerantly have my way till now.

Am I to oppose him? Oh, I don't know how
To act at all. I'm utterly perplexed.

MYSIS: *(aside)*
Where his perplexity will lead him next
Is what I'm frightened of. Now he's in a dither
And now's the time to get him talking with her,
While he's in doubt—or else with me about her.
It takes so little to decide the doubter.

PAMPHILUS: Who spoke there? Oh, it's you. Good morning, Mysis.

MYSIS: Good morning, sir.

PAMPHILUS: How is she?

MYSIS: At the crisis,
Poor creature, of her pains. And then today, sir,
Being when that other marriage was meant to take place, sir,
Originally, well, she frets. She's afraid even now
You might desert her.

PAMPHILUS: Oh, how could I? How
Let that poor girl who's laid her heart and life
In my hands, whom I've loved as my true wife,
Find I've deceived her? How can I see that child
Brought up to be so sweet and pure, defiled
By force of need? That's something I'll never do!

MYSIS: Oh, I'd not worry if it lay with you.
But—can you face force? That's what I'm afraid of.

PAMPHILUS: For heaven's sake, Mysis, what do you think I'm made of?
Or am I so ungrateful do you think,
So callous and inhuman that no link
Of love and everything we've shared could move me
To keep my word, no sense of shame reprove me?

MYSIS: Well, Pamphilus, she has deserved, none better,
That I do know, that you should not forget her.

PAMPHILUS: Forget her? Forget Glycerium? Oh, Mysis,
Those words are written in my heart that Chrysis
Used of her. I was summoned as she lay
Dying. And all you women were sent away.
We were alone. 'You see,' she said, 'Pamphilus dear,
How young and pretty is my sister here.
You know how little use is either of these
For keeping modesty or money. Please,
By your right hand I beg you, by your heart,
Your loyalty and your loneliness, never part,
Never desert her. I've loved you like a brother,
And she adores you. There never was another

Like you in all the world. She tried to do
What you wished always. Now I'm giving you
To her as husband, guardian, father, friend,
And all my worldly goods I here commend
To your safekeeping.' She took my hand, placed in it
Glycerium's hand, and almost the next minute
She'd gone. I took her sister into my care
And mean to keep her.

MYSIS: Well, I hope so, sir.
PAMPHILUS: But why have you left her?
MYSIS: I was on my way
To fetch the midwife.
PAMPHILUS: Hurry then! But stay!
Mind you don't say a word about my marrying.
We mustn't have her made worse, or miscarrying.
MYSIS: I take your point, sir. *(Exit)*

ACT II

*(The action continues without a break. Enter Charinus with
Byrria. Pamphilus ponders his own problems at the back of
the stage)*
CHARINUS: What's all this you say?
That she's being married, Byrria? Today?
To Pamphilus?
BYRRIA: That's right.
CHARINUS: But how do you know?
BYRRIA: Davus just told me, in the town-square.
CHARINUS: Oh!
With hope and fear my heart's been on the rack
So long that, now hope's gone, it just sinks back
Dazed, weak, worn-out.
BYRRIA: Now listen, sir, why not
Since what you want apparently can't be got,
Try wanting what you can get?
CHARINUS: I want her,
And nothing else.
BYRRIA: In my opinion, sir,
You'd do much better to concentrate attention
On getting her out of your system, and not mention
What's bound to make your hot blood hotter still.
CHARINUS: Oh, when we're fine and someone else is ill,

CHARINUS: We all give good advice with the utmost ease.
In my place you'd feel different.

BYRRIA: As you please.

CHARINUS: But look! There's Pamphilus. I'll not go under
Till I've tried every means.

BYRRIA: *(to himself)*   What means, I wonder,
Does that mean?

CHARINUS: I'll implore him, I'll appeal
As man to man, tell him just how I feel.
Surely I'll get him to postpone the date
Of the wedding for a week at any rate.
And meantime something will turn up—it will,
It must.

BYRRIA: *(to himself)*
Oh yes, the number known as nil.

CHARINUS: Well, Byrria, should I tackle him?

BYRRIA: Why not?
If he won't listen and weds, he'll know he's got
A co-respondent ready.

CHARINUS: Oh, to hell
With you and your low mind!

PAMPHILUS: *(seeing them)*   Charinus! Well,
How are you?

CHARINUS: How are you? I'm here to ask you
For your advice and help. Please come to the rescue!

PAMPHILUS: Advice? Help? I've no money for the latter,
No leisure for the former. What's the matter?

CHARINUS: You're getting married today?

PAMPHILUS: So they've just told me.

CHARINUS: Pamphilus, if you do, you now behold me
For the last time.

PAMPHILUS: How come?

CHARINUS: Oh, Lord, you tell,
Byrria, I can't say it.

BYRRIA: Right, sir.

PAMPHILUS: Well?

BYRRIA: Well, he's in love with your intended.

PAMPHILUS: Eh?
He must have different tastes from mine. But say,
Has there been anything more than love, my lad,
Between you?

CHARINUS: Oh, no, Pamphilus!

PAMPHILUS: Too bad!

CHARINUS: I love her. You're my friend. Unless you've got to,
Don't marry her, please!
PAMPHILUS: I'll certainly try not to.
CHARINUS: If you can't help, or if your heart is set
Upon this match—
PAMPHILUS: My heart!
CHARINUS: Don't do it yet.
Give me a few days to get out of sight.
PAMPHILUS: Now listen. You must know—for it's not right
To make a favour out of none—that match
I'm more concerned to miss than you to catch.
CHARINUS: You've saved my life!
PAMPHILUS: So go ahead. Plot, plan,
The two of you, contrive what means you can
To make her yours. I'll meanwhile be contriving
To make her not mine.
CHARINUS: Thanks!
PAMPHILUS: And look—arriving
Right on the dot comes Davus, whose advice
And brains I'm banking on.
CHARINUS: *(to Byrria)*   But you—what price
Your brains, except for knowledge not worth knowing?
That's right—just run away.
BYRRIA: Don't fret. I'm going. *(Exit)*
(Enter Davus)
DAVUS: God, what good news! Where's Pamphilus? Let me see him!
I'll fill his young heart with delight, I'll free him
From all the fears he's feeling at this minute.
CHARINUS: *(aside)*
He's pretty pleased at something.
PAMPHILUS: *(aside)*   Nothing in it.
He's just not heard of this disaster yet.
DAVUS: If he's been told by now that they're all set
To marry him—
CHARINUS: *(aside)*   Did you hear what he just said?
DAVUS: I bet he's scouring town for me, half-dead
With worry. Where do I start this hide-and seek?
This way or that way first?
CHARINUS: *(aside)*   Go on man, speak!
DAVUS: Well, here I go.
PAMPHILUS: Hey, Davus! Stop!
DAVUS: Now, who—?
Ah, the one man I want, sir. No, the two.

         You're both well-met.

PAMPHILUS: Davus I'm ruined!

DAVUS: Oho!

         Listen to me.

PAMPHILUS: I'm wrecked.

DAVUS: Yes, yes. I know

         Your worry.

CHARINUS: What about me? I'm sure my life

         Hangs on a thread.

DAVUS: I know yours too.

PAMPHILUS: A wife—

DAVUS: I said I know.

PAMPHILUS: Today—

DAVUS: I know, I said.

         Don't deafen me! You're worried that you'll wed

         This wench, you're worried that you won't.

CHARINUS: You've got it.

PAMPHILUS: That's it.

DAVUS: As far as real risk goes, that's not it.

         Trust me.

PAMPHILUS: Oh, put me out of my misery, Davus, hurry,

         For God's sake!

DAVUS: Oh, you're out of it. Don't worry.

         Chremes has got no wife in store for you.

PAMPHILUS: How do you know that, Davus?

DAVUS: Well, I do.

         Your dad got hold of me just now and said

         This day as ever was he'd see you wed,

         With a lot more that I've not time to tell now.

         I rushed down town at once to inform you. Well, now,

         Not seeing you, I went a bit higher, looked around—

         No sign of you. And then by chance I found

         Your friend's man, Byrria, and inquired of him.

         He hadn't seen you. This was getting grim.

         What next? And then it struck me, coming back,

         'The whole thing's fishy, father looking black,

         Not much food bought, then, out of the blue, a wedding—

         It doesn't hang together.'

PAMPHILUS: Where's this heading?

DAVUS: I headed for Chremes' house. To my delight

         I found the door deserted—

CHARINUS: Hey, you're right!

PAMPHILUS: Go on.

DAVUS: I waited, saw no one leave or enter,
No bridesmaids, decorations, seething centre
Of nuptial preparation.
PAMPHILUS: Yes, strange signs,
I grant.
DAVUS: And do they run on marriage-lines?
PAMPHILUS: No, I don't think they do.
DAVUS: Think, think, you say?
You haven't a clue! The thing's as clear as day!
Why, as I left the house, whom should I meet
But Chremes' boy, who'd brought, for him to eat,
An obol's worth of greens and fish that small—
CHARINUS: Davus, you're my deliverer!
DAVUS: Not at all.
CHARINUS: Why? He's not getting her, clearly.
DAVUS: Don't be silly!
It doesn't follow that Chremes, willy-nilly,
Will let you have her if Pamphilus doesn't get her.
Canvass the old man's friends, the sooner the better,
Enlist their aid.
CHARINUS: You're right. I'm off, then—though
That hope's proved hollow before. Still—cheerio. *(Exit)*
PAMPHILUS: What's father up to? What sort of play's he staging?
DAVUS: I'll tell you. If your father started raging
At you, because of Chremes' recent retraction,
Before he'd probably tested your reaction
To marriage, he would feel himself he might
Be wrong to treat you so—and he'd be right
To blame himself. Refuse, and he'll blame you rather.
Then—fireworks.
PAMPHILUS: I'll face anything.
DAVUS: He's your father.
It's tricky. She's all alone. And once he's found,
As I suspect he will, some legal ground,
He'll have her expelled from Athens at a wink.
PAMPHILUS: Expelled?
DAVUS: And quick.
PAMPHILUS: But, Davus, what do you think
I'd better do?
DAVUS: Just say, 'I will.'
PAMPHILUS: Will what?
DAVUS: What's the matter?
PAMPHILUS: Say I'll marry?

DAVUS: Yes, why not?
PAMPHILUS: Never!
DAVUS: Now don't say no.
PAMPHILUS: I do, I do.
            No argument.
DAVUS: But think what will ensue
            If you consent.
PAMPHILUS: Ensue? I'll be shut out
            At that door and shut in by this, no doubt.
DAVUS: No. This is what I think. Your dad'll say,
            'A marriage has been arranged for you today.'
            'Father, I will,' says you. What kind of row
            Can he raise then? And what he's fixed up now
            You'll all unfix, at no risk. Chremes won't,
            That's clear, give you his daughter now. So don't
            For that consideration fear or falter
            Or swerve off course, in case his mind should alter.
            It won't. You say, 'I will.' Your dad, who might
            Be spoiling for a row, will have no right.
            But don't start telling yourself, 'My way of life
            Alone will easily ward off a wife.
            No father-in-law will have me.' Why, your father
            Will find you a girl without a penny rather
            Than let his son go merrily to hell.
            But if he finds you take it calmly, well,
            You'll put him off his guard, and he'll not hurry
            To find another wife. Meanwhile don't worry.
            Something'll turn up.
PAMPHILUS: You think that?
DAVUS: I know it.
PAMPHILUS: Well, you mind where you're steering me.
DAVUS: Aw, stow it!
PAMPHILUS: All right. I'll say yes. But—we must take care
            He doesn't find I've got a child by—her.
            (Indicates Glycerium's house)
            I've said I'll rear it.
DAVUS: Oh, you're just beyond
            A joke!
PAMPHILUS: She begged it, as a pledge, a bond
            That I'd stand by her.
DAVUS: Oh, all right. Hey! Your dad!
            Mind, he must find you looking suitably sad.
            (Enter Simo)

SIMO: Well, I've come back to see if I can find
           What's doing, what's brewing.
DAVUS: *(aside)*   He's made up his mind
           That you'll refuse. Been in some quiet little place
           I bet, rehearsing, getting up his case.
           He hopes he's got an argument to rout you.
           So, lad, you'll need to have your wits about you.
PAMPHILUS: I hope I have.
DAVUS: Bah! You just say you'll wed
           And then you'll see. There won't be one word said.
           (Enter Byrria behind)
BYRRIA: *(to himself)*
           'Drop everything else,' my master said, 'and go
           And keep an eye on Pamphilus. Get to know
           Exactly what he's up to with this wedding.'
           So in his father's footsteps I've come treading.
           And there we have him! There's the hopeful youth
           Himself with Davus. Now we'll know the truth.
SIMO: *(aside)*
           Ah, there's the precious pair!
DAVUS: *(aside to Pamphilus)*   Look out!
SIMO: Well, lad!
DAVUS: *(aside)*
           Look round as though you hadn't seen him.
PAMPHILUS: Dad!
           It's you!
DAVUS: *(aside)* Well played, sir!
SIMO: As I said already
           I hope to see you married today.
DAVUS: *(aside)*   Now steady
           Our side! Out with our answer!
PAMPHILUS: For this proposal
           Or any other I'm at your disposal.
SIMO: Oh! Ah!
DAVUS: *(aside)* Struck dumb!
BYRRIA: *(aside)*   What's this?
SIMO: *(uncertainly)*   You know your place,
           Doing what I ask with such a very good grace.
DAVUS: *(aside)*
           What did I say?
BYRRIA: *(aside)*   My master's had his bride,
           From what I hear.
SIMO: Well, get along inside.

	Then, when the call comes, you'll be ready quick.
PAMPHILUS:	Yes, sir. I will, sir. *(Exit)*
BYRRIA:	*(aside)* Doesn't it make you sick?

You can't trust anyone! It's rightly reckoned
That Number One's first, and Two a pretty poor second.
I've seen the girl, and now I recollect
She was a good-looker. What can you expect?
I see why Pamphilus wanted her in bed
Rather than have my master there instead—
With her, I mean. Well, back I'll bear my tidings,
Though bearers find bad news can bring good hidings. *(Exit)*

DAVUS: *(aside)*

Ha! Simo thinks I've got some trick to play
And stayed on purpose.

SIMO: Well, what's Davus say?

DAVUS: Same as before, sir—nothing.

SIMO: Nothing?

DAVUS: No, sir.

Not a dicky bird.

SIMO: You surprise me.

DAVUS: *(aside)*   Quite a poser

I've set him. Got him worried.

SIMO: Can you answer

One question truthfully?

DAVUS: Of course I can, sir,

Just try me.

SIMO: Has my son got no objection

To this marriage—based, I mean, on his connection
With that young foreigner?

DAVUS: None, sir. Or, if so,

A couple of days will cure the wound, you know.
He's thought it out himself and come round.

SIMO: Good.

DAVUS: He loved, while youth allowed and while he could,
But even then he kept it dark, took care
Not to be compromised by that affair.
In fact, he played the game. Being due to wed
He's turned his heart towards his wife instead.

SIMO: He seemed to me a bit glum.

DAVUS: Not at that.

There's something, though, he's slightly niggled at.

SIMO: What?

DAVUS: A lad's whim—too trivial to tell, sir.

SIMO: What is it?
DAVUS: Nothing.
SIMO: Will you answer?
DAVUS: Well, sir,
He thinks you're being a bit mean.
SIMO: Me?
DAVUS: Yes, you.
'We've scarcely spent ten drachmae on this do—
On food, I mean. Would anyone', he said,
'Guess that my father's son is getting wed?
Which of my pals am I supposed to invite
To this reception?' And speaking, if I might,
Frankly, it seemed to me a little mean, too.
SIMO: Shut up!
DAVUS: *(aside)*   That shook him.
SIMO: I'll have the matter seen to.
(aside)
What is all this? What's the old evil-doer
Hatching? If trouble's brewing, he's the brewer.

ACT III

*(The action continues without a break. The maid Mysis
comes back with the midwife Lesbia, going towards
Glycerium's house. They do not notice Simo and Davus)*
MYSIS: Well, Lesbia, as I said, it is a rare case
To find a fellow being faithful—as in her case.
DAVUS: *(to Simo)*
The Andrian's maid.
SIMO: *(to Davus)*   You don't say!
DAVUS: *(to Simo)*   Yes, I do.
MYSIS: But Pamphilus—
SIMO: *(aside)*   Eh?
MYSIS: He's proved it.
SIMO: *(aside)*   Eh? What? Who?
DAVUS: *(aside)*
God strike him deaf or her dumb!
MYSIS: He's for rearing
The baby, boy or girl.
SIMO: *(aside)*   What's this I'm hearing?
Good grief, we're sunk if this is sober truth!
LESBIA: He sounds a decent, generous sort of youth.

MYSIS: One of the best. But come inside now, do, dear.
We mustn't keep her waiting.

LESBIA: After you, dear.
(They go into the house)

DAVUS: *(aside)*
This situation's going to take some saving.

SIMO: *(aside)*
What does this mean? Is my son mad—stark, raving?
A baby by that foreigner! . . . Ah, I've got it!
Oh, I was dense! I nearly didn't spot it.

DAVUS: *(aside)*
Spot what?

SIMO: *(aside)*   It's Davus' first move. It's a catch,
That's it—to frighten Chremes off the match.
They're going to fake a birth.
(A cry is heard from inside Glycerium's house)

GLYCERIUM: *(inside)*   Oh, Juno, save us!
Mother of Gods!

SIMO: So soon? How silly, Davus!
She hears me at the door and in hot haste
Gives tongue! Your episodes should be better spaced.

DAVUS: Mine, sir?

SIMO: Or were your actors in this scene
Jumping their cues?

DAVUS: I don't know what you mean.

SIMO: *(aside)*
I must say, if we'd really fixed our match,
And I'd been caught off guard by this same catch
I can imagine he'd have had some sport.
But now he risks the wreck. I'm safe in port.
(Lesbia comes out, talking loudly to someone inside)

LESBIA: Yes, Archylis, everything so far in this case
Is sound and normal, nothing out of place.
So have her washed. Then give her some of that stuff
To drink. I told you how much is enough.
I'll soon be back. *(To herself)* Well, it's a bonny boy.
Let's hope he lives to give his father joy.
He's such a nice chap, Pamphilus. Couldn't bear
The thought of wronging that sweet creature. *(Exit)*

SIMO: There!
Who, knowing you, wouldn't spot your hand in that?

DAVUS: What, sir?

SIMO: She couldn't give her little chat

On mother and child indoors. She must come out
And give the rest of the cast inside a shout.
Do you rate me so low, then? Do I seem
The sort to fall for such a bare-faced scheme?
Let's have some subtlety, please. Let's have it thought
You've some fear of my anger, if you're caught.

DAVUS: *(aside)* Well, it's yourself, not me, that's fooling you.

SIMO: Didn't I say? I warned you what I'd do.
And were you worried? Were you hell! Now, maybe,
I'm meant to think this girl has had a baby
From Pamphilus. Am I?

DAVUS: *(aside)*   Ah! I see his blunder
And my chance.

SIMO: Are you dumb?

DAVUS: No. I just wonder
Why you ask me. It's clear some little bird
Told you just what would happen.

SIMO: Not a word.

DAVUS: Don't say your keen brain guessed.

SIMO: Be funny, would you?

DAVUS: You must have heard from someone, sir. How could you
Suspect it otherwise?

SIMO: I knew my man.

DAVUS: That sounds as though you thought this was my plan.

SIMO: I know damn well it was.

DAVUS: You haven't got
My character right at all, sir.

SIMO: Have I not?

DAVUS: No, sir. Whatever tale I start to tell
At once you smell a rat.

SIMO: What should I smell?

DAVUS: Now I daren't breathe a word.

SIMO: One thing I'll bet
There's been no birth here.

DAVUS: You're dead right. And yet
For all that they'll be bringing out a baby.
I'm giving you good notice, sir. Then maybe
You'll not say this was any plot or plan
Of mine. I'd like to better, if I can,
Your bad opinion.

SIMO: Hum! What makes you think
They're going to do this?

DAVUS: I was tipped a wink—

Which I believe, with one thing and another.
Earlier on, she claimed he'd made her a mother,
But this was proved to be a fabrication.
And now, on seeing all the preparation
For a wedding at our house, our sly young woman
Sends off her serving-girl at once to summon
The midwife and to bring some borrowed brat—
The match, of course, being safe till you'd seen that.

SIMO: But why, as soon as you perceived their plan,
Didn't you tell my son?

DAVUS: Am I the man
Or am I not, sir, who first got the lad
Out of her clutches? We all know how mad
He was about her. Now he wants to wed.
So leave all this to me, and go ahead
And have your wedding, and God help—God speed it.

SIMO: No. You go in. Wait there. Get ready what's needed.
I'll follow.
(Davus goes into the house)
                        Well, this fellow's not cajoled me
Into complete belief, though what he told me
May all of it be true. But I don't feel
That matters most. What matters a good deal
Is that my son's committed. He's agreed
To marry. I'll see Chremes now and plead
With him for his agreement. If I win it
The wedding needn't wait another minute.
No time like the present. If Pamphilus tries to get out of it,
Now that he's given a promise, I've no doubt of it
Being justifiable then for me to compel him.
But look there!—just in time for me to tell him—
Chremes! Well, well, and how's the world been treating you?

CHREMES: *(entering)*
Ah, just the man!

SIMO: Same here. What good luck meeting you!

CHREMES: Simo, some folks have been at my house and said
They'd heard from you that your son's going to wed
My daughter, and the wedding is today.
I've come to see who's raving—you or they.

SIMO: Just listen a moment. I'll tell you all you seek
To know and what I'd like—

CHREMES: I'm listening. Speak.

SIMO: In the name of heaven and our old friendship, then,

That's grown as we have grown from boys to men,
For your only daughter's and for my son's sake,
Whom you've been given the chance to make or break,
Please help us, Chremes. Let the marriage planned
Take place.

CHREMES: I can't. Don't ask me. That demand
I simply can't accede to. Have I changed,
Do you suppose, since then, when we arranged
The match between us? If both benefit still,
Send for my daughter. But if more of ill
Than good seems sure for both, I beg you rather,
As though she were your daughter, I his father,
To think what's best for both sides.

SIMO: But I do.
That's just the point. I'd not ask this of you,
Did facts themselves not argue for it.

CHREMES: How?

SIMO: Glycerium and my son have had a row.

CHREMES: Really?

SIMO: I mean it—and on such a scale
I've hopes of parting them.

CHREMES: A likely tale!

SIMO: It's true, all right.

CHREMES: All right, and what's the moral?
Nothing renews love like a lover's quarrel.

SIMO: That's what I'm asking you to help forestall,
While we've still time, while honey's turned to gall.
Let's get him wed before his love-sick heart's
Been moved to pity by these women's arts
And false tears. Once tied down to a married life,
Once used to a decent home, a well-bred wife,
He'll pull himself, I hope, out of this mess.

CHREMES: That's your idea. I've doubts of its success.
He'll not stand by his vows, nor I stand by
And see them broken.

SIMO: You can't tell till you try.

CHREMES: Try, with my daughter's happiness at stake?

SIMO: But what's the worst loss that you stand to make?
We all hope it never happens, of course,
But what does it all add up to? A divorce.
While, if we do reform him, don't you see
How much you'll gain? First you'll have given me,
Your friend, a son back. Secondly you'll draw

A prize yourself, a steady son-in-law,
A good match for your daughter.

CHREMES: Have your way.
If you're convinced this could do all you say,
Well, I'm the last man in the world to thwart you.

SIMO: That's spoken like the man I always thought you!

CHREMES: But tell me one thing.

SIMO: Yes, what is it?

CHREMES: How
Exactly did you find they'd had a row?

SIMO: Davus himself, who's in their every plan,
Said so, and bade me do the best I can
To speed the wedding. Well, do you suppose
You'd catch him doing that, unless he knows
It's what my son wants? You shall hear it, though,
From his own lips. Hallo, in there! Hallo!
Tell Davus to come here outside.
(Enter Davus)

                                    Ah. There!
The man himself.

DAVUS: I was just coming, sir,
To see you.

SIMO: What about?

DAVUS: The bride-to-be.
Why's she not brought? It's getting dark.

SIMO: *(to Chremes)*   You see?
Davus, I've been a wee bit shy of you
So far, in case, as slaves, alas, will do,
Seeing my son's got a girl-friend, you might try
To trip me with some trick or other.

DAVUS: I?

SIMO: That's what I thought. And that unfounded fear
Made me hide something.

DAVUS: What, sir?

SIMO: You shall hear.
I trust you now—almost.

DAVUS: Ah, now you know me.

SIMO: We hadn't fixed this match.

DAVUS: No match? Well, blow me!

SIMO: No. It was all my bluff. You were being tested.

DAVUS: You don't say!

SIMO: Yes, I do.

DAVUS: I never guessed it.

           Well, fancy! What a super-subtle plan!

SIMO: Then, when I'd sent you in, up comes the man
I wanted—there!

DAVUS: *(aside)*   Don't say he's sunk us!

SIMO: So
I told him all that you'd told me.

DAVUS: *(aside)*   Oh, no!

SIMO: I wooed him for his daughter's hand and won it,
Not without difficulty.

DAVUS : *(aside)*   Hell! That's done it!

SIMO: What did you say then?

DAVUS: Me? Well done, I said.

SIMO: As far as we're concerned, we can go ahead.

CHREMES: I'll just go home and tell her to get dressed,
And then report back. *(Exit)*

SIMO: Davus, one small request.
Since you've done more than any other man
To make this match—

DAVUS: *(aside)*   Too true—

SIMO: Do all you can
To bring my son right round.

DAVUS: I'll try—you bet.

SIMO: Now, while he's been provoked's your chance.

DAVUS: Don't fret.

SIMO: Where is he, though?

DAVUS: At home, sir, I expect.

SIMO: I'll go and tell him what I've told you. *(Exit)*

DAVUS: Wrecked!
Ruined! I might as well go straight to the mill.
This is past praying for. If I'd sat still,
Everything would have been all right. But no,
I had to be smart and smash up the whole show.
Fooled my old master, hurled his hopeful son
Into the nuptial noose—that's what I've done,
And fixed the wedding for today—that's more
Than either of them ever bargained for.
But talk of the devil! Oh, I'm done, dished, dead!
A hill, a hill to jump off, on my head!
(Enter Pamphilus)

PAMPHILUS: Where is he? Where's that wretch, that—?

DAVUS: *(aside)*   This is it.

PAMPHILUS: And yet it serves me right, I must admit.
How dumb and helpless can you get? I gave

My life into his hands, a half-wit slave.
I'm paying for my folly. But he'll rue it.
He can't do this to me.

DAVUS: *(aside)*   If I can do it,
If I can get away with this little effort—well,
I'll get away with anything.

PAMPHILUS: What'll I tell
My father now, that, though I gave my word to,
I'm not prepared to marry? How'll I dare to?
How can I have the face? I just don't see
What I can do to save myself.

DAVUS: *(aside)*   Nor me.
God knows I'm trying. I'll say I've got a solution—
That may at least postpone due retribution.

PAMPHILUS: Ah, there!

DAVUS: *(aside)*   He's seen me.

PAMPHILUS: Come here, clever Dick.
Look at me—tripped and trapped by your damned trick!
Well, what have you to say?

DAVUS: I'll get you out.

PAMPHILUS: Will you indeed!

DAVUS: Indeed I will.

PAMPHILUS: No doubt—
The way you've done already.

DAVUS: No, I hope
For better luck next time.

PAMPHILUS: Ripe for a rope,
That's what you are! You want me to believe
That you can put this right, you retrieve
This wreck? I tried you once. Look where I'm heading
Out of safe harbour, hell-bent for a wedding!
Oh, wasn't this exactly my prediction?

DAVUS: Yes, sir.

PAMPHILUS: What are you fit for?

DAVUS: *(ruefully)*   Crucifixion.
But give me a breathing-space, just time to strike
On something.

PAMPHILUS: Time to strike you, as I'd like,
Is what I lack, by God. Time won't allow
Your punishment. I've myself to think of now.

ACT IV

CHARINUS: *(Enter Charinus)*

CHARINUS: *(to himself)*
Oh, it's past words, it's past belief to find
A human being with such a twisted mind,
A nature that gets pleasure out of pain
And mischief, making other's loss his gain.
Can it be true? It is. What's more, the worst
Are those who can't for shame say no at first,
But when their promises should be redeemed
They're forced to show they're not the men they seemed.
They face it out, though, bold as bold can be,
'Well, who are you? Or what are you to me?
Hell, charity begins at home. She's mine.
Give her to you? Why should I?' That's their line.
They gave their word, you say. Well, what about it?
Where shame would be appropriate, they're without it.
They're timid at the wrong time. Well, what now?
Shall I accost him, challenge him, have a row?
That's not much use you say. Ah, but it is.
It helps to ease my feelings and hurt his.
(He goes up to Pamphilus)

PAMPHILUS: Unwittingly, friend, unless the heavens have pity,
I've wrecked us both.

CHARINUS: Unwittingly? That's witty!
You've broken your word because you've found an excuse now
At last.

PAMPHILUS: At last?

CHARINUS: Ah, that smooth line's no use now.

PAMPHILUS: Look here—

CHARINUS: I told you of my love. That drew you.
I judged your heart by mine. I didn't see through you,
Worse luck.

PAMPHILUS: You've got it wrong.

CHARINUS: This was the cream
Of your delight, to play with love's young dream
And lead me up the garden-path. Well—keep her!

PAMPHILUS: Keep her! If you but knew! I'm deeper and deeper
Each moment in the mess. You've no idea.
I'm tied in knots by my damned hangman here
With his bright notions.

CHARINUS: Is it any wonder,

If you're the master that he studies under?

PAMPHILUS: Oh, you'd not talk to me like this if you but knew
My nature or my feelings.

CHARINUS: *(ironically)*   But I do.
Don't tell me. You and your father had a row,
And that's the reason he's so angry now.
Of course he wasn't able to compel you
To accept her hand.

PAMPHILUS: For heavens' sake! I tell you
You don't know half my troubles. No one's hand
Was ever offered to me. No one planned
A marriage in the first place.

CHARINUS: No, of course.
You've been coerced by overwhelming force—
Of your own feelings.

PAMPHILUS: Wait. You still don't know—

CHARINUS: I know you're going to marry her.

PAMPHILUS: No, no!
You'll drive me crazy. Will you listen at least
To what I have to say? He never ceased
Insisting I should say I would get married.
He urged and argued till his point was carried.

CHARINUS: Who?

PAMPHILUS: Davus.

CHARINUS: Davus?

PAMPHILUS: Damn him, yes!

CHARINUS: Why?

PAMPHILUS: Can't say.
I know it wasn't on my lucky day
I listened to him.

CHARINUS: Davus, is this true?

DAVUS: It's true enough.

CHARINUS: Why, you damned rascal, you,
Calmly admitting it! May Heaven send you
What Heaven knows you've earned, a nasty end, you—!
If his enemies wanted the poor man
Tied into nuptial knots, what other plan
Would they propose but this one? Tell me that.

DAVUS: I'll tell you this. I'm floored, but I'm not flat.

CHARINUS: Indeed?

DAVUS: This way we've met with no success.
So what? We'll try another way, unless
You're going to say, because the first shot missed,

This tangle can't be given a lucky twist.

PAMPHILUS: Oh, if you try, I see myself in clover,
Not tied to just one girl, but wed twice over.

DAVUS: Sir, as your man, I'm bound with all my might
To toil, moil, risk my skin, by day and night
For you. If things go contrary to plan,
Why, then, the master must excuse the man.
It's not my labour, it's the fruit that's lacking.
If you can manage better, send me packing.

PAMPHILUS: I'd like to! You restore the status quo,
That's all.

DAVUS: Okay.

PAMPHILUS: At once, though.

DAVUS: Half a mo!
That noise—Glycerium's door!

PAMPHILUS: Not your affair.

DAVUS: I'm on track.

PAMPHILUS: High time.

DAVUS: We'll soon be there.
(Enter Mysis from Glycerium's house, talking to Glycerium inside)

MYSIS: Now, dear, wherever Pamphilus may be,
I'll find him for you without fail, you'll see,
And fetch him here. You mustn't let that fret you.

PAMPHILUS: Mysis!

MYSIS: Who's that? Oh, you! I'm glad I've met you.

PAMPHILUS: What is it?

MYSIS: My young lady sends to say
Please, if you love her, to come straightaway
She's pining for a sight of you.

PAMPHILUS: Damnation!
This is a really frightful situation.
Look at the anguish your intrigues have meant
For her as well as me. Why has she sent?
She's heard that I was getting wed, that's why.

CHARINUS: A sleeping dog that could have been let lie,
If this dog could have done.

DAVUS: Yes, goad him, do,
In case he can't go mad on his own.

MYSIS: It's true.
That is the reason. Oh, it did so grieve her
To hear that news.

PAMPHILUS: Oh, Mysis, I'll not leave her.

Never, I swear, by all the blessed gods,
Not though I find it means my being at odds
With all the world else. She's the girl I chose
And wooed and won—the ideal match. And those
Who want us torn apart can go to hell.
Nothing but death shall part her from me.

MYSIS: Well,
I am relieved.

PAMPHILUS: No answer from the shrine
Of Phoebus is more firm than this of mine.
If I can manage not to have my father
Blame me for ruining this match, I'd rather.
If not, I'll do—what shouldn't take much doing—
Make him responsible for its ruin.
(to Charinus)
Now what do you think of me?

CHARINUS: Oh, you're a man—
In as big a mess as I am.

DAVUS: I've a plan—
Somewhere.

PAMPHILUS: That's great. When you start trying—wow!

DAVUS: This one will work. Just wait.

PAMPHILUS: I want it now.

DAVUS: Got it!!

CHARINUS: What is it?

DAVUS: Oh, it's not for you.
Don't think it. It's for him.

CHARINUS: Well, that might do.

PAMPHILUS: Well?

DAVUS: I've not time to tell you. I must hurry.
Will one day see this job through? That's my worry.
You two are in my way here. Clear off, do, sir.

PAMPHILUS: I'll go and see Glycerium. *(Exit)*

DAVUS: Good! And you, sir?
Where are you off to?

CHARINUS: *(resentfully)*   Well, if you want to know—

DAVUS: Of course. And now begins a tale of woe.

CHARINUS: Well, what's to happen to me?

DAVUS: Have you the face
To ask that? I've won you a breathing-space
At least as long as I put off this marriage.
Is that a contribution to disparage?

CHARINUS: But, Davus—

DAVUS: Well?
CHARINUS: If she could be my wife—
DAVUS: I never heard such rubbish in my life.
CHARINUS: But come to me at once if you've found a way—
DAVUS: Why should I when I haven't?
CHARINUS: Ah, but say
You find one later?
DAVUS: All right. If I do
I'll come.
CHARINUS: I'll be at home. *(Exit)*
DAVUS: Now, Mysis, you
Just wait out here a moment. I've a visit
To pay to your young mistress.
MYSIS: Why? What is it?
DAVUS: A matter of urgency.
MYSIS: All right. But hurry.
DAVUS: Oh, I'll be back in no time, don't you worry.
(Exit into Glycerium's house)
MYSIS: One can be sure of nothing, that's God's truth.
I thought she had a treasure in this youth,
A friend, a lover, and a man, prepared
For every situation. But, my word,
What misery he's made for her! There's more
Of bad about it now than good before
By a long chalk, I must say.
(Davus comes out of a house with a child)
                                But there's Davus
Just coming out. Eh, what's all this? God save us,
Where are you off to with that child?
DAVUS: Now, Mysis,
Get your whole bag of tricks out. It's a crisis.
MYSIS: What are you up to?
DAVUS: Take this child and set him
Outside our door.
MYSIS: What, on the ground?
DAVUS: Well, get him
Some greenery from the altar there and strew it
Under him.
MYSIS: But why me? Why can't you do it?
DAVUS: I want to be able honestly to swear,
If need be, that I never put him there.
MYSIS: Well, that's a novel scruple. You should worry
About an oath or two!

DAVUS: You'll have to hurry.
I want to explain my plan. Damnation!
MYSIS: What?
DAVUS: Enter bride's father. Drop first draft of plot.
MYSIS: What are you talking about?
DAVUS: I'm going to make
My entrance from the right. Now mind you take
Your cues at the right time and come in pat.
MYSIS: Well, though I'm sure I don't know what you're at,
If you've a plan and want me to support it
I'll stay and try. God knows I wouldn't thwart it.
(Davus goes out on one side as Chremes enters on the other)
CHREMES: All that was wanted for my daughter's wedding
I've now provided for, so back I'm heading
For Simo's house, to bid them send and summon
The bride. What's this? Good God! A child! You, woman,
Did you put this child here?
MYSIS: Oh, dear! Where's Davus?
CHREMES: Well, can't you answer?
MYSIS: Oh, he's gone! God save us!
He's left me, vanished!
(Davus comes in, as if from the town)
DAVUS: Lord, I never saw
Such crowds in the city! And the courts of law!
So crammed with clients! And the bread—what prices!
(aside)
I've dried up.
MYSIS: Why did you leave me here?
DAVUS: *(loudly)*   Why, Mysis,
Where's he from? What's the game? Who brought the brat?
MYSIS: You must be off your head to ask me that.
DAVUS: Whom should I ask? There's no one else in sight.
CHREMES: *(aside)*
Where can it come from?
DAVUS: *(seizing Mysis)*   Well?
MYSIS: Ow!
DAVUS: *(aside)*   Further right.
Move over.
MYSIS: You're crazy. Didn't you just before—?
DAVUS: *(aside)*
Answer my questions, not a syllable more!
(aloud)
Abuse me, would you? Where did you get that brat?

      (aside)
      Loud, now.
MYSIS: From our house.
DAVUS: Ha, ha! Listen to that!
      Your type will stick at nothing.
CHREMES: *(aside)*   Ah! I see.
      The Andrian girl's maid—that's who this must be.
DAVUS: Do we look mugs enough for that old trick?
CHREMES: *(aside)*
      I've come at the right moment.
DAVUS: *(aloud)*   Come on. Quick.
      Take that child off our doorstep. *(aside)* Not so fast, you.
      Don't move an inch from here just now.
MYSIS: Oh, blast you1
      You've got me scared stiff.
DAVUS: *(aloud)*   Am I talking to you
      Or not?
MYSIS: What do you want?
DAVUS: You don't know, do you?
      Come off it! Who's the father of that brat
      You dumped down on our doorstep? Tell me that.
MYSIS: You know.
DAVUS: *(aside)* Shut up about my knowing. Answer.
      (aloud)
      Whose is it?
MYSIS: It belongs to your young man, sir.
DAVUS: What young man? Who?
MYSIS: Why, Pamphilus.
CHREMES: *(aside)*   Eh?
DAVUS: What?
      Pamphilus' child?
MYSIS: Well, can you say it's not?
CHREMES: *(aside)*
      I didn't want this match, and I was right.
DAVUS: Outrageous!
MYSIS: What are you shouting for?
DAVUS: Last night
      I saw this brat being smuggled in.
MYSIS: Oh, you—!
      How dare you say a thing like that!
DAVUS: It's true.
      I spied the midwife's extra bulk and girth.
MYSIS: Thank God we had some witness of the birth,

Freeborn Athenians.

DAVUS: She doesn't know the man
For whom she's engineered this little plan.
'If Chremes sees that child laid at our door,'
She thinks, 'He won't be willing any more
To give his daughter's hand to Pamphilus.' Rot!
He'll damn well be more willing.

CHREMES: *(aside)* He will not!

DAVUS: Trick after trick! I hear you're spreading it round now
That she's Athenian born.

CHREMES: *(aside)* Eh?

DAVUS: 'He'll be bound now
By law to marry her.' That's the latest.

MYSIS: Well,
Wasn't she born here?

CHREMES: *(aside)* Hum! I nearly fell
Into a pretty kettle of fish.

DAVUS: *(pretending surprise)* Who's that?
Oh, Chremes, you, sir. Oh, you come just pat.
There's something you must hear.

CHREMES: Thank you, I've heard
Everything.

DAVUS: Everything, sir?

CHREMES: Yes, every word.
Right from the start.

DAVUS: You have? Well, it's appalling,
Isn't it? Why, this woman, she wants hauling
Off to the rack. *(To Mysis)* That's him. Don't think Davus
Is simply having fun and games.

MYSIS: God save us!
By all that's holy, now, I never lied, sir.

CHREMES: Quietly! I know all. Is Simo there?

DAVUS: Inside, sir.
(Chremes goes into Simo's house)

MYSIS: Don't touch me, rogue! If I don't tell her now—

DAVUS: Fool, don't you see what's happened?

MYSIS: Where? When? How?

DAVUS: That's the bride's father. I'd no other way
To tell him what I wished.

MYSIS: Why couldn't you say?

DAVUS: So that you'd act on impulse, from the heart.
Nature convinces more than conscious art.
(Enter Crito)

CRITO: This is the street where Chrysis lived, they say,
    Who, rather than stay poor the honest way
    At home, preferred to get rich here instead
    The not so honest way. Well, now she's dead,
    Her property comes to me. But there I see
    Someone to ask. Good day.

MYSIS: No! can it be?
    Not Chrysis' cousin, Crito. Yes!

CRITO: Why, Mysis!
    How are you?

MYSIS: Hope you're well, sir.

CRITO: And so Chrysis—?

MYSIS: Yes, gone, and left us in a sorry plight.

CRITO: How goes it? How do you manage here? All right?

MYSIS: Us, sir? So, so. We live as best we may,
    Since as we'd like, we mayn't, sir, as they say.

CRITO: Glycerium—has she found her parents here?

MYSIS: Oh, no such luck!

CRITO: Not even yet? Oh, dear!
    It's by an ill wind, then, that I was blown
    To Athens. I'd never have come here if I'd known.
    It was as Chrysis' sister that everyone knew her.
    She's got her goods. And if I tried to sue her,
    How easy, as a foreigner, I'd find it
    And how effective, I am well reminded
    By other cases. And she'll have, no doubt,
    Some friend as champion. For, when she set out
    From home, she was no child. Damned pettifogger
    They'll call me, beggarly inheritance-hogger.
    And anyway I wouldn't want to fleece her.

MYSIS: You're a good sort, a fine, old-fashioned piece, sir.

CRITO: Well, since I've come, take me to see her.

MYSIS: Right.

DAVUS: *(aside)*
    I'll follow, to keep out of Simo's sight. *(Exeunt)*

ACT V

(Enter, after a short pause, Chremes and Simo)

CHREMES: I've proved my friendship, and run risks for you
Often enough. Don't ask for more. I'm through.
Just to oblige you, I damned nearly wrecked
My daughter's life.

SIMO: But all that I expect,
And more than ever must insist be done,
Is that on one good service well-begun
In words your actions now should set the seal.

CHREMES: You're blinded with excess of fatherly zeal.
So long as your point's gained, you just can't see
Where charity ends, or what you're asking me.
For if you could, you wouldn't overwhelm me
With these unfair demands.

SIMO: Unfair? How? Tell me.

CHREMES: How can you ask? You talked me into giving
My daughter to a young man who's now living
With and for someone else, and wants no wife—
Condemning her, that is, to endless strife
And to a marriage neither safe nor sure.
Her tears, her sufferings were to work his cure.
You got your wish. I went your way, as long
As facts would let me. Now facts are too strong.
The girl's Athenian by birth, they say.
They've had a child. So—you can go your way
And I'll go mine.

SIMO: For God's sake, now, don't credit
Such a ridiculous rumour. Those who spread it
Have every interest in seeing my son
Made black as black can be. It's all been done,
Designed, directed, at our match, to stop it.
Deprive their game of motive and they'll drop it.

CHREMES: You're quite mistaken. I myself just now
Saw Davus and her servant have a row.

SIMO: No doubt.

CHREMES: With genuine expressions, though,
Neither aware that I was there.

SIMO: I know.
He'd warned me they'd be up to some such plot.
I'd meant to tell you. Somehow I forgot.

(Enter Davus, talking to someone inside Glycerium's house)

DAVUS: Be easy now.
SIMO: There's Davus now!
CHREMES: And where
        Has he just come from?
DAVUS: *(as before)*   You're in my good care
        And our new friend's.
SIMO: *(to himself)*   Now what's the rogue contriving?
DAVUS: *(to himself)*
        A most convenient visitor that, arriving
        Just in the nick.
SIMO: In the nick? Who? Gods and gallows!
        Whom does he mean?
DAVUS: *(as before)*   Our ship's now safe in shallows.
SIMO: I'll tackle him.
DAVUS: *(as before)*   The boss! What do I do?
SIMO: How are you, my fine fellow?
DAVUS: What, sir? You?
        And you, sir? Everything's ready now inside.
SIMO: You've done a good job haven't you?
DAVUS: Send for the bride
        Soon as you like.
SIMO: Of course. That's all we miss.
        (friendly)
        What are you up to, eh? What is all this?
DAVUS: Up to, sir? Me, sir?
SIMO: Pah! You heard me.
DAVUS: Me?
SIMO: Yes, you.
DAVUS: Well, I just stepped inside, you see—
SIMO: I do not wish to know that!
DAVUS: —with your son.
SIMO: What? He's in there? This is the end! We're done.
        You rascal, didn't you say they'd had a row?
DAVUS: They have, sir.
SIMO: Oh? Then what's he doing there now?
CHREMES: Wrangling, of course.
DAVUS: Oh, no. But if you please, sir,
        I've got a shocking story. Some old geezer
        Has turned up, cunning as the devil, bold
        As brass, yet looking worth his weight in gold,
        So serious, solemn, plausible.
SIMO: What plot,
        What tale have you got hold of?

DAVUS: His.
SIMO: Being what?
DAVUS: He says he knows for certain that by birth
       Glycerium's an Athenian.
SIMO: Heaven and earth!
       (shouting)
       Dromo! Hi, Dromo!
DAVUS: Dromo? What's that for?
SIMO: Dromo!
DAVUS: Now listen, sir.
SIMO: Say one word more—
       Dromo!
DAVUS: Please!
       (Enter Dromo, a large, burly slave)
DROMO: Yes, sir.
SIMO: Come on. Shoulder-high.
       In with him.
DROMO: Who, sir?
SIMO: Davus.
DAVUS: What for? Why?
SIMO: Because I say so. Seize him. Quick! Inside!
DAVUS: What have I done?
SIMO: In!
DAVUS: If you find I've lied,
       I'll let you kill me.
SIMO: I'm not listening, you—!
       I'll shake you!
DAVUS: Even if my story's true?
SIMO: Yes, even then. Now truss him up—you know—
       Calf-wise, and mind you keep him safe. There! Go!
       (Dromo hauls Davus off)
       Lord, if I live, I'll show what risks you run
       Cheating your master—the same goes for my son
       In there, by God.
CHREMES: Now, Simo, not so wild!
SIMO: Oh, don't you pity me? Such a dutiful child!
       Such labour lost on such a graceless son!
       What, Pamphilus, don't you blush for what you've done?
       Hi, Pamphilus, here!
PAMPHILUS: *(entering)*   Who wants me? Hell! My father!
SIMO: What's that, you—
CHREMES: No, face him with bare facts, rather.
       Leave the bad names.

SIMO: What name could be too bad
For this young good-for-nothing? So, my lad,
Glycerium's an Athenian?
PAMPHILUS: So I'm told.
SIMO: You're—! Oh, did you see anything so bold?
Does he care what he says, feel what he's done,
Show in his face one trace of shame? A son
So hardened as to flout his father's will
And laws and moral codes, determined still
To keep that girl and live in utter shame!
PAMPHILUS: Oh, I'm so wretched!
SIMO: Wretched's the right name,
You've found that out, eh? But it's then, not now,
Then, when you set your heart, no matter how,
On having your desires, it fitted best.
But what the hell! Why should I be distressed,
Why wear myself into a shadow, why
Plague my old age with your mad tricks? Am I
To pay for his faults? Let him have her—rather
Go hang with her. I've done.
PAMPHILUS: Oh, my dear father.
SIMO: Dear father! Do you need your father still,
With house, wife, child—all got against his will?
PAMPHILUS: Father, a word, please.
SIMO: What words have you got?
CHREMES: Now, Simo, hear him all the same.
SIMO: Hear what?
Why should I?
CHREMES: Listen to him none the less.
SIMO: All right, then, speak.
PAMPHILUS: I love her, I confess.
If that's a sin, I own it. In your hands
I place myself. Lay on me what commands
You like, what burdens. You want me now to marry,
Give up the girl I love. That cross I'll carry
As best I can. But, father, don't believe
I had that old man brought here to deceive.
Please let me fetch him out and prove that's so.
SIMO: Fetch him?
PAMPHILUS: Please, father.
CHREMES: Well, that's fair, you know.
Let him produce the fellow.
PAMPHILUS: Yes, please, father.

SIMO: All right.
      (Pamphilus goes into Glycerium's house)
                I can face almost anything rather
      Than find he's fooling me.
CHREMES: Ah, with one's son
      Light penalties satisfy, whatever he's done.
      (Enter Pamphilus and Crito)
CRITO: When each of three good reasons prompts me to it,
      You haven't got to beg this, lad. I'll do it
      For you, for Glycerium, and for truth's own sake.
CHREMES: Crito of Andros here? Yes. No mistake.
CRITO: How are you, Chremes?
CHREMES: What caused this rare visit?
CRITO: Oh, it just happened. This is Simo, is it?
CHREMES: Yes.
CRITO: Did you want to see me?
SIMO: Look here, you!
      You say Glycerium's an Athenian?
CRITO: True.
      Do you deny it?
SIMO: Come all ready, eh?
CRITO: For what?
SIMO: For what? You think you'll get away
      With this fine talk, enticing to their ruin
      Well-bred young men who don't know what they're doing,
      Inducing and seducing with soft soap
      Their soft heads.
CRITO: Are you crazy?
SIMO: So you hope
      To knit a sordid love affair together
      With nuptial knots?
PAMPHILUS: *(aside)*   Oh, dear! I'm doubtful whether
      Our friend will hold his ground.
CHREMES: Look, if you knew
      This gentleman, you'd see this can't be true.
      Why, he's the soul of honesty.
SIMO: Honesty, is it?
      Did honesty inspire this well-timed visit
      By one who never crossed our path before he
      Turned up for my son's wedding. A tall story!
PAMPHILUS: If I weren't scared of my father, I've a cue
      That I could give our friend.
SIMO: You swindler, you!

CRITO: What's that you said?

CHREMES: Don't mind him. That's his way.

CRITO: Then let him mend it. If he's going to say
Just what he likes to me, well, he'll be hearing
Things he won't like. Look! I'm not interfering
Or starting anything. It's your affair
How sensibly and patiently you bear
Your troubles. Whether what I say is so
Can soon be settled. Many years ago
A man from Attica, whose ship went down,
Was thrown up on the shore just near our town;
With him that girl, a child then. In his need
He turned to Chrysis' father first.

SIMO: Indeed?
He's telling a good tale.

CHREMES: Well, let him tell.

CRITO: With all this interruption?

CHREMES: Go on.

CRITO: Well,
Her father took him in. We were related,
And I was present when the stranger stated
He came from Attica. He breathed his last
In that same house.

CHREMES: His name?

CRITO: His name? Now, not so fast.

PAMPHILUS: *(aside)*
Don't say we're sunk.

CRITO: Well now, I think his name
Was Phania, but I know he said he came
From Rhamnus.

CHREMES: Heavens!

CRITO: Many others, too,
In Andros heard this.

CHREMES: May my hopes come true!
The child—did he say she was his own? Or not?

CRITO: No.

CHREMES: Whose?

CRITO: His brother's.

CHREMES: Mine! She's mine!

SIMO: Eh? What?

PAMPHILUS: Hey, Pamphilus, prick your ears up.

SIMO: Yours? How so?

CHREMES: I had a brother Phania.

SIMO: Yes, I know.
                   I knew him.
CHREMES: As a war-time refugee
                   From Athens he set out to join me
                   In Asia. Well, he couldn't leave behind
                   His niece. Now, after all these years, I find
                   What happened to him.
PAMPHILUS: I'm completely dazed.
                   First fear, then hope, then sheer delight. I'm mazed
                   By my so sudden stroke of luck. Oh, boy!
SIMO: Well, well, on every count I'm full of joy
                   That she should prove your child.
PAMPHILUS: You've said it, father.
CHREMES: There's only one small point that worries me rather.
PAMPHILUS: *(aside)*
                   Oh, bother that old bore with his small points!
                   Give him a bulrush and he'll look for joints.
CRITO: What's wrong?
CHREMES: Her name—
CRITO: Ah yes, when she was small
                   She had another.
CHREMES: What? Can you recall?
CRITO: I'm trying to.
PAMPHILUS: Oh, Lord! Must I allow
                   His memory to hold up my happiness now,
                   When I've the remedy? No! Sir, sir—the name
                   You want's Pasiphila.
CRITO: So it is!
CHREMES: The same!
PAMPHILUS: I've heard it from her scores of times.
SIMO: *(to Chremes)*   Well, you, sir,
                   I'm sure, know we're all glad at this.
CHREMES: I do, sir.
PAMPHILUS: Well, father?
SIMO: Well, events appear, my lad,
                   To have made us friends again, eh?
PAMPHILUS: Dear old dad!
                   And you, sir, Fortune having managed to mate us,
                   I take it you won't want to change our status?
CHREMES: No, a clear case—unless there's something your father
                   Would like to know.
PAMPHILUS: *(with a paying-out gesture)*

	About the—?
SIMO:	Yes, I would, rather.
CHREMES:	The dowry is ten talents.
PAMPHILUS:	Done!
CHREMES:	Let's go.

I must see my daughter. She won't know me, though!
Crito, come with me. *(Exeunt)*

SIMO: And I must see my daughter.
Isn't it time that someone went and brought her?

PAMPHILUS: You're right, dad. I'll give Davus that commission.

SIMO: You can't.

PAMPHILUS: Why not?

SIMO: He's got his own position
To think of. He's a bit tied.

PAMPHILUS: Tied?

SIMO: With rope.

PAMPHILUS: That's a bit hard.

SIMO: Well, it's not soft, I hope.

PAMPHILUS: Please set him free.

SIMO: All right.

PAMPHILUS: Without delay?

SIMO: I'm going. *(Exit)*

PAMPHILUS: Oh, what a lovely, lucky day!
(Enter Charinus)

CHARINUS: *(to himself)*
I've come along to find out how it goes
With Pamphilus. There he is!

PAMPHILUS: *(to himself)*   Well, I suppose
Some chaps might think I mightn't think this true.
But true's the way I want it. In my view
Gods live for ever just because they're sure
Of joy. My immortality's secure—
Unless some petty human irritation
Disturbs my happiness. Whom, of all creation,
Would I most wish to come upon the scene now
To share my news?

CHARINUS: *(to himself)*   What happiness does he mean now?

PAMPHILUS: There's Davus. No one better. My keen pleasure
No one but he could share in such full measure.
(Enter Davus)

DAVUS: Where's Pamphilus? Ow!

PAMPHILUS: Hi, Davus!

DAVUS: Who's that? Oh!

PAMPHILUS: It's me.

DAVUS: Oh, Pamphilus!

PAMPHILUS: Ah, you don't know
The strokes of luck I've had.

DAVUS: No, I do not.
I only know the unlucky strokes I got.

PAMPHILUS: Yes, I had heard.

DAVUS: That's life. Of my bad luck
You learn before I learn what good you've struck.

PAMPHILUS: My little Glycerium's found her family.

DAVUS: Fine.

CHARINUS: *(aside)*
What's that?

PAMPHILUS: Her father's a great friend of mine.

DAVUS: Who?

PAMPHILUS: Chremes.

DAVUS: Marvellous!

PAMPHILUS: Now no mischance
Can mar our marriage.

CHARINUS: *(aside)*   Is he in a trance,
Having a wish-fulfilment session, maybe?

PAMPHILUS: And then our child—

DAVUS: I know. The luckiest baby
Alive of course.

CHARINUS: *(aside)*   I'm saved if this is true.
I'll speak to them.

PAMPHILUS: Who's that? Charinus! You!
The man I wanted to meet!

CHARINUS: Congratulations!

PAMPHILUS: You've heard?

CHARINUS: The lot. And now your situation's
So satisfactory, spare a thought for me.
You're Chremes' blue-eyed boy, he's bound to agree
With anything you suggest.

PAMPHILUS: You're borne in mind,
And waiting for him to emerge I find
Distinctly tedious. Come along inside.
He's with Glycerium. Davus, we've a bride
To be brought over. So off home at the double,
And send an escort for her. What's the trouble?
What's keeping you?

DAVUS: *(groaning)*   I'm going.

(Pamphilus and Charinus go inside. Davus turns to the audience)

Don't hang about
Waiting for bride and bridegroom to come out.
The marriage ceremony will take place indoors—
And anything after it.

PRODUCER: So, please, applause!

ALTERNATIVE ENDING

PAMPHILUS: You're borne in mind.
But look! Just what I wanted, nicely timed!
The old man's coming out. Get out of the way
A minute.

CHARINUS: Davus, we'll withdraw.

DAVUS: Okay.

(Enter Chremes)

PAMPHILUS: Sir, I've been waiting for you, to discuss
Something which touches you much more than us.
In case you think I had forgotten, however,
Your other daughter, I've made some endeavour
And I believe I've found a husband here
Worthy of you and your child.

CHARINUS: *(aside)* Oh, dear!
Davus, my love, my life is now at stake!

CHREMES: Young man, the proposal that you're trying to make
Is nothing new to me, if I'd been ready
To entertain it.

CHARINUS: *(aside)* Oh, I'm done for!

DAVUS: *(aside)* Steady!

CHARINUS: *(aside)*
There's no hope!

CHREMES: Let me explain my objection.
It wasn't any sort of marriage-connection
With that young man.

CHARINUS: *(aside)* Eh?

DAVUS: *(aside)* Hush, and listen!

CHREMES: But rather
The friendship handed down to me and your father
By our own fathers made me very keen
To see our children keep it growing as green
As ever. But—I am by no means loth

Now chance allows me, to oblige you both.
She's his.

PAMPHILUS: Three cheers!

DAVUS: *(to Charinus)*   Go on, express your gratitude.

CHARINUS: Oh, sir, my best of friends, your generous attitude
Gives me more joy than I can say, not merely
Because you grant my wish. You show so clearly
That all the friendly feelings you first had
Were never changed. That really makes me glad.

PAMPHILUS: Well, naturally you'll now be keen to show him
All your respect, and then you'll really know him.

CHREMES: We were at odds, but I was well aware
Of your true character.

PAMPHILUS: I'm sure you were
From my experience of your wisdom.

CHREMES: There, now!
My daughter Philumena's hand I hereby declare now,
Together with ten talents dowry yours.
Anything further will take place indoors.

PRODUCER: Clap, please!

The Self-Tormentor

The Self-Tormentor

CHARACTERS

CHREMES: an old man
MENEDEMUS: an old man, his neighbour
CLITIPHO: a young man, son of Chremes
CLINIA: a young man, son of Menedemus
SYRUS: a slave of Chremes
DROMO: a slave of Menedemus
BACCHIS: a courtesan
ANTIPHILA: a young woman
SOSTRATA: wife of Chremes
CANTHARA: old nurse in Chremes' household
PHRYGIA: a maid of Bacchis

PROLOGUE

*(spoken by the actor manager, Lucius Ambivius Turpio, who acts the part
of Menedemus in the play)*

'Why has the author given a young man's task,
The prologue, to an old man?' you may ask.
I'll start there, then say the rest of my piece.
A quite fresh play, from its fresh source in Greece,
Entitled *The Man Who Punished Himself* is what
We're about to produce—except its single plot
Has been made a double one. I've said it's new,
I've given its name. I'd give the author's too,
And that of the original Greek poet,
Did I not think you mostly already know it.[1]
Now I'll explain why this task's fallen to me
In brief. What the author's written is really a plea
And not the usual prologue. He has made you
His court, and me the counsel meant to persuade you,
If only his apt thoughts and skill in framing them

1 Menander.

In words are matched by my power in proclaiming them.
First for the spiteful rumours spread, which say
Our author's rarely written a Roman play
But often with Greek plays made one of two,
This he admits he's done and means to do,
Being unrepentant. He has precedents set him
By certain eminent authors, which should let him,
He feels, do as they did. As for the item
That old hack[2] harps upon ad infinitum,
About our man so very suddenly trying
His hand at writing and allegedly relying
On his friends' powers and not his own abilities,
The judgement's yours. Your wisdom and your will it is
Which shall prevail. To them I'm now appealing.
Let fair words, not unfair ones, sway your feeling.
Be fair yourselves. Give scope for growth to those
Who give *you* chances of seeing some new shows
Free from old faults. By which I do not mean
To excuse the playwright who recently had a scene
In which a slave ran amok in a public street
And everyone fled before him. Do we treat
Madmen as masters? Of that author's blunders
Our playwright promises to report fresh wonders
Next time he has a new play to produce,
Unless the opposition cease their abuse.
Please listen, please be fair, and please—be quiet.
Allow me to present you—not a riot,
But static-dramatic art. Those roles uproarious
Let me exchange for something less laborious,
No record runs of slaves, no record hungers
Of hangers-on, no mercenary flesh-mongers,
Angry old men or shameless sharks. My trust is
Knowing me, you'll acknowledge it's no more than justice
To lighten my load a little at this stage.
Writers of new plays never spare my age.
To me they run with all the real hard stuff,
And try some other troupe with tasks less tough.
This play is one of words, well-chosen—a test
Which may decide what suits my talents best.
So—make me an example to the rest,
Self-punished perhaps. And let our young men learn
It's *your* praise, not their own, they've got to earn.

2 Luscius of Lanuvium.

*Scene: a country road near Athens, showing the houses of Chremes and
Menedemus with doors opening on to the road and plots of cultivated
ground behind and at the side of each house.*

ACT I

> *(The time is towards evening. Menedemus is working hard
> with a mattock. Enter Chremes)*

CHREMES: Though our acquaintance is of recent date,
Beginning, indeed, when you bought the adjoining estate
To mine, and nothing more has passed between us,
Yet what I see of your character, Menedemus,
And the mere fact—which comes a very close second
To real friendship, or so I've always reckoned—
Of our being neighbours, makes me—well, so bold,
So intimate, as to ask, aren't you too old
To work like this? Your means can't really demand it.
Then why, for God's sake? I don't understand it.
What's it all for? You're sixty—more, my guess is—
And surely no man in these parts possesses
A finer farm—that soil's worth a pretty penny—
You've plenty of slaves. Yet, as though you hadn't any,
You take on every sort of task and fairly
Slave-drive yourself. I never leave so early
Or come back so late but you're to be found
Whenever I come past this piece of ground
Digging and ploughing, fetching and carrying hard,
Never a moment's respite, no regard
For your own comfort. You can't be doing it for fun.
One *can* get sick seeing how little's done
By the slaves. But, damn it, the trouble you're now taking
To do the job yourself, if spent on making
Your labourers do it, would go further.

MENEDEMUS: Sir,
Are you so free, with so much time to spare
From your own business that you bother so
With things that don't at all concern you?

CHREMES: *(complacently)*   No.
But I'm a man, and what any human being
Does or experiences I can't help seeing
As my concern. Regard me as either adviser
Or questioner, ready to learn if your way's wiser,
Or put you right.

MENEDEMUS: I go the way I must.
Go yours, and do as *you* think right and just.
CHREMES: Must any man punish himself like this?
MENEDEMUS: Yes, I!
CHREMES: I'm sorry if you're really in trouble. But why?
What have you done to hate yourself like this?
MENEDEMUS: Oh, God!
CHREMES: What? Tears? Come now. Whatever's amiss,
Out with it. Trust *me*, now. Count on my aid—
Cash, comfort, advice—what's needed. Don't be afraid.
MENEDEMUS: You want to hear?
CHREMES: I do, for the reason I gave.
MENEDEMUS: All right.
CHREMES: But wait. Down tools! Stop being a slave
For a minute.
MENEDEMUS: No!
CHREMES: But why—?
MENEDEMUS: Please let me be.
I don't want to be left one moment free.
CHREMES: I'm not going to allow it, I tell you straight.
MENEDEMUS: This isn't right.
CHREMES: *(wresting the tools from him)*
                       Good God, man, what a weight!
MENEDEMUS: No worse than I deserve for what I've done.
CHREMES: Now tell me all about it.
MENEDEMUS: I have one son,
In his late teens. Have, did I say? I had.
Now whether I have a son or not, poor lad,
I just don't know.
CHREMES: How's that?
MENEDEMUS: The tale's soon told.
A young girl, with her mother, who was old
And penniless, arrived from Corinth. She came,
He saw, and was conquered completely. In all but name
They were man and wife. Of all this never a word
Was said to me. When, in the end, I heard,
I treated him with no trace of fellow-feeling,
The sympathy that's really needed in dealing
With love-sick youth, but in the forceful way
Fathers so often use. Day after day
I nagged at him. I said, 'Do you hope, my lad,
To be allowed, as long as I, your dad,
Am still above ground, to lead this sort of life,

Keeping that wench as though she were a wife?
If you think *that*, you couldn't be more wrong.
Clinia, you don't know me. You're mine, as long
As you behave decently. Otherwise, my son,
I'll have to make up my mind what's going to be done
With you. Your trouble, Clinia, is too much leisure.
At your age I'd no eyes for amorous pleasure.
Need drove me to Asia. I earned my bit of laurel
And made my fortune fighting.' I was so moral!
Result—the poor lad beaten down by dint
Of heavy, one-string harping took the hint.
Age, obviously, was more experienced, wiser
Than youth, his father a well-informed advisor.
So—off to be a soldier of the king
He went, to Asia.

CHREMES: What?

MENEDEMUS: Without saying a thing
To me, and now he's been three months away.

CHREMES: You're both to blame. Yet that act did display
Conscience, and enterprise, in your young man.

MENEDEMUS: Some friends, to whom he had confided his plan,
Told me. I came home, miserable, half out
Of my mind with worry, full of sickening doubt.
I sat down. Slaves ran up at once, to draw
My shoes off for me. Other slaves I saw
Bustling about to get the couches laid,
The dinner ready, all rushing to my aid,
All anxious to relieve my sorrow. The sight
Of all this set me thinking. 'Is it right',
I asked myself, 'for all these people here
To be so concerned for my sake, their sole fear
That there could be some comfort I might lack?
Must all these women work to clothe my back?
Shall I, alone at home, have all this done,
This spent, on me, while there's my only son,
Who ought to have as much—to tell the truth,
More, since it can be more enjoyed by youth,
Driven out by my intolerance? If I do,
All ills that flesh is heir to are my due.'
No sooner said than done. I sold out quick,
Stripping my house of every stitch and stick.
My servants, man and maid, in one clean sweep,
Apart from those who were able to earn their keep

By farm-work, I dispose of, advertised
The house itself for sale, and realized
Round about fifty talents. Then I bought
This land, and here I work—hard. For I thought
By suffering to make the wrong I did
Less by that much. I feel I must forbid
Myself all leisure till I know the boy's
Back safe, if ever that happens, to share my joys.

CHREMES: You're obviously by nature not made to act
The heavy father. And your son, with tact
And proper treatment, would prove a biddable youth.
You never knew each other—that's the truth—
Not properly, I mean. And in such cases
Life on both sides is built on a false basis.
You never let him see how much you cared,
And he for his part simply never dared
Confide in you entirely, as a son
Should with a father. If that *had* been done,
All this would never have happened.

MENEDEMUS: There, you've hit it.
I went completely wrong there, I admit it.

CHREMES: But, Menedemus, I see every ground
To trust and hope you'll have him safe and sound
At home again, and soon.

MENEDEMUS: God send it so.

CHREMES: He will, you may be sure. And now, you know,
If you don't mind, it's Dionysus' feast.
Do come and spend today with me at least.

MENEDEMUS: I can't.

CHREMES: Why not? Do give yourself a break.
That's the line your son, if he were here, would take.

MENEDEMUS: No, I've doomed *him* to danger and hard work.
It isn't right that I myself should shirk.

CHREMES: You're adamant?

MENEDEMUS: Adamant.

CHREMES: Well, good-bye.

MENEDEMUS: Good-bye. *(Exit)*

CHREMES: I'm sorry for him. He really made me cry.
My neighbour Phania's late. I must remind him
He's coming to dinner, if only I can find him.
(Goes off for a moment to Phania's house, returns)
Well, no reminder was needed, it seems. They said he
Had been at my house quite a time already.

I'm keeping my own guests waiting. I must go in.
But what's happening at our front door? Quite a din!
I'll step aside and see who's coming out.
(He does so. Clitipho comes out, talking to someone inside)

CLITIPHO: Look, Clinia, there's nothing to worry about.
They're still not even late. You'll see her arrive
With your messenger in no time. Why contrive
To punish yourself with pointless fears? Don't fret!

CHREMES: *(aside)*
Who's my son talking to?

CLITIPHO: *(aside)*   My dad! Well met!
I'll tackle him. Dad, you're the man we want!

CHREMES: How so?
What has made *me* so welcome?

CLITIPHO: Well, do you know
Our neighbour, Menedemus?

CHREMES: Yes, my lad.

CLITIPHO: You know he has a son?

CHREMES: I'd heard he had . . .
In Asia.

CLITIPHO: No, dad. At our house.

CHREMES: What? How?

CLITIPHO: I met him when he disembarked just now
And brought him home to dinner. He and I
Have been firm friends since we were that high.

CHREMES: Why,
What wonderful news! I only wish I'd pressed
His father harder, and made him be my guest.
And then, before anyone else, I'd have been able
To serve his fine surprise at my own table.
But what am I saying? There's still time.

CLITIPHO: No, wait!
I wouldn't do *that*.

CHREMES: Why not?

CLITIPHO: He's in such a state,
He doesn't know what to do. He's just got here
A minute ago. He's full of doubt and fear
Of his father's anger, and how his girl-friend feels
Towards him now. You see, he's head over heels
In love. That started it. That's what made him go
And leave home in the first place.

CHREMES: Yes, I know.

CLITIPHO: He's sent a slave down to the city just now
To fetch her. I sent Syrus with them.

CHREMES: And how
              Does he see his situation?
CLITIPHO: Pretty grim.
CHREMES: Indeed? You'll not find many as lucky as him.
              His family and country are safe. And what on earth
              Does *he* lack of what men call assets? Birth,
              Wealth, friends, relations—he's every ground for gratitude.
              But all these assets depend on our own attitude—
              They're blessings if you know how to enjoy them,
              Mere plagues if you can't properly employ them.
CLITIPHO: But Menedemus is such an old curmudgeon,
              What I fear is that we'll see him, in high dudgeon,
              Going off the deep end with his son.
CHREMES: What? Him?
              (aside)
              But wait. It'll pay to paint him stern and grim.
CLITIPHO: What are you muttering to yourself?
CHREMES: Just pondering
              What a fool your young friend was, to go a-wandering,
              Whatever had happened at home. His father *might*,
              No doubt, have been more strict than he felt right.
              He should have been ready to take it, all the same.
              Who *would* he be patient with, in heaven's name,
              If not a parent? Do you expect the father
              To live according to the son's rules rather
              Than the other way around? It's really absolute rot
              To call *that* man tyrannical. He's not.
              The sins of the fathers to the sons—at least
              Of any father who's not an absolute beast—
              Boil down to one old story. They draw the line
              At too much womanizing, and too much wine.
              They're careful with the cash. But in all cases
              Their aim is building character, on a sound basis.
              You just look round, and you'll see, when a sordid passion
              Gets hold of a man, how it tends to mould and fashion
              His whole being. Take good note. Wise men learn sense
              From others' experience—and at others' expense.
CLITIPHO: I'm sure you're right.
CHREMES: Well, I'll just step inside
              And see what sort of a meal we're going to provide
              Tonight. And, noticing the time of day,
              I wouldn't advise you to stroll far astray.
              (He goes into his house)

ACT II

CLITIPHO: What jaundiced judges old men are of youth!
Born old is how they want us—that's the truth—
Grey from the cradle, strangers to all pleasure
Young blood craves, with strait-jackets made to measure,
The measure of *their* desires—of present date,
Not as they were once. Well, I hereby state,
If ever I have a son, he'll find his father
Open and easy with him, ready rather
To face and to forgive a fault or two
Than doing what you've just seen *my* father do—
Take someone else's case, to show what he's thinking
In *my* case. Damn it, though, when he's been drinking,
What tales he tells about his past—oh, brother!
But now he says, 'Get knowledge from another,
Profit from his experience.' Fine finessing!
He little knows what deaf ears he's addressing.
My girl's nagging has more point. *That* stings me,
Her everlasting 'Give me', 'Get me', 'Bring me',
Imperatives leaving one painfully embarrassed
For answers. Never was a man so harassed!
Clinia has his troubles. His girl's some claim
To decent breeding, though, some sense of shame.
She's not a hardened pro. Mine's a prime floozy,
A flaunting extravagant queen, changeful and choosy.
What can I give her? Sweet nothings, like 'Sure, honey'—
I haven't the nerve to admit I've got no money.
She's a real Tartar, a type I've never met
Before in my life, nor has my father—yet.
(Clinia comes out from Chremes' house, talking to himself)
CLINIA: If I had any luck in love, I know
Those women would have got here hours ago.
Yes. I'm afraid that, while I've been away,
They've ruined her. So many things point that way,
So many doubts add up to one dark truth—
Temptation, circumstances, her own youth,
Her being in charge of such an unprincipled mother,
Whose pleasure's profit, now she has no other.
CLITIPHO: Now, Clinia!
CLINIA: Oh, what misery!
CLITIPHO: You take care!
Someone coming out from your father's could find you there.

CLINIA: Yes, yes. But I've a horrible premonition—
CLITIPHO: Still making up your mind on mere suspicion
        Before you know!
CLINIA: If there were nothing wrong,
        They'd be here now.
CLITIPHO: They will be, before long.
CLINIA: How long is your 'before long'?
CLITIPHO: It's quite far,
        Remember. And you know what women are
        Dressing; their fussing and fiddling takes a year.
CLINIA: I feel like death.
CLITIPHO: Wake up and live! They're here!
        There's Dromo, look—and Syrus.
        (The two slaves enter, talking to each other, and not at first
        noticing the two young men)
SYRUS: Fancy that!
DROMO: Yes, and what's more—
SYRUS: What's more, with all our chat,
        The girls have got left.
CLITIPHO: *(to Clinia)*   Do you hear? She's found.
CLINIA: Yes, yes, I hear, I see, I'm safe and sound!
DROMO: Well, but with so much luggage that's scarcely odd,
        And all those maids too!
CLINIA: Maids! Where from, by God?
CLITIPHO: Search me.
SYRUS: We shouldn't have left them with that load.
CLINIA: Hell!
SYRUS: Jewellery, clothes—*and* they don't know the road
        And it's near dusk. We should have taken more care.
        Go back and meet them. Quick! Don't stand and stare!
        (Exit Dromo)
CLINIA: Oh God! From what a heaven of hope I fell!
CLITIPHO: *Now* what's the trouble?
CLINIA: Don't you see, man? Hell!
        Maids, jewels, clothes—where did she get them? How?
        I left her with one half-sized slave.
CLITIPHO: Ah, now,
        Now I do see her.
SYRUS: Cor, who'd expect such a spate of them?
         Our house'll simply collapse under the weight of them.
        It's mountains they'll be eating, seas they'll be drinking!
        Our old man'll be misery's self, I'm thinking.
        But there are the lads I'm looking for.

CLINIA: God in heaven!
So much for loyalty! For your sake I was driven,
Antiphila, idiot that I was, to roam
Far from my native land, while you at home
Were on the make, leaving me high and dry.
You made my name mud, led me to defy
My father's will—oh, God, the shame, the pain
I feel, to think of it! He tried in vain
To warn me of their ways. I wouldn't hear.
He wanted to wean me from her. But no fear!
I'm weaned now, yes. But when he might have blessed me
For obeying him, I wouldn't. What possessed me?
Who could be more unhappy?

SYRUS: He's been misled,
Apparently, by some of the things we said.
Look, Clinia, you've got some quite wrong notion
About your girl. She's lost none of her devotion
To you. She's still the girl she's always been—
That is, if seeing's believing.

CLINIA: What do you mean?
Explain! There's nothing I desire more strongly
Than to have proof that I suspect her wrongly.

SYRUS: First, to get everything straight, that old witch said
To be her mother wasn't. What's more, she's dead.
That much I overheard her clearly state
En route to the other girl.

CLITIPHO: What other?

SYRUS: Wait,
First let me finish the tale I'd started to tell,
Then I'll come back to *her*.

CLITIPHO: Hurry up, then!

SYRUS: Well,
We came to her house just now and Dromo knocked,
And some old crone came out. As she unlocked,
Dromo, with me on top of him, rushed right in.
She barred the door again, and went back to spin.
Now was our opportunity to discover
What sort of life in the absence of her lover
Your girl had led, her regular routine.
Our coming so unexpectedly on the scene
In the first place made it possible to find out
The pattern of her daily life, past doubt,
And that in turn's the clearest way to tell

A person's fundamental character. Well,
We found her busy weaving. A plain black dress,
In mourning for the old woman who'd died, I guess.
No jewellery—got up simply as women are
Just for themselves, no muck out of a jar
All over her face. Hair a bit loosely spread
And thrown back carelessly behind her head.

CLINIA: Stop, Syrus, don't for God's sake make me dizzy
With heights of false hope!

SYRUS: The old crone was busy
Spinning the wool. A single slave-girl sat
To help at the loom, a ragged little brat,
Horribly dirty.

CLITIPHO: If he's telling the truth,
And I believe him, then, my love-sick youth,
You're the luckiest lad alive. The girl's being seen
So horribly dirty must, with the other things, mean
Her mistress's morals needn't be suspected—
Not when the go-between is so neglected.
Paving your way to a mistress via the maid
With presents is the oldest trick in the trade.

CLINIA: Go on, for God's sake. But mind—no flowers of invention,
Swindling me sweet. What did she say at the mention
Of *my* name?

SYRUS: When we told her you were back
And asking her to come round here, quite slack
The thread slipped from her fingers, and her face
Was bathed in tears. No mystery in the case!
Heart-sickness for the sight of you is what she feels.

CLINIA: I don't know whether I'm on my head or my heels
For joy, God help me! After that fog of fear!

CLITIPHO: Which, I well knew, was groundless. But look here,
Syrus. The time has come for you to tell
The other girl's identity.

SYRUS: Very well.
We've brought your Bacchis along too.

CLITIPHO: You've what?
Where to, you rogue?

SYRUS: To our house, sir. Why not?

CLITIPHO: My father's?

SYRUS: That's what I said.

CLITIPHO: Have you no shame,
No fear, no scruples?

SYRUS: Faint heart never won fame,
Or name, or dame, without danger.
CLITIPHO: Danger? You've said it!
What are you after? Some crazy kind of credit
For hazarding my whole future? One slip from you
And I'll be done for! Clinia, what can one do
With such a dolt?
SYRUS: But—
CLITIPHO: But what?
SYRUS: If I may,
I'll explain.
CLINIA: Let him speak, Clitipho.
CLITIPHO: Okay.
SYRUS: (slowly)
The matter, as I see it, is sort of—
CLITIPHO: Hell!
It's a sort of long-winded tale you're going to tell!
CLINIA: Syrus, he's right. Come to the point. Quit stalling.
SYRUS: I can hardly hold my tongue, sir. It's appalling,
This petty persecution by Clitipho.
CLINIA: Let's hear him, and keep quiet for heaven's sake.
SYRUS: (rapidly)   So
You want to woo a wench, you want her won,
You want the cash to keep her. But risks run
In winning you don't want. You're wise, my lad—
That's if it's wise to want what can't be had.
Risks and rewards a man must take and lose
Together. You've two alternatives. So choose.
I'm sure my plan's a good one, though, risk-proof;
We'll get the other girl under your father's roof
Safely and easily. The money you promised to give her
My plan will simultaneously deliver,
A boon you've begged for, till you've stunned me stiff,
Deaf, dazed. What more do you want?
CLITIPHO: If it's possible—
SYRUS: If!
The only way to find out is to try it.
CLITIPHO: All right, all right. Let's have your plan. I'll buy it.
SYRUS: Well, we'll pretend your girl-friend's his.
CLITIPHO: I see.
That's clever. And who's his girl-friend going to be?
Is she to be counted his as well, in case
Keeping one woman isn't enough disgrace?

SYRUS: No. *She*'ll go to your mother's apartments.

CLITIPHO: Oh?
Why there?

SYRUS: It'd take me too long, Clitipho,
To explain my reasons. Take it from me, they're sound.

CLITIPHO: Rubbish! I can't see any convincing ground,
Any good reason for taking *that* chance.

SYRUS: Wait!
I've another plan, if *that* risk seems too great,
One that you'll both admit to be quite free
Of any risk.

CLITIPHO: Ah, that's the plan for me.
Out with it.

SYRUS: Right. I'll just go and meet your dame,
And tell her to go back the way she came.

CLITIPHO: What—what do you mean?

SYRUS: That'll free you from all fear.
You can sleep at ease, as they say, on either ear.
(Starts as if to go)

CLITIPHO: Oh, what shall I do?

CLINIA: Do? With a heaven-sent boon—

CLITIPHO: Syrus! Speak, man!

SYRUS: Act, man! You'll be wishing soon
You had, when it's too late.

CLINIA: Such boons it's as well
To make use of while you can. You never can tell—

CLITIPHO: Look, Syrus!

SYRUS: Talk away, I'm off.

CLINIA: You never
Can tell, I was saying, if such a chance will ever
Come back or not.

CLITIPHO: You're right. Hi, Syrus, Syrus!

SYRUS: Did you call, sir? *(aside)* Our young blood's started to fire us!

CLITIPHO: Come back.

SYRUS: I'm back. You want to say something? Or just
'I don't like this plan either'?

CLITIPHO: No, I entrust
Myself, the management of my love affair
And my good name to your judgement. So beware,
Judge, of being judged.

SYRUS: Why give me that warning? As though
I'd less at stake than you have, Clitipho.

You must be joking. If we make one slip,
You've got a warning waiting, I've the whip.
Small chance of my being slack! But ask your friend
If he's prepared to play up and pretend
Your lady friend is his.

CLINIA: Of course I'll do it.
The way things are, we're simply driven to it.

CLITIPHO: I knew you'd prove a friend in need.

CLINIA: Take care
She doesn't slip up, though.

SYRUS: No fear of *her.*
She's well-drilled.

CLITIPHO: But one thing surprises *me*—
The ease with which you got her to agree.
She's adept at saying no to any suggestion
From any quarter.

SYRUS: That was simply a question
Of proper timing. I turned up to discover
A madly pleading military lover
Wanting one night. And naturally her game
Was to let him cool his heels and fan his flame
By showing to yourself all possible favour.
But mind—don't ruin us all with rash behaviour.
You know your father's lynx-eyes, and I know
Your lack of self-control. So, Clitipho,
No double-talk, no sighs, and no neck-wriggling
To see her, no throat-clearing, coughing, giggling.

CLITIPHO: You'll find me perfect.

SYRUS: Just be careful, eh?

CLITIPHO: You'll be amazed at me yourself.

SYRUS: I say!
These girls have followed quite quickly in our track.

CLITIPHO: Where are they? What do you mean by holding me back?

SYRUS: She isn't yours now.

CLITIPHO: Once home she isn't, I know.
But meanwhile—

SYRUS: Makes no odds.

CLITIPHO: Oh, let me go!

SYRUS: No.

CLITIPHO: Just one moment.

SYRUS: Can't be done.

CLITIPHO: Just one kiss!

SYRUS: Just be a clever boy, and clear out of this!

CLITIPHO: I'm off. And him?

SYRUS: He stays.

CLITIPHO: The lucky devil!

SYRUS: Off!

(Exit Clitipho towards town. Enter Bacchis and Antiphila)

BACCHIS: You're a nice kid, really, on the level—
And lucky, keeping yourself as pure and sweet
In feeling as in face. The men you meet
Must fall for you, of course. Our little chat,
Coming along, has put me wise to *that*.
And when I just look at our different lives—
Mine, yours, and any kid like you who contrives
To keep to herself a bit, well, it's no wonder
Our sort and yours should end up poles asunder.
While decency's your best policy, pure profit,
The kind of men *we* deal with put you off it.
Our faces are our fortune. When they fade,
Men wander elsewhere. And, unless we've made
Some slight provision for that probable end,
We're left alone in the world, without a friend.
Your sort decides to spend your lives together
With *one* mate, some male bird of the same feather,
And marriage based on mutual give and take
Provides a bond no shock will ever shake.

ANTIPHILA: Well, I can't speak for others. I've tried, I know,
To make his happiness mine.

CLINIA: *(aside)*   Ah, so much so
That you, and none but you, have made my heart
Find its way home. And when we were apart
All other hardships that I had to bear,
Compared with missing you, were light as air!

SYRUS: *(aside)*
I'm sure they were.

CLINIA: *(aside)*   Oh, Syrus, it's too hard!
That heavenly disposition, and I'm barred
From being its sole owner, with no interferences
Of any sort.

SYRUS: *(aside)*   Well, judging by appearances,
Your father'll make lots of trouble still.

BACCHIS: Who's that young fellow ogling us?

ANTIPHILA: *(seeing Clinia)*   I'm ill!
Help! Hold me tight!

BACCHIS: For heaven's sake, what's upset you?

ANTIPHILA: Oh dear, I'm faint, I feel queer!
BACCHIS: I don't get you!
You've gone so strange!
CLINIA: Antiphila!
ANTIPHILA: Is it true?
Do I see Clinia or not?
BACCHIS: See who?
CLINIA: Oh, my sweet, lovely girl!
ANTIPHILA: Oh, Clinia, dear!
CLINIA: How *are* you?
ANTIPHILA: Glad to see you safe back here.
CLINIA: Antiphila, do I really hold you fast,
So long imagined, in my arms at last?
SYRUS: In! Our old man's been waiting ages past.
(All go into Chremes' house)

ACT III

(Early the next morning. Chremes comes out of his house)
CHREMES: There's the day breaking. Well, I'd better go
And knock my neighbour up, and let him know
From me before anyone else about his son
Being back. The young man doesn't want that done
I know. But when I see the old fellow grieving
So bitterly, so tormented by his leaving,
How can I hide this great, unhoped-for joy
When telling it can't possibly harm the boy?
No, no. My cue's to help him all I can.
It's only right and fair for an elderly man
Like me to try and stand by another old-stager,
Just as my son, with his friend and fellow-teenager,
Appears to be offering every sort of aid
And co-operation.
MENEDEMUS: *(coming out)*   Surely I was made
With positively morbid force in feeling things,
Or else what people say about Time's healing wings
Is false. I feel more deeply every day
About my son. The longer he's away
The greater grows my love and sense of loss.
CHREMES: Ah, there, he's just come out. I'll go across.
Good morning, Menedemus. Man, I've news!
The very sort yourself would soonest choose!

MENEDEMUS: About my son?
CHREMES: That's it. He's safe and sound.
MENEDEMUS: But where, my good friend, where can he be found?
CHREMES: Why, at our house.
MENEDEMUS: My son?
CHREMES: That's where he's staying!
MENEDEMUS: He's here?
CHREMES: Sure.
MENEDEMUS: Clinia?
CHREMES: Isn't that what I'm saying?
MENEDEMUS: Then, Chremes, what are we waiting for? Let's go!
Let's see him.
CHREMES: Well—he doesn't want *you* to know
He's back yet. No. He's keeping out of sight,
Afraid his last exploit of sudden flight
Could have increased your harshness.
MENEDEMUS: Didn't you say
How I feel now?
CHREMES: No.
MENEDEMUS: Why not?
CHREMES: And betray
How meek and mild you've turned? The worst thing out
For both of you would be that, beyond a doubt.
MENEDEMUS: Oh, I can't help it. I'm so tired, so sick
Of being the heavy father!
CHREMES: You're too quick
To jump both ways. More prodigal now than's proper,
Too strict before. Both ways one comes a cropper.
You frowned on him for wanting to frequent
That wench's house when she was well content
With little, grateful for the least help given.
He was scared off. Unwillingly she was driven
To get her living from the town at large.
Now that her keep's become a crippling charge,
You're ready to give all. God, you'll be stripped!
Why, just to show how well she's now equipped
For that, ten slave-girls has that modest maiden
Brought with her, everyone of them well-laden
With clothes and jewellery. I tell you, if her lover
Were a Persian satrap, he would soon discover
He couldn't stand the pace. Still less could you.
MENEDEMUS: Is *she* at your house?
CHREMES: Is she—? Oh, too true

She is! A single supper's all I've treated
Her and her entourage to—which, repeated,
Would ruin me. The wine we've watched her wasting,
To take one item only, just with tasting!
'This brand', she says, 'is rather rough, old fellow.
Could I have something just a shade more mellow?'
She had me opening every jar and cask,
Gave us no rest. That was *one* night. I ask
What's going to happen to *you*, friend, when they start
Eating you up non-stop. Trust me, my heart
Bled for your property. Face the prospect! Ponder it!

MENEDEMUS: Oh, let him do what he likes, take, use it, squander it—
If I can keep him, I'm resolved, resigned to it.

CHREMES: Well, if you really *have* made up your mind to it,
I think it's vital not to let your son
Know that you're purposely paying for his fun.

MENEDEMUS: How should I act, then?

CHREMES: Any other way
Than that royal road to ruin. You could pay
Through someone else—or let his fellow diddle
The money out of you. Some sort of fiddle
Is, incidentally, being secretly plotted
Already by those rogues. Oh, yes, I've spotted
Syrus in whispered conference with your man,
And both reporting back on some bold plan
To their young masters. If you have to choose,
Waste one whole talent *my* way, rather than lose
One mina by the other. It's not mainly
A matter of money now. Your plan is plainly
To let him have *that*—but don't risk too much!
For once he finds your state of mind is such
You'd sooner part with life and all beside
Than let him leave you, you'll have opened wide
Windows to every wickedness and vice,
And made your own life miserable. The price
Of too much liberty is moral ruin.
Whatever takes his fancy he'll be doing
Without regard at all for wrong and right.
And then you'll suffer doubly at the sight
Of son *and* substance ruined. But—decline
To let him have it, and he'll take the line
Which he perceives gives him the greatest hold,
Threatening to leave at once the paternal fold.

MENEDEMUS: That sounds convincing. Yes. I really think
You must be right.

CHREMES: I haven't slept a wink,
Working out feasible ways and means to win you
Your son back.

MENEDEMUS: Oh, your hand, friend! Pray continue
The good work.

CHREMES: At your service.

MENEDEMUS: Do you know
What I'd like done immediately?

CHREMES: Why, no.
What, then?

MENEDEMUS: Well, as you've spotted they've some trick
In preparation, make them try it—quick!
I'm longing to help him—in secret. I can't rest
Till I've set eyes on him.

CHREMES: I'll do my best.
One little bit of business I must clear
Out of the way first. Two of my neighbours here,
Simus and Crito, having made the suggestion
That I should arbitrate in some boundary question,
I told them I'd look into it today.
I must cry off. I won't be long away.

MENEDEMUS: By all means. Thank you very much. *(Exit Chremes)*
                                Dear God,
How curious human nature is! How odd
That each of us sees more clearly, judges better
Somebody else's business! Do feelings fetter
Mind in our own affairs so much, the pleasure
Or pain involved being powerful beyond measure?
Well, take my case—how infinitely wiser
Than I myself is this new-found adviser!

CHREMES: *(returning)*
Well, now, that's that. I've made myself quite free
To give my time to your affairs. Let's see.
I must get hold of Syrus, and set about
Instructing him. Hallo! Who's coming out?
Someone from our house? Get off home, then—quick!
We mustn't let them see us being so thick.
(Exit Menedemus. Enter Syrus)

SYRUS: *(to himself)*
Run hither and thither, quicksilver money, yet

Catch you I must. So now to spread the net
For my old bird.
CHREMES: *(to himself)*   They're at it, then! I knew it!
Clinia's slave's too slow. He couldn't do it,
So Syrus gets the job.
SYRUS: *(to himself)*   Who's that, right near me?
The devil! Now we're done for! Did he hear me?
CHREMES: Syrus!
SYRUS: Sir!
CHREMES: Do I find you—?
SYRUS: Fit, sir? Fairly.
But I'm surprised to see you up so early,
Considering what you put away last night.
CHREMES: A trifle!
SYRUS: Trifle! Sir, it was a sight!
An eagle's old age, as they say.
CHREMES: Enough.
You needn't—
SYRUS: No, sir. Smashing bit of stuff,
That girl, eh? Had a way with her.
CHREMES: *(feelingly)*   She had.
SYRUS: You felt it? And good-looking, eh?
CHREMES: Not bad.
SYRUS: Not a patch on the old sort, true, but as they go, sir,
By modern standards, pretty good. You know, sir,
I'm not surprised at Clinia's being smitten,
But he's got such a miserly, mean, hard-bitten
Beast of a father here next door. You've met him?
As if he wasn't stiff with the stuff, he let him
Leave home for want of funds. Oh, yes, it's true.
Perhaps you didn't know?
CHREMES: Of course I do.
Dull-witted slave, fit for grain-grinding!
SYRUS: Who?
CHREMES: Why, Clinia's fellow.
SYRUS: *(aside)*   Syrus, I feared for *you*!
CHREMES: Letting that happen!
SYRUS: What ought he to have done?
CHREMES: Found ways and means, got money for the son,
To treat her with, from the father by some trick,
So saving, in spite of his teeth, that sour old stick.
SYRUS: You're joking.
CHREMES: No! It was his duty.

SYRUS: *You*
        Approve of boss-bamboozling slaves?
CHREMES: I do—
        In certain circumstances, mind.
SYRUS: Sure, sure.
CHREMES: It could be, in extremis, the sole cure.
        It might have kept his only son from straying
        Abroad in this case.
SYRUS: *(aside)*   I don't know if he's saying
        All this in sober earnest or subtle jest—
        I know it eggs me on, adds extra zest.
CHREMES: Now what's he waiting for? For his young master
        To quit again because the girl spends faster
        Than he can find funds? Has he no plan, no plot
        To milk the old man?
SYRUS: No, sir, he's a clot.
CHREMES: Then, for the lad's sake, you should lend a hand.
SYRUS: I could, of course—at your express command.
        I know the tricks of the trade.
CHREMES: Then they can use you.
SYRUS: Lies aren't my game.
CHREMES: Get on with it. I excuse you.
SYRUS: Well, sir. I hope you'll bear those words in mind
        If ever by any chance anything of this kind
        Should happen to—boys will be boys, you know—
        Your son.
CHREMES: I'll never need to, I hope.
SYRUS: Quite so—
        I hope you won't. And I'm not mentioning this
        Because I've noticed anything amiss
        In that direction. It's in case—I mean,
        Look what they're like at that age! You've just seen.
        And—I could lead you such a lovely dance,
        If need arose.
CHREMES: If need, by any chance,
        Arose—I'd reconsider our position.
        Meanwhile attend to your immediate mission.
        (Exit into house)
SYRUS: Well, what do you know—? A golden opportunity,
        Carte blanche to bluff him blind, complete immunity!
        He's never served me sauce so much to taste—
        But who's that coming out in such hot haste?
        (Enter from the house Chremes and Clitipho)

CHREMES: What's the idea? This really is too strong,
As morals or as manners!

CLITIPHO: *(sulkily)*   Why, what's wrong?

CHREMES: Didn't I see you put your hand just now
Into that Bacchis person's bosom?

SYRUS: *(aside)*   Wow!
That's torn it! That's wrecked us, right enough.

CLITIPHO: What, me?

CHREMES: I saw it. I'm not blind. Don't bluff.
You take fine liberties, letting your fingers stray
So freely! No. To have your friend to stay
And then start fiddling with his girl is quite
Beyond excuse. Yes, and at wine last night
How free you were!

SYRUS: *(aside)*   He was, too.

CHREMES: How offensive!
Why, damn it, I got more and more apprehensive
Where it was going to end. I know these lovers.
Things you think harmless their jealousy discovers
A grievance in.

CLITIPHO: But Clinia trusts me, father,
Not to go *that* far.

CHREMES: Does he? Well, I'd rather
You kept your distance. Your presence anyway checks
The very natural promptings of—well, sex.
I can put myself in his place. I'd not confide
To *any* friend *all* my secrets. With some of them pride,
With others sheer embarrassment's the bar,
They'd find I'd been a fool. Or gone too far.
I understand his feelings. And when and where
To respect them is a matter of savoir-faire.

SYRUS: What's this I hear?

CLITIPHO: They'll drive me round the bend!

SYRUS: Is this your loyalty towards a friend?
Is this the way you show up Syrus' teaching?
This your fine self-control?

CLITIPHO: Oh, do stop preaching!

SYRUS: Very pretty!

CHREMES: I'm ashamed of him. What next?

SYRUS: I'm sure you are, with good cause. He's got *me* vexed!
As well.

CLITIPHO: You've got me mad!

SYRUS: I'll tell you this flat—

CLITIPHO: Not to go near them?

CHREMES: There's more ways than that
Of going near people!

SYRUS: *(aside)*   Damn it, he's so rash,
He'll spill the beans before I've got the cash.
(aloud)
Sir, if you'll take my very humble tip—

CHREMES: What is it?

SYRUS: Tell him to take a cooling-off trip.

CLITIPHO: Where to?

SYRUS: Wherever you like. But give them air.
Go for a nice long walk.

CLITIPHO: A long walk? Where?

SYRUS: As if you hadn't got the whole world to walk in!
To, fro, wherever you like.

CHREMES: It's sense he's talking.
I second the motion.

CLITIPHO: The shove, eh? Damn and blast you,
Syrus! I'll give you tips!

SYRUS: Eh, not so fast, you!
Remember, keep those hands from straying! Ow!
Oh, would you? *(Exit Clitipho)*
         How—that's what I wonder—
Is that boy going to end, do you suppose?
God help you—for you'll need his help, God knows,
Watching and warning, yes, and punishing too, now
And then.

CHREMES: *(impatiently)*
        I'll watch him.

SYRUS: The watching is up to you now.

CHREMES: I'll keep my eye on him.

SYRUS: That would be wise.
He listens less and less when I advise.

CHREMES: Yes, yes. But, Syrus, about that little affair
We talked about, have you got anywhere,
Hit on a promising plan? Or not yet? Eh?

SYRUS: You mean about that trick we'd planned to play?
Well, I've just hit on something.

CHREMES: Stout chap! Well?

SYRUS: Let me work out the tale I have to tell
By stages.

CHREMES: Start!

SYRUS: This Bacchis is a stinker.

CHREMES: I think she's that all right.

SYRUS: What would you think her,
If you but knew the half? Wait till you've heard
What's now been hatched out by that little bird.
There was an old woman living here, who'd come
From Corinth. Bacchis lent her a large sum—
A thousand drachmae. She died, and left behind
A teenage daughter, who was duly assigned
To Bacchis as a sort of guarantee
For the recovery of the debt.

CHREMES: I see.
A pledge.

SYRUS: Quite so. She's here now. Bacchis brought her.
That girl now with your wife's the old woman's daughter.

CHREMES: Yes. Well?

SYRUS: Well, Bacchis reckons to recover
The money out of Clinia. He, her lover,
Must take the girl as a matter of course. The price
Will be one thousand drachmae.

CHREMES: Very nice!
So 'must's' the word?

SYRUS: 'Must' is, sir. Can you doubt it?
And maybe 'will'.

CHREMES: How will you set about it?

SYRUS: Me? Go to Menedemus, sir, and pitch
A yarn about this girl's being really rich,
High-born, a Carian captive, with a ransom
In prospect that would make his profit handsome.

CHREMES: No go.

SYRUS: Why not?

CHREMES: Imagine me replying
As Menedemus—'Off with you! I'm not buying.'
What's your next line?

SYRUS: You've hit him off to a T, sir.
'Why aren't you buying?'

CHREMES: 'Don't want her.'

SYRUS: 'Oh, but please, sir,
Explain. I'm so surprised.'

CHREMES: 'I will.' But wait!
Who's set our front door rattling at that rate?

ACT IV

(No pause in the action. Sostrata and the nurse come out of Chremes' house, not noticing the others.)

SOSTRATA: You know, dear nurse, unless I'm out of my mind,
This *must* be what I think—and what a find!
The ring left with that poor mite—

CHREMES: *(aside)*   What on earth
Is she going on about?

SOSTRATA: —exposed at birth.
Do *you* think it's the same?

NURSE: I told you so
The moment that you showed it me.

SOSTRATA: I know.
But did you look at it with sufficient care?

NURSE: I certainly did.

SOSTRATA: Well, you go in to her
And tell me when she's finished her bath. I'll stay
And wait here till my husband comes. *(Exit nurse)*

SYRUS: I say!
It's you she wants. You'd better find out why.
She looks as if any minute she might cry.
There must be a reason. What? She has me scared.

CHREMES: Much ado about nothing, take my word.

SOSTRATA: *(seeing him)*
Oh, husband darling!

CHREMES: Yes, wife darling?

SOSTRATA: My dear,
You're the very person I wanted.

CHREMES: Well, I'm here.
What is it?

SOSTRATA: Please believe this first—I wouldn't
Ever dare do a thing you said I shouldn't.

CHREMES: So I'm to start by swallowing that, despite
It's sheer improbability? All right.
(to himself)
She *must* feel guilty, trying to forestall
Judgement like that!

SOSTRATA: My dear, do you recall
How I was pregnant once, and you forbade
My rearing a girl, if that was what I had?

CHREMES: Don't tell me. You had her reared.

SYRUS: *(aside)*   That's one live boss more

For me, and for my master one dead loss more.
SOSTRATA: No, but—there was a woman from Corinth here,
A decent old body. I handed the baby, my dear,
To her to get rid of.
CHREMES: Oh, what brains! Poor brat!
SOSTRATA: Oh, dear, what have I done?
CHREMES: *You*—ask me *that* !
SOSTRATA: If I did anything wrong, it was unwitting,
Unconscious.
CHREMES: Even without yourself admitting
As much, I can believe that! Do you ever
Do anything witting, conscious or clever?
On any count you chose the worst expedient.
First, if you'd chosen—by chance—to be obedient,
You should have had the child destroyed. In fact
You faked her death in words, but by your act
Left hope of life. Of course, of course, you'll plead
A mother's tender heart. Okay! Agreed!
A pretty future you proposed to give her!
What was your plan? All *you* did was deliver
Your child into the hands of that old witch,
To sell, for all you knew, or else get rich
Out of her earnings. Doubtless, my dear wife,
You thought, 'Provided I can save her life,
Nothing else matters.' Oh, it's hopeless dealing
With people like you, deficient in all feeling
For principles of right and wrong, vice, virtue,
Good, bad, or even what's going to help or hurt you,
Blind to all else but what you choose to see.
SOSTRATA: Dear husband, I did wrong. I quite agree.
But try to be, *because* you *are* more sensible,
More understanding. My folly's indefensible.
But let your fairness plead for it, my dear.
CHREMES: Well, I'll forgive you this time—though I fear
My tolerance is no good teacher. Well,
What was the tale you had begun to tell
That started all this?
SOSTRATA: With the disposition
We women have towards silly superstition,
When giving the old woman our child, I took
A ring from off my finger and said, 'Look,
Lay this beside the child. Then, should it die,
It'll have something of ours.'

CHREMES: *(ironically)*   And so thereby
You saved your conscience and your child.

SOSTRATA: And now
Here is the ring!

CHREMES: You got it back? But how?

SOSTRATA: The girl that Bacchis brought—

CHREMES: I don't understand this.
What tale are you trying to tell me?

SOSTRATA: —happened to hand this
To me, when going to the bath, just to take care of it.
At first I wasn't very much aware of it,
But then I noticed, recognized it—and flew
Outside to tell you.

CHREMES: Hum! And what would *you*
Make out of all this—or make up—with respect to her?

SOSTRATA: I don't know. I hoped, perhaps, if you went direct to her
And asked where she got the ring, we'd have a clue, maybe.

SYRUS: *(aside)*
Hell! I spy more than enough hope. She's our baby,
If this is true.

CHREMES: The old woman—no doubt she's dead?

SOSTRATA: I don't know.

CHREMES: What did she say at the time?

SOSTRATA: She *said*
She carried out my orders.

CHREMES: What was her name?
We'll make inquiries.

SOSTRATA: Philtera.

SYRUS: *(aside)*   The same!
She's found, I'm lost. I've had it. It's all too clear.

CHREMES: Come on inside.

SOSTRATA: Oh, this is more, my dear,
Than I had dared to hope. I rather feared
You'd be as firm as then about having her reared,
Not wanting to own her.

CHREMES: Life often won't allow
A man to be as he wants. As things are now,
I like the idea of a daughter. *Then*, I confess,
There was nothing in the world I wanted less.
(Exeunt into house)

SYRUS: This, if I judge the situation rightly,
Means trouble. My forces are boxed up pretty tightly,
Unless I can make sure he doesn't discover

It's really Clitipho who's Bacchis' lover.
We needn't hope for money, or think to cheat
Or chisel anyone. There I accept defeat.
In fact, I'll hold a triumph, I'll give thanks,
If I come off without exposing both flanks.
But fancy having a prize so fine and fat
Snatched from one's jaws in a minute, just like that!
Sheer agony! But where do we go from here?
What's the next move? The slate's wiped clean, that's clear.
But patient thought beats the best problem-setter.
Suppose I tried—? No good. But if—? No better.
One might, of course—It can't be done . . . it can!
Three cheers for me! I've found a first-rate plan!
That runaway money, I really do believe,
In spite of life's little tricks, I shall retrieve.
(Enter Clinia from Chremes' house)

CLINIA: I feel that nothing now can intervene
To cloud my sky so suddenly serene.
Whatever my father's wishes now, I'm ready
To bow to them. I'll be more staid and steady
Than ever he expects.

SYRUS: *(aside)*   I was right, it's clear.
The girl's been recognized, from what I hear.
(aloud)
Well, you've had a nice turn-up for the book. I'm glad.

CLINIA: You've heard the lovely news?

SYRUS: Trust me, my lad.
I was very much on the spot then.

CLINIA: Did you ever
Hear of a stroke of luck like this?

SYRUS: No, never.

CLINIA: It isn't half as much for myself, I swear,
I feel so much up in heaven, as for *her*.
There's no place too exalted for her virtue!

SYRUS: I'm sure you're right, sir. But, if I could divert you
Just for one moment, Clinia, into lending
A hand to secure a similar happy ending
For Clitipho's love-life, what Chremes still mustn't guess is
Bacchis is his.

CLINIA: Who says the gods don't bless us?

SYRUS: Calm down!

CLINIA: Antiphila my wife! What bliss!

SYRUS: Must you keep interrupting me like this?

CLINIA: I'm so happy. I can't help it. You must bear with me.
SYRUS: I do.
CLINIA: I feel as though she's right up there with me!
SYRUS: Oh, it's vain pains I take, lost time I'm spending.
CLINIA: Go on. I'm listening.
SYRUS: But you're not attending.
CLINIA: I will attend.
SYRUS: I said, what we've still to do
Is get your friend Clitipho in harbour too.
If you merely move out, leaving Bacchis here
Behind you, it'll soon be crystal-clear
To our old man that her boy-friend's Clitipho.
But, if you take her with you when you go,
The secret'll be safe.
CLINIA: But, damn it, man,
That's the best way to ditch my marriage plan!
With her there, how can I approach my father?
Can you suggest what I could say?
SYRUS: Yes, rather!
CLINIA: All right—what fiction could I feed him?
SYRUS: Why,
I'm not proposing that you tell a lie.
Just feed him facts, without disguise or cover.
CLINIA: What? Do you mean—?
SYRUS: Say, 'I'm Antiphila's lover.
I want to marry her. This other dame
Is Clitipho's.'
CLINIA: Just like that? A fine, fair game,
Straight, loyal, simple. By what subtle means
Do I persuade him not to spill the beans
To your old man?
SYRUS: You don't. You get your dad
To tell him the whole story.
CLINIA: Are you mad?
Or drunk? You realize you'll be simply driving
Poor Clitipho to ruin?
SYRUS: I'm contriving
My masterpiece. This is my finest hour.
A demonstration of my gifts, my power
Of pulling the wool. I'll tell those two old buffers
The simple truth, and prove the prince of bluffers.
When your old man tells ours that it's *his* son
Who's keeping Bacchis, and has always done,

                    You'll see—he won't believe it all the same!
CLINIA: Yes, and my marriage? By your little game
          That's down the drain. As long as your old man
          Believes that Bacchis is my girl, he'll ban
          My marriage with his daughter. But my fate,
          I daresay, seems a matter of small weight.
          So long as you can help *him*, that's enough.
SYRUS: Damn it, do you suppose I want this bluff
          Kept up for life? *One* day, while I extract
          The cash, and then—full-stop. And that's a fact.
          Not an hour longer.
CLINIA: But will one day do?
          Suppose his father finds the truth?
SYRUS: Oh, you
          And your supposing! Suppose I said, 'Suppose
          The sky should fall!'
CLINIA: I'm scared. God only knows
          What's right.
SYRUS: Scared? Right? As if you weren't well able,
          As soon as ever you wish, to cut the cable
          And blow the gaff!
CLINIA: All right. Where's Bacchis? Get her.
SYRUS: Ah, look! She's coming out. What could be better?
BACCHIS: *(entering with Phrygia)*
          That Syrus has a nerve, the way he's lured me
          With promises. Ten minae, he assured me,
          I'd get. If I discover he's been cheating me,
          He'll waste his wits imploring and entreating me
          In future to come over. I'll refuse.
          Or I'll agree, make a date, give him good news
          For him to carry back to his young master,
          Get *him* agog with hope, heart beating faster,
          Then—I'll not go. Next time I'll do the cheating,
          Get my own back on Syrus' back—with a beating.
CLINIA: *(aside)*
          Fine promises she's making you—eh, what?
SYRUS: You think she's joking, don't you? Well, she's not.
          I'll have to mind my step.
BACCHIS: *(seeing them)*   Asleep, no doubt?
          I'll rouse them! Which house did that fellow point out
          To us as being Charinus', Phrygia, eh?
          You heard him.
PHRYGIA: Yes, of course.

BACCHIS: You heard him say
That house next-door to the farm there, on the right?
PHRYGIA: Yes, I remember.
BACCHIS: Off, then—run. Tonight
Being Dionysus' feast, there's a spot of revelry,
And the captain's at Charinus'.
SYRUS: *(aside)*   Now what devilry
Is this dame up to?
BACCHIS: When you see him, say
I'm here against my will, watched night and day,
But that, by hook or crook, I'll slip away.
I'll come across at any rate.
SYRUS: *(aside)*   *I'll* come a cropper
At that rate. Bacchis, wait! Where's she off to? Stop her!
BACCHIS: *(to Phrygia)*
Run!
SYRUS: Look, the money's waiting.
BACCHIS: Then I'll wait
Of course.
SYRUS: Yes, well, of course you'll get it straight.
BACCHIS: Just as you like. You can't say I've been pressing.
SYRUS: No, but—you know what?
BACCHIS: What? Don't keep me guessing.
SYRUS: You've got to move next door with all your—retinue.
BACCHIS: What are you up to now, you crooked old cretin, you?
SYRUS: Just coining cash for you to have the run of.
BACCHIS: What makes you feel I'm fair game to make fun of?
SYRUS: We've got good grounds.
BACCHIS: Some new transaction in view?
SYRUS: Oh, no, we're simply seeing you get your due.
BACCHIS: Let's go.
SYRUS: This way. Hi, Dromo!
DROMO: *(entering from Menedemus' house)*
                                    Who called?
SYRUS: Me,
Syrus.
DROMO: Oh, what do you want?
SYRUS: Kindly see
That all this lady's maids without delay
Are moved from our house over to your place.
DROMO: Eh?
What for?
SYRUS: No questions, please. Let each take out

Exactly what she brought with her. Now no doubt
Our old man'll have high hopes that by their going
He'll be relieved of much expense—not knowing
What great loss from this little gain will come
Mind—what you know you don't know, see?

DROMO: I'm dumb.

*(Exeunt Clinia, Dromo, Bacchis, Phrygia and her other
maids in procession from Chremes' house to Menedemus'.
Chremes himself emerges to see the last of them disappear)*

CHREMES: Poor chap! What a crushing blow! My heart's just bleeding.
Poor Menedemus—I mean it. Fancy feeding
That woman and her hungry horde! It's true
He may notice nothing for a week or two,
Having longed so much to see his dear son. Still,
When once he does take in that daily bill,
That boundless waste invading hearth and home,
He'll wish once more to see his dear son roam.
Ah, good. There's Syrus.

SYRUS: *(aside)*   Why should I delay?
Let's tackle him.

CHREMES: Syrus!

SYRUS: Oh, three cheers! Hurray!

CHREMES: What does that mean?

SYRUS: It means, sir, you're the answer
To Syrus' secret prayers. Yes, you're the man, sir!

CHREMES: Don't tell me you've managed something with Menedemus.

SYRUS: You mean on the general lines agreed between us?
No sooner said than done.

CHREMES: Dead earnest?

SYRUS: Dead
As can be.

CHREMES: You deserve a pat on the head.
Oh I insist. And—anything I can do
To pay you back, any time—

SYRUS: If you but knew
The subtlety of my invention here.

CHREMES: Oho!
Success has gone to your head, I think.

SYRUS: No, no.
I'm telling nothing but the simple truth.

CHREMES: Well, let me hear.

SYRUS: You shall. That hopeful youth
Next door has told his father that the one

Who's had an affair with Bacchis is your son,
But that, to keep the whole thing hidden from you,
He brought her as his.

CHREMES: It's too good to be true!

SYRUS: Say that again.

CHREMES: It's really rich!

SYRUS: And how!
If you only knew! But let me give you now
The cream of the joke, sir. He proceeds to tell
His father that he saw your daughter, fell
In love at first sight and wants to marry her!

CHREMES: Eh?
You mean the daughter I've just found today?

SYRUS: Yes, and he'll ask his dad to ask her hand
From you.

CHREMES: Why? Damn it, I don't understand.

SYRUS: Oh, you are slow.

CHREMES: I must be.

SYRUS: Well, for their wedding
He'll pump his father—you see now where we're heading?

CHREMES: To buy her—?

SYRUS: That's it. Knick-knacks, jewellery, clothing.

CHREMES: He'll not get me, though, marrying or betrothing
My daughter to him.

SYRUS: Why not?

CHREMES: Why not? What a question!
A boy who's got—!

SYRUS: As you please, sir. My suggestion,
Of course, was not to give her for keeps, but just
As bluff, sir.

CHREMES: Bluff be blowed! No. If you must
Brew that hell's broth, you needn't imbrue me in it.
Betroth my child, not meaning for a minute
To marry her in earnest!

SYRUS: I just thought, sir—

CHREMES: Then think again.

SYRUS: A trap that could have caught, sir,
So beautifully! If you'd not been so whole-hearted
In urging me to act, I'd never have started
To move in that particular direction.

CHREMES: Quite.

SYRUS: I'm not quarrelling, though, with your objection.

CHREMES: Oh, but I'm very keen you should endeavour

To get the money, not by these means, however.
SYRUS: Okay. I'll look for some other way instead.
Changing the subject—remember what I said
About the money your daughter owes to Bacchis?
It's got to be paid. And we all know what your tack is—
The strictly straight. You're not the man to cry,
'What's that to do with me? It wasn't I
Who got the money or asked for it to be lent.
What? Mortgage my daughter without my consent?'
There's truth in that old saying that the heights
Of wrong are reached by standing on one's rights.
CHREMES: I'll not do that.
SYRUS: 　　　　　No, even if others can,
You can't. The world regards you as a man
Of substance and position.
CHREMES: 　　　　　　　In fact I'll go
Myself and pay the money.
SYRUS: 　　　　　　　You? Oh, no!
You send your son.
CHREMES: 　　　　Why?
SYRUS: 　　　　　　　Isn't he Bacchis' lover—
In Menedemus' eyes? Let him discover
Your son doing this, that tale's made more believable—
(aside)
And my ulterior objectives more achievable.
(aloud)
Talk of the devil! He's here. So in you go
And fetch the money.
CHREMES: 　　　　　Yes, I'll do that. (Exit)
CLITIPHO: (entering) 　　　　　　　　Oh!
The least exertion, if your heart's not in it,
Becomes a drudge. Take me now, at this minute.
This strolling round—it's not work, but it's killing me.
And one suspicion, first and last, is filling me
With dread—that once again I'll get the shove,
Banned, barred from Bacchis. All the powers above,
Gods, goddesses, the lot of them, damn you,
Syrus, and your bright brains, that have to brew
Trouble and tricks of this sort all day long
To torture me!
SYRUS: 　　　　Oh, go where you belong!
Your capers nearly put me in the cart.
CLITIPHO: And don't I wish they had, with all my heart!

You've earned it.

SYRUS: Earned it? Me? Well, now I'm glad
I heard you speak your mind before you had
The money I was going to give you.

CLITIPHO: Well,
What do you want to hear me saying? Hell!
You go and bring my girl right under our roof,
And then it's hands off—I'm told to hold aloof.

SYRUS: I can't be angry with you. Do you know
Where she is now?

CLITIPHO: At our house.

SYRUS: No, sir.

CLITIPHO: Oh?
Then where?

SYRUS: At Clinia's.

CLITIPHO: That's the end.

SYRUS: Oh, is it?
Don't worry. You'll be paying her a visit
In just two ticks, primed with that promised money.

CLITIPHO: You're mad. Where from?

SYRUS: Your dad.

CLITIPHO: Are you being funny?

SYRUS: Events will show. Watch.

CLITIPHO: Syrus, you're a honey,
A darling! And I've the devil's own luck.

SYRUS: Your dad!
He's coming out. Now, no surprise, my lad,
No wondering why or wherefore. In this matter
Humour his mood, do as he says, don't chatter.

CHREMES: *(entering)*
Where's Clitipho?

SYRUS: *(prompting)*   'Here, father'—go on.

CLITIPHO: Here.

CHREMES: *(to Syrus)*
You've put him wise?

SYRUS: To everything—pretty near.

CHREMES: Then take this and deliver it.

SYRUS: Go on. Grab it.
Don't stand there like a stone.

CLITIPHO: Sure, sure. Let's have it.

SYRUS: Come on, now, quick! We'll be right back. Just wait.
There's nothing over there to keep us late.
(Clitipho and Syrus go with the money into Menedemus' house)

CHREMES: Ten minae I've paid for my daughter. That can count
As cost of rearing. But the same amount
Follows for outfit. Then what's gone before
Demands a sequel—say, two talents more
For dowry. What unfair, daft things are expected now
By custom! My affairs must be neglected now
While I go looking for some hopeful lad
To give my hard-earned wealth to. It's quite mad!

MENEDEMUS: *(entering)*
I feel myself the happiest of men
Seeing my son has found his wits again.

CHREMES: *(aside)*
That's what he thinks!

MENEDEMUS: Ah, Chremes, just the man, now!
Are you prepared to salvage—for you can now—
My son, myself, my family?

CHREMES: Sure. Just say
The word. What is it?

MENEDEMUS: Well, you've found today
A daughter.

CHREMES: Well?

MENEDEMUS: My son wants her for wife.

CHREMES: You're marvellous!

MENEDEMUS: What do you mean?

CHREMES: Upon my life!
Have you forgotten all we said just now
About them hatching plots and planning how
To get you giving them money?

MENEDEMUS: Yes, I know—

CHREMES: Well, this is it.

MENEDEMUS: What do you mean? How so?
Chremes, it can't be. You see, that girl that's staying
With us—well, she's your son's.

CHREMES: That's what they're saying,
And you believe each single word that's said.
Their story now is that he wants to wed,
So that, as soon as I promise her, you'll provide
The wherewithal for him to buy his bride
Clothes, jewellery, and her every other need.

MENEDEMUS: Of course you're right. Then doubtless he'd proceed
To give it to his girl-friend, eh?

CHREMES: You bet.

MENEDEMUS: Oh, dear, my joy was all illusion. Yet

I'd swallow anything not to lose him now.
So what do I say? I mean, in telling him how
You took his marriage proposal. I mustn't let him
See he's been seen through. That might—well, upset him.
CHREMES: Upset him! You're soft. You simply spoil your son.
MENEDEMUS: Oh, let me be. Help me, since I've begun
This game, to carry it through.
CHREMES: Well, if you must,
Tell him we had a meeting and discussed
This marriage.
MENEDEMUS: Yes, and then?
CHREMES: Say I agreed,
To give her, and was very glad indeed
To have him as a son-in-law. And add,
If you so wish, that they're engaged.
MENEDEMUS: I'm glad.
That's what I hoped.
CHREMES: So he can straight away start
His act of asking, while you play your part
In giving, both sides under the false heading
Of money for an entirely mythical wedding,
Since that's apparently what you desire.
MENEDEMUS: It is.
CHREMES: I guess you'll very quickly tire
Of that game. And in any case you'll dispense
Your cash in driblets if you've any sense.
MENEDEMUS: Of course.
CHREMES: Go in, then. Find what he's proposing
To ask you for. I'll be at home, supposing
You should require me.
MENEDEMUS: Oh, I shall. Don't doubt it.
Whatever happens I'll tell you all about it.
(Both go into their own houses)

ACT V

(A little time has elapsed. Enter Menedemus)
MENEDEMUS: To cuteness and keen sight I don't pretend,
But my new guide, philosopher and friend—
He beats me hollow. All the terms in stock
For dullness—lead-head, donkey, doorpost, block,
Fit me. But for his denseness they're too small,

He's several sizes thicker than them all.
(Enter Chremes talking back to his wife inside)

CHREMES: All right, all right! Our daughter's found. Don't deafen
With your thanksgivings all the gods in heaven!
My wife must measure their minds by hers and hold them
Impervious to all matter till it's told them
A hundred times. But what can be delaying
My son and Syrus?

MENEDEMUS: Who is that you're saying
Is being delayed by something, Chremes?

CHREMES: Well,
At least you're back, Menedemus. Did you tell
Your son—?

MENEDEMUS: Oh, yes. Exactly as you said.

CHREMES: And he?

MENEDEMUS: Was just like any would-be-wed,
Delighted.

CHREMES: Ha! That's rich!

MENEDEMUS: Oh, is it? Why?

CHREMES: Syrus knows all the tricks! He's devilish sly!

MENEDEMUS: Is he?

CHREMES: Plots, plays, players' faces—a master of make-up!

MENEDEMUS: You mean my son's delight was feigned?

CHREMES: Pure fake-up!

MENEDEMUS: Yes, well, I had the same idea as you.

CHREMES: He's an old fox!

MENEDEMUS: He is—if you only knew.

CHREMES: Eh, what?

MENEDEMUS: Just listen.

CHREMES: Wait. What have you lost
By this little game? I mean, the total cost.
When the engagement was announced, no doubt
Friend Dromo lost no time in throwing out
Some hints of items needed by the bride,
Clothes, jewellery, and maids, to be supplied
From your side—yes?

MENEDEMUS: No.

CHREMES: No?

MENEDEMUS: That's what I said.

CHREMES: Your son himself, then?

MENEDEMUS: Not him. To be wed
Was all he wanted, and at once, today.

CHREMES: Well, you surprise me. What did Syrus say?

Had he no comment?

MENEDEMUS: None.

CHREMES: I don't get this.

MENEDEMUS: Now you surprise me. There's not much you miss.
That sly fox Syrus, faking your son's face, too—
And his behaviour—leaving no hint or clue
Of her being Clinia's!

CHREMES: What's that?

MENEDEMUS: I'm not counting
Mere hugs and kisses—trifles—not amounting
To anything.

CHREMES: How far could faking go
Further than that, if I might ask?

MENEDEMUS: Oho!

CHREMES: What is all this? Well? Tell me.

MENEDEMUS: Oh, I'll tell.
We have a small back-room inside there. Well,
Into that room a sofa was conveyed,
And on that sofa coverlets were laid.

CHREMES: And then?

MENEDEMUS: And then—no sooner said than done—
Into that room went Clitipho, your son.

CHREMES: Alone?

MENEDEMUS: Alone.

CHREMES: That's bad.

MENEDEMUS: Straight after him
Bacchis went in.

CHREMES: Alone?

MENEDEMUS: Alone.

CHREMES: That's grim.

MENEDEMUS: Once in, they shut the door.

CHREMES: Did your son see?

MENEDEMUS: Oh yes. My son was standing there, with me.

CHREMES: She—she—she's Clitipho's! It's sheer ruin!

MENEDEMUS: But why so?

CHREMES: Her? In my house? We've less than a week's supplies! Oh!

MENEDEMUS: Are you so worried because your son attends
To his friend's wants?

CHREMES: His what? His *female* friend's!

MENEDEMUS: That's if she is—

CHREMES: If! If! Who'd be so kind,
So meekly tolerant as not to mind
His girl-friend underneath his nose being—

MENEDEMUS: Oh,
          Why not? The better to fool me, you know.
CHREMES: Yes, have your fun. I've earned it. Oh, I'm mad
          At my own cloddishness! The clues I had,
          Which made the whole thing clear, if I'd not been
          A stock, a stone! The signs I'd heard and seen!
          But if I live they'll pay for this.
MENEDEMUS: Now steady!
          Don't take it out of yourself. Aren't I already
          A warning example of what not to do?
CHREMES: Oh, I'm beside myself with rage!
MENEDEMUS: What? You?
          You can say that? For shame! So good a guide
          To others, so wise in the world outside,
          At home so helpless?
CHREMES: Oh, what's to be done?
MENEDEMUS: Why, what you said I failed in. Make your son
          Feel you're his father, dare to tell you all,
          Ask your advice, appeal to you, not call
          Outsiders in and leave you out.
CHREMES: No, rather
          Let him go where he likes, not bring his father
          By running riot here to rack and ruin!
          Good god, if I go on the way I'm doing,
          Paying his bills, I'll be reduced indeed
          To digging, in dead earnest.
MENEDEMUS: Take good heed,
          Or you'll be heading for trouble. Yes, my friend,
          You'll first appear too harsh, then in the end
          Forgive him—with a bad grace and no gratitude.
CHREMES: You don't know how I feel.
MENEDEMUS: If that's your attitude—
          But what about your daughter? Will you let her
          Marry my son? Or have you something better
          In mind for her?
CHREMES: No, no, I'm satisfied
          With son-in-law and family.
MENEDEMUS: And the bride
          Will bring as dowry—how much shall I say?
          I mean, to him . . . Well, how much?
CHREMES: *(thoughtfully)*   Dowry, eh?
MENEDEMUS: That's what I said.
CHREMES: Quite so.

MENEDEMUS: You needn't fear
It's being too small. Money's no object here.

CHREMES: Well, measuring my means, I meant to give her
Two talents. But—if you really want to deliver
From ruin my estate, my son and me,
Just tell your son the dowry's going to be—
My every penny.

MENEDEMUS: What game is this you're playing?

CHREMES: But—ask him what Chremes is up to. Keep on saying
You just don't understand it.

MENEDEMUS: Well, that's true.
I don't see what you're up to.

CHREMES: Well, I do.
He's running rank and wild. I'm going to chop him
Right down to size and see if that'll stop him.
He'll be at his wit's end.

MENEDEMUS: Yes, but where does it get you?

CHREMES: Please! Let me follow my feelings.

MENEDEMUS: Sure, I'll let you.
You want this done, then?

CHREMES: Yes, I want it done.

MENEDEMUS: Well, then, I'll do it.

CHREMES: Yes—and please bid your son
Make ready to come at once and fetch my daughter.
(Menedemus goes indoors)
Meanwhile my son will get his due—cold water,
Well-frozen words, the medicine wise men give
Free youth. But as for Syrus—if I live
I'll lick him into shape. I'll make sure yet
That Chremes is a name he'll not forget,
Not till his dying day. I'll disabuse him
Of this idea that I'm just here to amuse him.
Good God, he wouldn't dare to make so free
With one weak widow as he's made with me!
*(Menedemus, Clitipho and Syrus all come out from
Menedemus' house)*

CLITIPHO: But, Menedemus, is it really true
That Father, like a bolt out of the blue,
Has cast me off, disowned me? What have I done,
God help me, that's so heinous for a son?
Don't they all do it?

MENEDEMUS: It's far worse, I know,
For you, who've felt the full weight of this blow.

But honestly my dismay is scarcely less.
I can't give reasons. I can't even guess.
I can assure you, though, come what may,
You have my heart-felt sympathy.

CLITIPHO: Did you say
My father was outside the house?

MENEDEMUS: Yes—there.
(He goes back into his own house)

CHREMES: So, Clitipho, you find I'm being unfair?
I've not forgotten you, though, in what I've done,
You and your folly. Having seen my son
So utterly feckless, putting first what's pleasant
Today, without one thought beyond the present,
I've planned to keep you out of want, but placed it
Out of your power to get my wealth and waste it.
It should have come to you. You wouldn't let it.
And so your next-of-kin has had to get it.
It's in his care and charge. Your feeble mind
Is in good hands. With him you'll always find
Food, clothes, a roof that's ready to receive you—

CLITIPHO: Oh, no!

CHREMES: I thought this better than to leave you
The property yourself, which meant bestowing
The lot on Bacchis.

SYRUS: *(aside)*   It's a hurricane, all unknowing,
I've raised, no wind, God help me!

CLITIPHO: I might as well die!

CHREMES: First learn what it is to live. Then you can try
The other, if life's no good.

SYRUS: Sir, if I may—

CHREMES: Proceed.

SYRUS: I want safe conduct.

CHREMES: Say your say.

SYRUS: It's wrong, sir, mad, that what I did amiss
Should hurt your son.

CHREMES: Syrus, keep out of this.
No one's accusing you. So you've no need
Of sanctuary or kind friends to intercede.

SYRUS: But what—?

CHREMES: I'm not annoyed with you—or you.
And so you mustn't be vexed at what I do.
(Goes into house)

SYRUS: Gone? I had something to ask him.

CLITIPHO: What?

SYRUS: Oh, merely
Where my next meal is coming from. Yours clearly
Is at your sister's. It seems I'm just a stranger.

CLITIPHO: Just think of it coming to this, of being in danger
Of actually starving!

SYRUS: While there's life there's hope.

CLITIPHO: Of what?

SYRUS: Of excellent appetites.

CLITIPHO: You dope!
We're in this mess, and all you do's make fun,
Not plans to help.

SYRUS: I do, though. I'd begun
Before he'd finished. And one idea I got—

CLITIPHO: Yes?

SYRUS: Hush! I'd nearly worked it all out.

CLITIPHO: What?

SYRUS: Suppose—you're not their son?

CLITIPHO: Not theirs? You're mad.

SYRUS: No, listen to my line of thought, my lad,
Then judge. When they'd no other pride and joy
Nearer their hearts, you were their blue-eyed boy.
They gave you everything. But now—they've found
A genuine daughter, and, with that, good ground
For getting rid of you.

CLITIPHO: That could make sense.

SYRUS: Do you really think your faults gave such offence?

CLITIPHO: No, no, I don't.

SYRUS: That's one point. Here's another.
When he's done wrong, a boy's best friend's his mother.
If ever his father's unfair to him, it's she
Who takes his side. Well, that's not happened—see?

CLITIPHO: By God, you've hit it! But what am I to do?

SYRUS: Ask them if what we suspect is true.
Out with it. Then you'll either, if I'm wrong,
Wring both their hearts, or find where you belong.

CLITIPHO: You're right. I'll do it now. *(Exit into house)*

SYRUS: I reckon I had
The right idea there, firmly giving the lad
That wrong idea. The firmer and the wronger,
The sooner he'll make peace with his dad, the stronger
His bargaining position. He may be heading—
No thanks to Syrus then!—for a suitable wedding.

Ha! Chremes coming out—I'd better run.
I wonder why, considering all I've done,
He hasn't hauled me off to hard labour
Long since. Shall I seek sanctuary with our neighbour?
Perhaps he'll take my part. Yes, yes, that's it.
I don't trust our old man one little bit.
*(Goes into Menedemus' house. Enter Chremes and Sostrata
from their house)*

SOSTRATA: Dear husband, take care, please, or else you'll do
Our son some real harm. I'm surprised that you
Could ever have been so silly.

CHREMES: Ah, dear wife,
Always the perfect woman! All my life
Whatever's been my wish, you've been agin it,
And if I asked you at this very minute
Where am I wrong, what reasons you suppose me
To have, you wouldn't know. Yet you oppose me
With idiotic self-assurance.

SOSTRATA: Oh!
So I don't know?

CHREMES: All right, all right, you know—
Rather than have that rigmarole repeated.

SOSTRATA: Was ever woman so unfairly treated,
Expected to keep mum on such a matter?

CHREMES: Expected nothing! Go on—natter, chatter,
I'll do what I intend to do, none the less.

SOSTRATA: You will?

CHREMES: Yes.

SOSTRATA: Don't you see, though, what distress
You're causing? He suspects himself to be
A foundling!

CHREMES: Does he?

SOSTRATA: Oh, it's true. You'll see.

CHREMES: What, you admit it, do you?

SOSTRATA: Heaven forbid!
Admit I didn't bear him, when I did?

CHREMES: You'd have no difficulty, never fear,
In proving him yours, whenever you wished, my dear.

SOSTRATA: You mean because of the way I discovered our daughter?

CHREMES: No! I mean proper proof, proof to hold water—
Likeness of character. There you'll prove with ease
That he's your product. You're as like as peas.
The boy's no faults beyond what you have too,

No woman could bear such a son but you.
But there he comes—our sober, serious youth,
As anyone would swear who knows the truth.

CLITIPHO: *(entering)*
Mother, if ever I have given you joy
And made you glad to hear me called your boy,
Remember it now when I'm so desperate. Please
Have pity on me. Set my mind at ease,
All that I'm asking, all I want to hear
Is who my parents are.

SOSTRATA: Oh, please, my dear,
Do put out of your mind this mad mistake!
Not ours!

CLITIPHO: Well, am I?

SOSTRATA: Oh, for pity's sake,
How can you ask? You're ours, I'll take my oath,
Sure as I hope that you'll survive us both.
So if you love your mother, let me hear, child,
No more of these wild words.

CHREMES: And if you fear, child,
Your father, never let me see or smell you
At your old tricks.

CLITIPHO: What tricks?

CHREMES: What tricks? I'll tell you,
If you must know—you scurvy little scamp,
You lazy, guzzling, good-for-nothing tramp!
Believe these are your names, and then you may
Believe you are my son.

CLITIPHO: Why, that's no way
To talk to one's own son.

CHREMES: If from my head
You had hopped out, much as Minerva's said
To have emerged from Jove's, I'd still be loth
To let your graceless doings disgrace us both.

SOSTRATA: Oh, Heaven forbid!

CHREMES: I don't know about Heaven,
I'll do my best. You seek what you were given
By providence—parents. What is wanting rather
You won't seek—ways and means to help your father,
Preserving what his hard work won, not smuggling
Under my nose, by some smart bit of juggling,
Your—but your mother's here. Shame must forbid it
Being mentioned. You'd no shame, though, when you did it.

CLITIPHO: *(aside)*
  Oh, God, I'm utterly disgusted now
  With all I am and do—ashamed. But how,
  How can I make things up?
MENEDEMUS: *(entering)*   Oh, it's too bad,
  The way that Chremes is punishing that lad
  Too cruel. I had to come and try my hand
  At mediation. Good, good! There they stand.
CHREMES: You've not acknowledged that dowry for my daughter
  In writing, or sent anyone to escort her
  To your house. Hurry up!
SOSTRATA: Please, husband dear,
  Don't do it.
CLITIPHO: Dad, forgive me.
MENEDEMUS: Don't you hear?
  Forgive him. Be persuaded.
CHREMES: To bestow
  My goods on Bacchis open-eyed? Oh, no!
MENEDEMUS: We'll not allow this, Chremes.
CLITIPHO: For my life's sake,
  If that means anything, pardon me!
SOSTRATA: For your wife's sake,
  Please, please!
MENEDEMUS: Come, Chremes, don't be so unbending—

CHREMES: You bar as wrong and bad what I'm intending—
  So—as you wish—
MENEDEMUS: It's the only right and good thing.
CHREMES: I'll do it, provided it's an understood thing
  He does what I think right and proper.
CLITIPHO: Yes, rather!
  Anything. Say the word.
CHREMES: Get married.
CLITIPHO: Father!!
CHREMES: Did you say 'anything'?
SOSTRATA: Come, I'll pledge my word
  The boy will do his duty.
CHREMES: I've still not heard
  The boy himself say so.
CLITIPHO: Oh, this is grim!
SOSTRATA: Come, dear, don't dilly-dally.
CHREMES: It's up to him
  The choice is all his.

SOSTRATA: Oh, he'll choose the wife.
MENEDEMUS: It's hard, of course, the start of married life,
           While you're still new and green, but there's nothing to it,
           Once you've got over that.
CLITIPHO: All right, I'll do it.
           I'll marry, Father.
SOSTRATA: There's my dutiful boy!
           I'll fit you with the perfect wife, a joy,
           A treasure. Oh, you'll find it no hard labour
           To love her. Yes, the daughter of our neighbour,
           Phanocrates.
CLITIPHO: Oh, no! I can't! She's hideous—
           Green eyes, red hair, spots, snub nose—
CHREMES: He's fastidious!
           He really feels about it.
SOSTRATA: Well, I've another
           Proposal for you, my dear.
CLITIPHO: No thank you, mother.
           I have in mind a girl who ought to do,
           Since I must marry.
CHREMES: You have, eh? Good for you.
CLITIPHO: The daughter of Archonides here.
SOSTRATA: Agreed.
CLITIPHO: There's one thing more.
CHREMES: What's that?
CLITIPHO: If I might plead
           For Syrus, let his service in my cause, please,
           Be pardoned.
CHREMES: Done!
PRODUCER: (to audience)   Good-day to you. Your applause, please.

The Eunuch

The Eunuch

CHARACTERS

PHAEDRIA: a young man, son of Laches
PARMENO: his slave
THAIS: a courtesan
GNATHO: a hanger-on, attached to Thraso
CHAEREA: a young man, brother of Phaedria
THRASO: a soldier
PYTHIAS: a maid of Thais
CHREMES: a young man, brother of Pamphila
ANTIPHO: a friend of Chaerea
DORIAS: a maid of Thais
DORUS: a eunuch
SANGA: a cook, slave of Thraso
SOPHRONA: Pamphila's old nurse
LACHES: an old man, father of Phaedria and Chaerea

PROLOGUE

If there is any author whose one plan
Is just to please as many as he can
If there be one who feels unfairly got at,
This prologue's no first act of war. Being shot at
We answer, but that enemy fires first,
That hack translator making best things worse
With good Greek plays into bad Latin rendered.
Menander's *Ghost* was what he lately tendered,
And what a ghost!—while in the comedy named
The Find he lets the man from whom it's claimed
Give arguments showing why the gold is his
Before the plaintiff demonstrates how it is
He got the gold, and how it found its way
Into his father's tomb. Let him not say
Falsely secure, 'What digs now can he dog me with?
I'm a dead horse—he's nothing left to flog me with.'
Stop, then, your vicious nagging and venomous stinging

I've lots of other charges I'm not bringing,
Unless his present pin-pricks should persist,
In which case he shall hear the whole long list.
But—when the officials for the games contracted
For this, our present offering, to be acted—
Menander's *Eunuchus*—what does he do
But somehow get a special permission to view?
In the official presence we began,
Till he cried out, 'Stop thief!' and added 'This man
Thought he'd a catching plot, but it's not caught us!
There's an old play by Naevius and Plautus,
The Flatterer, from which the parasite's role,
As well as the captain's, has been lifted whole.'
The fault, if any, lies in not perceiving
This 'fact' put forward, not in deliberate thieving,
As you yourselves will be able to judge in a minute.
Menander has a play called *The Flatterer*. In it
There is a parasite, Colax, and moreover
A boastful captain. That he took these over
From that play for his *Eunuch*—*that* our poet
Does not deny, but says he did not know it
To have been turned into a Latin play
Entire by anyone, not till this day.
If making use of characters much the same
As someone else has used is, in this game,
'Not done' somehow, why is it rather 'done'
To write of slaves forever on the run,
Bombastic captains, parasites always eating,
Old men whom their own slaves are always cheating,
Matrons being virtuous, mistresses being vicious,
Children supposedly suppositious,
Mankind being amorous, angry or suspicious?
In fact there's nothing one can find to say
That's not been said before—which fact, I pray,
You'll bear in mind and make allowance due
If what the ancients did the moderns do.
In peace now hear our piece. Weigh word and action,
See if our *Eunuch* gives *some* satisfaction.

Scene: a place in Athens, with streets leading off towards the market, the harbour and the country. On the right is the house of Thais, a courtesan, on the left that of Laches.

ACT I

(Enter Phaedria and Parmeno, his slave, from Laches' house)

PHAEDRIA: What shall I do? Not go?—despite the woman's
Deigning to send an extra special summons?
Shall I be done with her sort, mocking and slighting me,
Shutting the door in my face, then re-inviting me?
Back there? Not though she begged me on her knees!

PARMENO: That would, sir,
Be the best and boldest course to take—if you could, sir.
But, if you start and can't stick to that tack,
But find you just can't stand it and creep back,
Unasked, an unconditional surrender,
Which tells the world your feelings are too tender
To hold out longer, you'll be doomed, dished, done with,
A beaten foe, a butt for her to have fun with.
Now, while there's time, before it is too late,
Reflect and re-reflect on your true state.
A thing which lacks all rational base and bounds
Defies all management based on rational grounds.
Love is a tale of discord, loud and long,
Suspicion, outright rage, outrageous wrong,
Truces and treaties, war and peace. In fact
In love's uncertain world to want to act
On any certain method is as bad
As want to be—methodically mad.
You run the gamut *now* of rage—'Ha! Me!
With *her*, when I had "no", while he and she—!
Never! I'd sooner die! She'll have to learn
Who she's dealing with!' Bold words, sir, words that burn,
And yet one tiny tear, one liquid lie,
With much hard rubbing wrung from one bright eye,
Will quench that fire. What's more she'll even make it
All *your* fault, after all—what's more, you'll take it.

PHAEDRIA: It's sickening! It's degrading! I can see
That she's a bitch who's made an ass of me.
I'm fed up—yet on fire. I know what I'm doing
But rush with open eyes on obvious ruin.
What remedy?

PARMENO: Buy back your freedom, man,
From this slave-driver, as cheaply as you can.
If that's not practical, then at any price,
To end these agonies.
PHAEDRIA: That's your honest advice?
PARMENO: If you've any sense. Bear like a man the trouble
Love brings, but don't, like a donkey, bear double.
(Thais comes out of her house)
Talk of the devil! Parmeno, there's your mildew,
Your seven years' blight, when plenty might have filled you.
THAIS: *(to herself)*
I'm so afraid that Phaedria's offended,
And hasn't taken at all as I intended
My not admitting him yesterday.
PHAEDRIA: Oh, I'm shivering
At the sight of her. Parmeno, I'm quaking, quivering,
Quite cold all over!
PARMENO: Don't worry. She's hot stuff.
Go near, and you'll get warmer soon enough.
THAIS: Who's that spoke? . . . Oh, good gracious, Phaedria dear.
It's you! But why were you just standing here?
Why didn't you come right in?
PARMENO: The door's been barred on us
Remember?
THAIS: Phaedria, won't you speak?
PHAEDRIA: You'll pardon us
Not noticing the welcome on your mat,
The preferential treatment.
THAIS: Don't talk like that!
PHAEDRIA: Like what? Oh, Thais, Thais, why the devil
Can't we make love the same way, on one level?
If what hurt me hurt you, there'd be more sharing,
Or if *you* could do as you like without me caring.
THAIS: This wasn't done—I swear by all above—
Because there's any man I like—no, love—
More than yourself. I beg you, Phaedria dear,
Don't, don't torment yourself! As things stand here,
I had no choice.
PARMENO: No doubt, our poor, dear Thais
Locked Phaedria out for pure love, as the way is.
THAIS: That's what you think of me, Parmeno? Very well, then,
But can you guess why I sent for you? . . . I'll tell then.
PHAEDRIA: Tell on.

THAIS: But first—can Parmeno keep mum?
PARMENO: What me? Sealed lips! The dumbest of the dumb.
          But—it's on one condition that I seal them.
          True secrets are quite safe. I never reveal them.
          But fables, fictions, fibs, I'm a perfect sieve with,
          Leak left and right. Those secrets I can't live with.
THAIS: My mother, by birth a Samian, was living
          At Rhodes.
PARMENO: On that you need have no misgiving.
          I won't tell.
THAIS: There she had a present made her,
          A little girl, brought to her by a trader,
          Kidnapped from here, from Attica.
PHAEDRIA: You mean
          Of free Athenian birth?
THAIS: She *may* have been.
          I think she was. Her father's name and her mother's
          She knew, but not her birthplace. That clue and others
          She was too young for. All remained a mystery.
          One fact the trader could add to her history,
          Something the pirate selling her did tell,
          That she'd been kidnapped near Cape Sunium. Well,
          My mother took her in, looked after her, taught her
          All that she could, and reared her as her daughter;
          And with most people she naturally passed
          As my young sister. I came to Athens at last,
          With the only man I'd ever had an affair with,
          Who left me all I have in the world.
PARMENO: And therewith
          You've told two leaking lies.
THAIS: How?
PARMENO: You—make do
          With *one* man and what he could give! Not true.
          This lad has done his part in giving, and paying.
THAIS: Fair point! But let me finish what I was saying.
          This lover, whose attentions so upset you,
          The captain, went off to Caria. Then—I met you,
          And what you've meant to me ever since you know,
          How I've confided in you.
PARMENO: Parmeno
          Can't keep *that* in.
THAIS: Who says I'm lying? Oh,
          Listen you two. Not long ago my mother

Died out in Rhodes there. Her tight-fisted brother
Seeing the girl had good looks and can play
The harp, smells money in it, puts her straight away
On sale in the market, sells her. Who should be,
By pure chance, there, but my new boy-friend! He
Unwitting, unawares, buys her—for *me*!
But, finding on his return, I've another friend—
Yes, *you*—invents excuses without end
For not delivering her at once, declaring
That, if he were only sure of my preferring
Himself, and had no fear that to surrender
The girl would mean good-bye to me, he'd send her
At once. That's what he fears, he *says*. My guess
Is that he's turned his eyes on *her*, no less.

PHAEDRIA: No more?

THAIS: You mean—? Oh, no, I've made inquiries
Of her. But, Phaedria dear, my one desire is
On many grounds, to get her back again.
First, we were brought up as full sisters. Then,
I've hopes of restoring her, for my own ends
To her family. I'm alone here. I've no friends
In Attica, no connections. If I can do
Someone a good turn, I may get a few.
Please help me. Don't make it harder. Let him play
The leading part with me, for just one day
Or two . . . Well, aren't you answering?

PHAEDRIA: What can I answer?
When you—you woman—?

PARMENO: Spoken like a man, sir!
Don't stand for any nonsense!

PHAEDRIA: Perhaps I fail
To fathom the full purport of your tale.
'A little girl was stolen somehow or other
In Attica, brought up as ours by my mother
And called my sister. That girl I must get',
You say, 'and restore her to her family.' Yet—
What does it all boil down to? I'm locked out,
And he's let in. And why? Can anyone doubt
You're crazy about him, and scared now, in case
This bought slave-girl might slip into your place
In your big hero's heart?

THAIS: Me? Scared of that?

PHAEDRIA: Well, then, what else can you be worried at?

Is he the only man that gives you things?
When have you ever found my poor purse-strings
Drawn tight against you? You tell me, first, you're set on
A little dark-skinned girl. I go and get one,
Giving it top priority. Then you're mad keen
On having a eunuch, since nobody but a queen
Would normally have one. Yesterday I took care
Of that too—twenty minae for the pair.
I don't forget—in spite of your cold shoulder;
And my reward, it seems, is to find it colder.

THAIS: Oh, Phaedria, stop it! Though my purpose *is*
To coax that girl into my hands from his,
And though I think I can achieve that end,
Rather than risk a rift with my best friend
I'll play it as you wish.

PHAEDRIA: If I were sure
You were sincere in this, I could endure
Anything in the world!

PARMENO: *(aside)*   He's on the brink!
He'll break his neck for one word and a wink!

THAIS: Me not sincere! When was there anything yet
You asked for, even in fun, and failed to get?
And can't I get a concession out of *you*,
Even for two days?

PHAEDRIA: If it *is* just two,
But see it doesn't turn into a score.

THAIS: Oh, no, it won't be more than two, or—

PHAEDRIA: Or?
Or nothing!

THAIS: Two days, then. You *do* agree?

PHAEDRIA: I'll have to do what suits you, I can see.

THAIS: Oh, you're so kind, I can't help loving you!

PHAEDRIA: Well,
I'll go off to the country. Two days' hell
I'll have there. But my mind's made up. I'll go,
To humour Thais. But look, Parmeno,
Have those two creatures brought across.

PARMENO: Aye, aye.

PHAEDRIA: And so, dear Thais, for these two days, goodbye,
Good luck to you.

THAIS: Dear Phaedria, same to you!
Now, unless there's anything else that I can do—

PHAEDRIA: Anything else? Yes, Thais. Keep your heart

At least while the captain's with you, worlds apart.
All day, all night, love *me*, think, dream about me,
Be waiting, longing, hoping, lost without me.
Dote on me, and be all mine—yes, the whole of you.
Give, as I give, the very heart and soul of you.
(Exit with Parmeno into Laches' house)

THAIS: Oh, dear, I can't help feeling he does doubt me.
Other women have given him these ideas about me.
My conscience is clear. There's been no double dealing
On *my* part. I never had the kind of feeling
I have for Phaedria with any other.
All I've been doing was for this girl, whose brother,
I do believe, I've managed to unearth
At last, a lad of what they call high birth;
And he's arranged to come and see me here.
I'll go inside and wait for him to appear.
(Exit into house)

ACT II

(A few minutes have passed. Enter Phaedria and Parmeno)

PHAEDRIA: Well, as I said, deliver them.

PARMENO: As you say, sir.

PHAEDRIA: With care.

PARMENO: Okay.

PHAEDRIA: And speed.

PARMENO: Okay, okay, sir.

PHAEDRIA: That's all quite clear, then?

PARMENO: Clear, sir? Need you ask?
As if it were so difficult a task!
I wish gifts could be got with half the ease
I'll find in losing—and it's dead loss—these.

PHAEDRIA: A dearer loss goes with them—my poor heart.
Don't fret so.

PARMENO: I'm not fretting. I'll play my part.
Will that be all, sir?

PHAEDRIA: Do your best to grace
Our gifts with good words. Go all out to displace
My wretched rival!

PARMENO: That goes, sir, without saying.

PHAEDRIA: I'm going down to the farm—and there I'm staying.

PARMENO: Good, sir.

PHAEDRIA: But, look here—
PARMENO: Yes, sir?
PHAEDRIA: Would you say
I'm capable of conquering my yearning,
No risk of my—well, prematurely returning?
PARMENO: You? No, sir. You'll return. You'll either do it
At once, or sleepless nights will drive you to it.
PHAEDRIA: I'll dig myself dog-tired, then willy-nilly
I'll sleep.
PARMENO: You'll lie, dog-tired, awake.
PHAEDRIA: That's silly!
God, I've gone soft! This weakness I must strive
To master. Why shouldn't I, if I must, survive
Even *three* whole days without her? Well, I ask you!
PARMENO: Three days? Eternity! Think—three days would task you
To the uttermost.
PHAEDRIA: I'm determined! *(Exit)*
PARMENO: Gods above!
What sort of sickness is this being in love,
That makes a man you knew a perfect stranger?
For who more sober, serious, less in danger
Of indiscretions than *he* used to be?
Hallo! Who's that approaching? Oh, I see—
The captain's creeper-upper, *and* he's got
The girl, their gift for Thais. Whew! She's hot.
That shape will show *us* up with our moth-eaten
Old eunuch. She's got even Thais beaten.
*(Gnatho enters with a young girl and attendant maid. He does
not see Parmeno and soliloquizes)*
GNATHO: Ye gods! The difference between man and man,
When one can't use his wits and the other can!
What prompted this particular observation?
I met a man of my own rank and station,
A decent sort, with property, which he'd duly
Eaten and drunk away, just like yours truly.
I saw a sick man, old before his time,
A ruin overgrown with rags and grime.
'Good Lord!' I said to him, 'You do look bad!
But why?' Says he, 'Well, I've lost all I had,
So I'm reduced to the plight you now perceive me in,
Which old friends and acquaintances happily leave me in.'
I scanned him and myself, and felt such scorn—
'Good grief!' I cried. 'So crushed, faint-willed, forlorn?

Did your wits fly out of the window with your wealth?
We started even. Now look at me—radiant health,
Rose-cheeked, sleek-skinned, and good clothes on my back.
I've everything, and nothing, nothing lack,
And nothing own.' Says he, 'I haven't your luck,
A nature that can bear being mocked and struck.'
'That's how you think it's done? You're miles astray,'
Said I. 'Maybe that method used to pay,
But there's another way to catch birds now,
And I claim credit for discovering how.
Some men, without reason, reckon they're cock of the walk
At everything under the sun. These birds I stalk,
Not to raise crows of mirth at my expense:
I smile my wonderment at wit immense,
I praise their every word, and if today's
Should contradict last night's word, still I praise,
Denying whatsoever *they* deny,
And whatsoever *they* say, so say I—
A thriving business, built on orders strict
Issued by me myself—'Don't contradict.'

PARMENO: *(aside)*
A clever fellow! Many a simple fool
Might learn to be a madman in his school.

GNATHO: *(continuing)*
Chatting like this, we'd reached the market-place;
Running to meet me came, with smiling face,
Dealers in fine fare, all of them, butchers, bakers,
Whale-mongers and sprat-mongers, sausage-makers,
Who, while my own estate was still intact,
Made money out of me, and still do, in fact,
Now it's defunct. I'm greeted, hailed, invited
To dinner. At the sight of me they're delighted.
Well, that poor famished fellow, when he sees
I'm so admired and earn my bread with ease,
Begs to be taught the sort of thing I'd told him.
'Who knows? Some day,' I thought, as I enrolled him,
'As with philosophers, Plato and the Platonics,
All hangers-on may bear the name Gnathonics!'

PARMENO: *(aside)*
The fruits of idleness and another's bread!
Just look at him!

GNATHO: Well, I'd better go ahead
And deliver this girl to Thais, and invite her

Along to dinner tonight . . . Ah, there's that blighter,
Parmeno, from the opposition party.
Standing outside. He doesn't look too hearty
So we're all right. Their welcome has been chilly,
That's obvious. I'll make the poor sod look silly.

PARMENO: *(aside)*
That girl's the gift meant to make Thais surrender
To them entirely.

GNATHO: *(to Parmeno)*   May Gnatho humbly tender
Greetings to Parmeno with great good will?
How are we getting on?

PARMENO: We're standing still.

GNATHO: Ah, so I see. Have *you* seen something to peeve you?

PARMENO: Yes, you—believe it or not.

GNATHO: Oh, I believe you.
But nothing else?

PARMENO: No. Why?

GNATHO: You're looking glum.

PARMENO: Not in the least.

GNATHO: Don't be down-hearted. Come,
How do you like this little slave-girl, eh?

PARMENO: Not bad.

GNATHO: *(aside)*
I've got him on the rack!

PARMENO: *(aside)*   You're wrong, my lad!

GNATHO: How do you think she will appeal to Thais?

PARMENO: You mean we're cut out? I expect, as the way is
With everything, ups and downs.

GNATHO: Why, Parmeno,
I'm really giving you six months' rest, you know—
No rushing round, staying up till the cocks are crowing—
In fact I'm filling your cup to overflowing.

PARMENO: Oh, thanks.

GNATHO: Don't mention it. It's my way with chaps
I like—

PARMENO: How charming!

GNATHO: I'm keeping you. Perhaps
You were on your way somewhere else.

PARMENO: No. I was *not*.

GNATHO: Then you can do me a small service, what?
Present me at court.

PARMENO: At Thais'? The door's there,
And it's wide open, now you're bringing *her*.

GNATHO: Well, is there anyone that you'd like sent out?
PARMENO: Just let these two days pass. Oh, now, no doubt,
            The luck's all yours. Doors open when you flick them
            With your little finger. But I'll soon see you kick them
            Twice or three times for nothing, never fear.
            *(Gnatho takes Pamphila and the girl into Thais' house, then
            re-emerges)*
GNATHO: Well, Parmeno, are you still standing here?
            Posted to guard the game, in case some poacher,
            Some go-between from the captain, should approach her?
PARMENO: Oh, very clever! You need such strokes of wit,
            No doubt, to be what the captain calls a hit.
            (Exit Gnatho)
            But there's my master's younger son, I see,
            Heading this way. Now why on earth should *he*
            Have come home from the harbour? He's meant to be doing
            Guard duty down there. Oh, there's trouble brewing.
            He's in a tearing hurry wherever he's bound for—
            And what's he lost that he keeps looking round for?
CHAEREA: *(entering)*
            She's lost—and so am I! Hell! Where's she gone to?
            What track or trace or lead can I get on to?
            Whom can I ask? My one hope is, no place
            On earth can hide for long that lovely face.
            I blot all other women out. I'm through now
            With common or garden beauties.
PARMENO: *(aside)*   Number two now
            Raving of love! My poor old man! This brother
            If he gets going, will make him call the other
            Mere child's-play, chicken-feed, beside the dish
            These flames will cook for us.
CHAEREA: What don't I wish
            On his damned doddering head who so delayed me,
            And mine for bothering, letting him persuade me
            To stop! Ah, Parmeno.
PARMENO: Well, what's your worry?
            What's happened? Where have you come from? What's the hurry?
CHAEREA: I've lost myself. I don't know where I've been.
            I've forgotten where I'm going.
PARMENO: What do you mean?
CHAEREA: I'm madly in love.
PARMENO: *(aside)*   Just what I was afraid of.
CHAEREA: So now's the time to show the stuff you're made of.

You know you've often assured me I'd discover
Your talents when I came to you as a lover
In need of help—that's when you'd had the profit
Of my pillaging of the pantry.
PARMENO: Oh, come off it!
CHAEREA: It's true. And she's well worth what wit you've got in you.
So prove your promises, strain every sinew.
This girl's not just a girl like so many others
In Athens where the sole aim of all mothers
Is slimness, sloping shoulders, strait-laced breast;
So any poor girl robuster than the rest
Mamma will nickname 'Boxer', dock her rations,
And forms that Nature nurtured Art refashions
On bulrush lines—lines that land boy-friends—frightful!
PARMENO: While yours—?
CHAEREA: Looks—two whole worlds away—
PARMENO: Delightful!
CHAEREA: Firm figure, full of—sap, face quite unpainted.
PARMENO: Her age?
CHAEREA: Sixteen.
PARMENO: Life's bloom, pure and untainted—
CHAEREA: That bloom you've got to pluck me—beg, steal, force—
No matter how, she must be mine.
PARMENO: Of course.
The owner of this paragon's—?
CHAEREA: Anyone's guess.
PARMENO: Birth, country of origin?
CHAEREA: Ditto.
PARMENO: Present address?
CHAEREA: Unknown.
PARMENO: Where did you see her, then?
CHAEREA: Just now,
Here in the street.
PARMENO: And how did you lose her?
CHAEREA: How?
That's just what I was cursing myself about
On my way here. Who ever fell in and out
Of luck like that?
PARMENO: What went wrong?
CHAEREA: Hell, damnation!
PARMENO: What happened?
CHAEREA: Happened? Do you know a relation,
An old friend of my father's, by the name

	Of Archidemides?
PARMENO:	Sure.
CHAEREA:	Well, he's to blame.

He blundered into me when I was hot
On the girl's tail.

PARMENO: A bit of a bore.

CHAEREA: A what?
One might call lots of things a bit of a bore.
This was a stunning blow. Six months or more
I'll swear I never saw the man till then,
When I least wanted it to happen, and when
I best could do without him. The hand of fate!
Uncanny, what?

PARMENO: It was.

CHAEREA: From miles off straight,
Straight up to me, bent half-double, he came flying,
Jaw dropping, quivering like a jelly, sighing,
'Hi, Chaerea! Hi!' So there I stood, stopped dead.
'There's something you could do for me,' he said.
'What?' 'I've a case coming on tomorrow.' 'Well?
What can I do?' 'Just this. Be sure to tell
Your father that I count on his support,
So will he please remember to be in court
Tomorrow morning?' . . . while he talked, time passed.
'Well, if there's nothing else,' I said at last.
'No thanks.' I ran, looked round where beauty beckoned
And saw her turning in that selfsame second
Into our street—here.

PARMENO: *(aside)* Talk about selfsame!
The girl they sent to Thais!

CHAEREA: When I came,
She'd vanished.

PARMENO: Was she alone, quite unattended?

CHAEREA: She'd a maid in tow, and a toady type.

PARMENO: Search ended!
It's her. Give up the game. You're dished, you're done.

CHAEREA: Your mind is running on something else.

PARMENO: Mine's run
Where yours did.

CHAEREA: You've seen her? You know her? Well, go on!

PARMENO: I've seen her, and I know her, and where she's gone.

CHAEREA: What, Parmeno? You know *who* she is and *where*?

PARMENO: She's been delivered to Thais' house, right there,

A present from an admirer.

CHAEREA: Who on earth
Is able to afford a present worth
That much?

PARMENO: Why, Phaedria's rival, Captain Thraso.

CHAEREA: My brother's up against it then?

PARMENO: You'd say so,
If you could see the sort of gift he's got
To match that.

CHAEREA: What's *he* giving?

PARMENO: A eunuch.

CHAEREA: What?
That horrible, hoary half-man that my brother,
God help him, went and bought yesterday?

PARMENO: None other.

CHAEREA: With *that* gift he'll get flung out on his ear.
I never knew, though, that Thais lived so near.

PARMENO: She's not been there long.

CHAEREA: Fancy me, all the same,
Not having seen her! Is she all they claim—
I mean, with regard to her good looks?

PARMENO: She is.

CHAEREA: But nothing like *my* girl?

PARMENO: *(shrugging)*   One's yours, one's his.

CHAEREA: Oh, Parmeno, you *must* make sure I get her.

PARMENO: We'll see. I'll be the aider and abetter
As best I can. Anything else right now, sir?

CHAEREA: Where are you off to?

PARMENO: Going back to the house, sir,
To fetch for Thais that eunuch and the rest,
As per your brother's orders.

CHAEREA: Oh, how blest
That eunuch is, to be a gift being sent
Inside there!

PARMENO: What do you mean?

CHAEREA: You know what I meant!
To have a fellow-slave like that to share
Your quarters with, to be all day with *her*
To look at, talk with, eat with at one table,
And sometimes sleep—quite near!

PARMENO: One might be able
To bless *you*.

CHAEREA: What on earth do you mean by blessing me?

PARMENO: Dress you in his gear—

CHAEREA: What's the point of dressing me—?

PARMENO: And send you in his place—

CHAEREA: I begin to spot it.

PARMENO: And pass you off, in fact, as him.

CHAEREA: I've got it!

PARMENO: The blessings you were counting you'd be able
         Yourself to sample, share the selfsame table,
         Be near her, touch her, have a bit of fun,
         Sleep with her not far off. It could be done.
         Not one of them in there has ever met you,
         No one knows what you look like. And I bet you,
         Your age and looks being—what they are, you'd do
         Quite nicely for a eunuch.

CHAEREA: Good for you!
         That's not a bad idea. No—it's the best
         I ever heard. Let's go, let's get me dressed
         For the part at once. Lead on.

PARMENO: What are you doing?
         I was just joking.

CHAEREA: Rubbish!

PARMENO: You'll be my ruin.
         Stop pushing! There, you've made me stumble. No!
         This won't do. Wait, now, wait.

CHAEREA: Come on, let's go.

PARMENO: You're serious?

CHAEREA: Sure.

PARMENO: But aren't you being too hot
         And hasty, don't you think?

CHAEREA: I reckon not.
         Let go of me.

PARMENO: You know this little pack
         Of trouble's going to land on my poor back.

CHAEREA: Come on!

PARMENO: It's a real rogue's game we're getting committed to.

CHAEREA: Rogue's game? The sort of house I'll be admitted to
         Harbours the torturers of our youth. They treat us
         Like dirt. I'll pay a debt we owe. They cheat us
         Day in, day out. So I'll cheat *them*. Would you rather
         Have me, for instance, cheat instead my father?
         That's something everyone, if they knew, would blame,
         But all the world would call *these* birds fair game.

PARMENO: All right, if you're resolved. Go on. But don't

Hereafter put the blame on *me*.

CHAEREA: I won't.

PARMENO: You're *telling* me to do this, are you?

CHAEREA: Telling you?
No, Parmeno, commanding and compelling you.
The onus of this act I shall not shirk.
Come on.

PARMENO: And heaven help this woeful work!
(They go into Laches' house)

ACT III

(Thraso enters with Gnatho)

THRASO: So Thais thanked me very warmly—what?

GNATHO: Ecstatically!

THRASO: She was pleased, then?

GNATHO: Yes, but not
So much with the gift, as with its being from you.
That's her real triumph, her great dream come true.
(Parmeno comes out of Laches' house)

PARMENO: *(aside)*
I've come to keep watch. When the coast is clear,
I'll smuggle him in. Hallo! The captain's here.

THRASO: I've always had this gift of reaping gratitude.

GNATHO: I've noticed that.

THRASO: Well, take His Majesty's attitude.
Whatever I did, most grateful. Not the same
At all with others.

GNATHO: Ah, the fruit of fame
That others plant with works, the men of wit—
Like you—with words graft on themselves—

THRASO: That's it.
Graft, as you say.

GNATHO: And grow, like you—

THRASO: Quite, quite—

GNATHO: The apple of the royal eye.

THRASO: That's right.
Trusted with all his troops, plans—

GNATHO: You *are* clever!

THRASO: Yes, and if ever sick of people, if ever
Fed up with business, wanting a holiday from it,
Wanting a sort of—

GNATHO: I know—a place to vomit
Vexations sitting on his royal chest—

THRASO: That's it—he'd get me alone, as his sole guest.

GNATHO: A man of really remarkable taste!

THRASO: True, true.
Not a man for every comer—the chosen few.

GNATHO: *(aside)*
No comers at all, if he consorts with *you*!

THRASO: Oh, they're all envious. Busy bunch of backbiters—
I know what they say, and I don't give a damn. Poor blighters,
They're green with it, especially one poor sod,
The O.C. Indian Elephants. By God
He met his match when he went out of his way
To annoy me. Know what I said? 'I say,
Strabo,' I said. 'Are you so bloody fierce
Because you're king of the beasts?'

GNATHO: Oh, that would pierce
Right to the bone! So sharp! So smart! What *could* be
More pointed? How did he take it?

THRASO: Dumb.

GNATHO: He *would* be.

PARMENO: *(aside)*
God help us! Don't that wretched idiot there
And this damned rascal make a precious pair?

THRASO: But the real beauty, of course, the absolute winner
Was the young man of Rhodes I floored at that dinner—
I must have told you.

GNATHO: Never. Oh, do tell!
(aside)
I've heard it more than a thousand times now.

THRASO: Well,
We had this Rhodian, regular white-arsed bunny-boy,
At dinner with us. And he starts being the funny boy
With *my* girl, giggling at *me*. 'Well, well! Our bunny dares,'
Says I, 'with *hims* on his own tail, to hunt *hers*!'

GNATHO: Oh, it's too bad!

THRASO: What?

GNATHO: Hers! What could be neater,
Smarter or smoother? A genuine world-beater!
So that's *your* crack. *I* thought it was quite old.

THRASO: You mean you've heard it?

GNATHO: Oh, it's often told,
And always reckoned as a first-rate crack.

THRASO: Oh, well, it's mine.

GNATHO: But what a nasty smack
In the eye for that poor, innocent young man, sir!

PARMENO: *(aside)*
God rot him!

GNATHO: What did he do by way of answer?

THRASO: He was utterly lost. The whole room rocked with laughter,
And everyone fought shy of me thereafter.

GNATHO: I'm sure they did.

THRASO: But listen. What would you say is
My right move? Should I clear myself with Thais
About this girl, since I seem to be under suspicion
Of being smitten?

GNATHO: No. That, in your position,
Would be the worst thing possible. You should try
To strengthen her suspicion.

THRASO: Should I? Why?

GNATHO: Look, if she mentions Phaedria, sing his praises,
You know very well how it burns your guts.

THRASO: Like blazes!

GNATHO: Well, here's the sole cure for that sort of sickness.
She lets fall Phaedria's name. With lightning-quickness
You bring in Pamphila. She says, 'Let's send
For Phaedria and have fun.' Then you pretend
We *must* hear Pamphila sing. Should she exclaim
On Phaedria's fine figure, you do the same
For Pamphila, topping praises, tit for tat—
Gall to her!

THRASO: If she fancied me, Gnatho, *that*
Would work, I daresay.

GNATHO: Work! But look at the state
You've got her in already. She can't wait
For your presents. She loves *them*. And by steady stages
She's come to love *you*. She's done that for ages:
For ages it's been easy enough to sting her.
She's always afraid the fruits of love you bring her
May, if she angers you, go elsewhere instead.

THRASO: You're dead right. It never entered my head.

GNATHO: That's rich! You never gave your mind to the question,
Or you'd have certainly bettered the suggestion.

THAIS: *(coming out)*
I thought I heard the captain's voice round here.
Ah, there he is. Good morning, Thraso dear.

THRASO: Thais, my treasure, how's the world treating you?
          Well, lovely, did my lute-girl sweeten you
          A soupçon for me?
PARMENO: *(aside)*   What a charming touch
          To start a visit with!
THAIS: Sweeten? Oh, yes, as much
          As your own sweet deserts.
GNATHO: Well, time for supper!
          Why are we waiting?
PARMENO: *(aside)*   The super backer-upper,
          Sub-human crawling creep!
THAIS: Whenever you please.
          I don't mind.
PARMENO: *(aside)*   Well, I'll stroll up, quite at ease
          As though I'd just come out. *(aloud)* Ah, Thais, you!
          Going anywhere?
THAIS: Oh, Parmeno, I *do*
          Thank you for what you did. I'm just going—
PARMENO: Well?
THAIS: *(aside)*
          Can't you see *him*?
PARMENO: *(aside)*   Sure. I'm as sick as hell
          At the sight of him. Phaedria's presents are to hand here
          Whenever you're ready.
THRASO: Why do we have to stand here?
          Why don't we get on?
PARMENO: Sir, I humbly petition
          That *we* may have a chance, with your permission,
          To meet this lady, talk with her, and deliver
          Whatever presents we may desire to give her.
THRASO: Fine presents, as good as any of ours, no doubt!
PARMENO: The event will show.
          (He shouts to someone in Laches' house)
                              Hi! Tell 'em to come out!
          You know the couple I mean. We haven't all day!
          (A black girl comes out)
          Ah, there. Step forward. She comes all the way
          From Aethiopia.
THRASO: Hum! Three minae's worth.
GNATHO: Oh, not that much.
PARMENO: Hi, Dorus! Where on earth—?
          (Chaerea comes out in eunuch's dress)
          Come over here. How's that for a eunuch now?

The bloom of youth, the free lad's frank, clear brow!
THAIS: I must say he's good-looking.
PARMENO: Ha! Would you say so,
Gnatho? Can you find fault with him? Or you, Thraso?
Their silence sings his praise. He's a lad of parts—
Test him—athletics, literature, all the arts
A boy of free birth is supposed to have mastered—
I'd back him up to the hilt.
THRASO: I'd back the smooth bastard
And without a drink to whet me.
PARMENO: Of course the donor
Of these gifts doesn't claim to be the sole owner
Of you and of your time and have your door
Locked to the world for his sole sake. No more
Does he tell tales of battle, or boast scars.
He never, like a certain person, puts bars
On your free choice. But if, when his appearance
Fits time and taste, and means no interference
With what you're doing, you'll welcome him, he's content.
THRASO: 'My master's a beggarly bum' is what that meant.
GNATHO: He's the sort of servant no man could endure
Who could afford a better, of that I'm sure!
PARMENO: You shut your gob! You—you're the dregs of dregs,
Of all the creatures crawling upon two legs!
If you can bring yourself to flatter *that*,
You'd go to the gutter for a good meal—rat!
THRASO: Look, are we off?
THAIS: Wait. I'll just take these two
Indoors and tell my maids what they've to do.
I'll be right back. *(Exit into the house)*
THRASO: *(to Gnatho)*   I'm off. You wait for her here.
PARMENO: *(ironically)*
Of course it doesn't do for a brigadier
To be seen abroad with his lady-friend.
THRASO: I'll waste
No words on you. With your master you're well-placed.
GNATHO: Ha, ha!
THRASO: What's the joke?
GNATHO: Your retort, sir— and what you said
To the Rhodian also came into my head.
Here's Thais emerging.
THRASO: Cut ahead, then, hurry,
See everything's ready at home.

GNATHO: I will, don't worry. *(Exit)*
(Thais enters with Pythias and two other maids)
THAIS: Now, Pythias, that's clear, I hope. Or is it?
If Chremes does decide to pay us a visit,
Ask him to call back later—tomorrow, say—
But, if that's inconvenient, to stay
And wait for me here. But if he simply can't,
Bring him to join us. Don't forget.
PYTHIAS: I shan't.
THAIS: Wait, wait. I'd something else on the tip of my tongue.
Ah, yes, look after that girl. She's very young.
And see that all of you stay in tonight.
THRASO: Let's go.
THAIS: *(to maids)* You two bring up the rear, then. Right? *(Exeunt)*
(Enter Chremes)
CHREMES: The more I think, the more I'd back my guess
That Thais means to land me in a mess,
Trapping and sapping since she first bade me call!
'Call? On what business?' you'll ask me. None at all.
I didn't even know her. On my arriving
She found some plausible reason for contriving
To keep me. She'd been offering up a prayer
And sacrifice, she said, and had an affair
Of weight to discuss with me. I smelt a rat
From then on. Very friendly and free she sat
Beside me, tried a little light talk. That task
Proving too much, she suddenly switched, to ask
How long my father and mother had been dead.
I answered, 'Quite a time.' Had we, she said
A farm at Sunium? How far from the shore?
It's taken her fancy, I reckon, and, what's more,
She hopes to wheedle it out of me. I'll resist her,
By God! Then—had I lost a little sister
At Sunium by kidnapping? Was she alone?
What was she wearing? Would she at once be known
If she turned up? Why on earth does she bother *me*
With all these questions? Unless she means to *be*
My little lost sister, which she might contrive,
She's nerve enough. But my sister, if she's alive,
Is only sixteen, no more, while she, I'd say, is
A year or two older than myself. Now Thais
Sends a fresh summons, earnestly imploring me
To come. Let *her* come—to the point, stop boring me!

I'm not coming for a third time, that's flat. Hi, there!
Hallo! Is anyone in? It's Chremes.

PYTHIAS: *(coming out)*   Why there!
How sweet! You dear boy!

CHREMES: *(aside)*   What was I just saying
About traps, eh?

PYTHIAS: Thais left word, begging and praying
You'd come again tomorrow.

CHREMES: I'm off today
To the country.

PYTHIAS: Please come back.

CHREMES: I can't, I say.

PYTHIAS: Then come inside and wait till her return.

CHREMES: No fear!

PYTHIAS: Why not, dear Chremes?

CHREMES: Go and burn!

PYTHIAS: Well, if you're so determined, would you mind
Stepping across to the place where she's just dined—
Please, Chremes?

CHREMES: Oh, all right.

PYTHIAS: Dorias, come here! *(Enter Dorias)*
Quick, take this young man to the captain's, dear.
(Pythias goes back into the house. Dorias escorts Chremes off.
Enter Antipho)

ANTIPHO: Yesterday, at the harbour I and a few
Of the other lads agreed to have a do
Tonight, the usual thing. Each paid his sub
To Chaerea, making him caterer for the club,
And fixing the time and place where we would dine.
The time's past; at the place fixed there's no sign
Of preparations. As for Chaerea, well,
He's simply vanished; how, why, I can't tell,
Can't guess. The others have given me the task
Of finding him. And so I've come to ask
If he's at home. But who on earth's that, just leaving
Thais' place? Is it or isn't it? Seeing's believing.
It is! But what's the idea of this fancy-dress?
What devilry is he up to? I can't guess.
He has me beat. But whatever the purpose in it,
Perhaps I'll learn by stepping aside one minute.

CHAEREA: *(coming from Thais' house)*
Is anyone about? No, nobody here.
Am I being followed? No. The coast's all clear.

Can I at last give vent to my delight now?
Oh, I could be content to die outright now,
Rather than let life mar this moment's bliss
With any after miseries! But how's this?
Would you believe it? No one madly curious
Dogging my footsteps, making me quite furious
With endless questions, what's up, what do I mean
Jumping about with joy, and where I've been,
And where I'm going, and why, and where I've got
This dress, and whether I've gone mad or not.

ANTIPHO: *(aside)*
I'll go and give him what he seems to miss
So very much . . . Hi, Chaerea! What's this?
Jumping like mad? Why the rig-out? Why the joy?
What's the idea? Are you all right, old boy?
What are you goggling for? Have you gone dumb?

CHAEREA: Day of delights! Dearest of friends! Chief chum!
The one man in the world I wanted to meet!

ANTIPHO: But what's going on? Please tell me, I entreat—

CHAEREA: No, no, it's I who am entreating *you*
To listen. You know my brother's flame?

ANTIPHO: I do.
That is, if you mean Thais.

CHAEREA: The same, no other.

ANTIPHO: Yes, I remember—

CHAEREA: This flame that warms my brother
Was given a girl. And what a girl! But why
Should I proclaim or praise her beauty, I
Whose taste and eye for choosing charms you know?
Well, she completely bowled me over.

ANTIPHO: Oh!
Did she indeed?

CHAEREA: She did. Yes, Antipho,
Wait till you see her. You'll be just as struck.
In short, I fell madly in love. By great good luck
We'd got a eunuch that my brother had bought
For Thais as a gift, but not yet brought
Across to her house here. I, not slow to adopt
A hint that Parmeno, my man, had dropped—

ANTIPHO: What hint?

CHAEREA: Be quiet, and you'll hear quicker. Why,
He hinted, shouldn't this half-man and I
Change clothes, and I give orders to be sent

To Thais in his place?

ANTIPHO: You mean, he meant
That you should take the eunuch's place?

CHAEREA: Correct!

ANTIPHO: But what did you expect to gain?

CHAEREA: Expect
To gain? Why, I expected to be near her,
Near to the girl I loved, to see, to hear her.
Was that an aim or object to be slighted?
I'm sent, accepted, welcomed. Thais, delighted,
Delivers the little girl into safe hands—

ANTIPHO: Not yours?

CHAEREA: Mine.

ANTIPHO: Taking no risks, eh?

CHAEREA: And commands
That no *man* shall go near her. I alone
Must stay right by her, the two of us on our own
In an inner room. Eyes dropped, I bashfully bow.

ANTIPHO: Poor boy!

CHAEREA: She adds, 'I'm off to supper now,'
And takes her maids along, leaving just a few
Looking after the girl. They all, like her, were new.
Promptly they started making preparations
For the girl's bath. I added exhortations
To speed. She meanwhile in her bedroom sat
And gazed at a picture on the wall. Now *that*
Showed how old Jupiter, as the tale is told,
Dropped in on Danae as a shower of gold.[1]
I started gazing too, and, as the game
That he had played of old seemed much the same
As I was playing, well, my pleasure rose
Each moment higher. There, I thought, he goes,
A god made man, and down his neighbour's tiles
Steals like cat-burglar and with gilt beguiles
The fair and guiltless maid. And what a god!
'He that shakes highest heaven with his nod.'
Should I not ape him, up to mere man's measure?
Of course I would, and with the greatest pleasure!

---

1 King Acrisius, on learning that he was destined to be killed by the son born to his
daughter, Danae, kept her firmly imprisoned. Jupiter broke in and his child by
Danae, Perseus, eventually killed Acrisius. Euripides and Naevius wrote tragedies
on the theme.

As I was meditating thus, they sent
To say the bath was ready. Off she went,
Was bathed, brought back and put to bed. I stand
Awaiting orders. A girl comes, fan in hand,
And says, 'Hey, Dorus! We're going to bathe. You fan her.
You can bathe after us, if you want.' With manner
Most sullen I accept.

ANTIPHO: I'd loved to have seen you,
You with your brazen face, fan held between you!
I bet you looked an absolute ass.

CHAEREA: Before
She got the words half out, they're at the door,
All dashing for the bathroom, with the din
That's only made when mistresses aren't in.
Meanwhile my little lady falls asleep.
I stealthily, through the fan-sticks, take a peep
At her, and half-squinting at the same time peer
All round the room to see the coast is clear.
It is. And so—I softly slide the bolt.

ANTIPHO: And then?

CHAEREA: And then? Oh, don't be such a dolt!

ANTIPHO: I stand rebuked.

CHAEREA: Well, was I going to miss
A chance in a million offered me like this?
Beyond all hope, so longed-for, and so short
The time? Why, then, I would have been the sort
Of freak I was supposed to be!

ANTIPHO: You're right.
But say, what's happened about our do tonight?

CHAEREA: All fixed.

ANTIPHO: Good lad! Where? At your house?

CHAEREA: Oh, no,
At the freedman, Discus's.

ANTIPHO: Quite far to go.
Less time to lose. You'll have to shed that gear.

CHAEREA: Where, damn it? I can't go back to our house, for fear
My brother may be in, and my father too,
Back from the country.

ANTIPHO: The nearest place for you
To change is *my* place. Let's go there.

CHAEREA: Okay.
Let's go down to your place. On the way
I want to discuss with you a possible plan

For getting that girl for good.

ANTIPHO: Good? I'm your man. *(Exeunt)*

ACT IV

Dorias enters, with a casket, on her way home)

DORIAS: *(to the audience)*
From what I've seen of him, God help us all,
That crazy captain's bent on having a brawl.
He'll use brute force on Thais, I'm afraid.
You see, when Chremes, the brother of our new maid,
Arrived, she asked the captain please to tell
His servants to admit the young man. Well,
He fumed but daren't refuse. She followed this line
By saying, 'Ask him, please, to stay and dine.'
She did this with the sole aim of detaining
This lad, as there was no time for explaining
The facts she wanted to about her sister.
The captain scowled, but didn't dare resist her.
The young man stayed, the two of them started talking,
The captain felt he'd seen a rival walk in
Under his very nose. Resolved to annoy
My mistress—tit for tat—he shouts, 'Hi, boy!
Fetch Pamphila. Let's live it up a bit!'
Cries Thais, 'That's something I just won't permit,
Her at a party.' He wouldn't let it rest.
They had a row. She, feeling herself hard-pressed,
Slipped off her jewellery, without his seeing,
And gave it me to carry home, that being
Her secret signal that she means to beat,
As soon as possible, her own retreat.
(She goes into Thais' house. Phaedria enters)

PHAEDRIA: I set off for the farm. But on the road
As often happens, when one has a load
Of worry on one's mind, I started thinking
Of this and that, my spirits steadily sinking.
In short, while pondering like this, I passed
Our farm-house unawares. And when at last
I noticed, I was miles out. Back I started,
Fed to the teeth. Then, coming where my path parted
From the main road, I stopped and thought, 'Ye gods,
Two days alone, without her, here? What odds?
It's nothing. Nothing? If the hand's no hope

Of handling, shan't the scanning eye find scope?
The first is barred, the second at least's allowed.
And loving even from the edge of the crowd
Is better than nothing.' I purposely passed our farm—
(Pythias and Dorias rush out excitedly from Thais' house)
Why's Pythias flying out in such alarm?

PYTHIAS: God help us, where'll I find that filthy crook?
Such bare-faced crime! Lord, tell me where to look!

PHAEDRIA: *(aside)*
What's happening at Thais'? Trouble, I'm afraid.

PYTHIAS: Insult to injury! He rapes the maid,
Then rips her dress in two and tears her hair!

PHAEDRIA: *(aside)*
What's this?

PYTHIAS: I wish I'd got him here. I'd tear
His eyes out in two ticks—the beast!

PHAEDRIA: *(aside)*   It's clear
Things have been happening in my absence here.
I'll tackle her. Hey, what's up? What's the to-do?
Who are you looking for?

PYTHIAS: Oh, Phaedria, you,
You ask that! Get out! Go where you belong,
You and your precious presents!

PHAEDRIA: Why, what's wrong?

PYTHIAS: That eunuch you wished on us—he hasn't half played
Hell's games round here! He's gone and raped the maid
The captain gave us.

PHAEDRIA: What?!

PYTHIAS: It's true, God knows.
We're sunk.

PHAEDRIA: You're drunk.

PYTHIAS: Lord, make my deadliest foes
As drunk as I am now.

DORIAS: But, Pythias dear,
What sort of monster *was* this creature here?

PHAEDRIA: You're mad. How could a eunuch—?

PYTHIAS: Don't ask *me*
What sort—his acts are plain for all to see.
The girl's in tears. Ask why, she won't, daren't say.
Your precious present's vanished. And I pray
I may be wrong, but my suspicion is
He's got away with portable goods not his.

PHAEDRIA: That gutless type would never get far, I guess.

I can't imagine where he's gone—unless
Perhaps he made for home.

PYTHIAS: Well, please, please go
And see if he's there.

PHAEDRIA: Oh, I'll soon let you know. *(Exit)*

DORIAS: Never in all my life have I heard tell
Of such an outrage—honestly, Pythias!

PYTHIAS: Well,
I should have been more careful. I'd heard, in fact,
They're keen enough on women, but can't act.
I'd have locked that fellow in, not left him at large,
And never put that young girl in his charge!
(Phaedria enters, dragging in Dorus, dressed in Chaerea's clothes)

PHAEDRIA: Come out of it, you treacherous trash! What's that?
Resist me, would you? Randy, runaway rat!

DORUS: Spare me!

PHAEDRIA: Look how he screws his face up! Louse!
What were you up to, sneaking back to the house
And changing all your clothes? What's that you say?
Look, Pythias, another minute's delay,
And I'd have missed him—not a shadow of doubt.
He'd made all preparations for clearing out.

PYTHIAS: Oh, Lord, you've got him, then?

PHAEDRIA: You bet I've got him!

PYTHIAS: Oh, good for you!

DORIAS: Yes, good for you! God rot him!

PYTHIAS: Where is he?

PHAEDRIA: Where? He's not a sight you can miss!

PYTHIAS: Sight? Where? What *are* you talking about?

PHAEDRIA: Why, *this*!
This fellow here!

PYTHIAS: And who may *he* be?

PHAEDRIA: Eh?
This creature sent across to you today.

PYTHIAS: But this—why this is someone none of us knows
Or has ever seen.

PHAEDRIA: Not seen?

PYTHIAS: Did you suppose
The fellow sent across was that thing there, then?

PHAEDRIA: I never had another.

PYTHIAS: You can't compare them.
Oh, no. The young lad that your servant brought

Was good-looking, not like a slave.

PHAEDRIA: That's what you thought,
Because of a rag or two of colourful dressing
We'd rigged him up in. He's less prepossessing
Now that he's taken it off again—that's all.

PYTHIAS: Talk sense! As if the difference was that small!
We had a young lad sent, a sight for sore eyes—
The sort, in fact, to give pleasure even to *your* eyes.
This is a—weasel-coloured, withered, hoary,
Crabbed, worn-out creature.

PHAEDRIA: That's a staggering story!
Do I or don't I know what I did? You've brought me
To doubt it. *You*—did I buy you?

DORUS: Yes, you bought me.

PYTHIAS: Tell him to answer this, then.

PHAEDRIA: Ask away.

PYTHIAS: Did you come here to Thais' house today?
(Dorus shakes his head)
No? But that other came, with Parmeno,
That lad who must have been sixteen or so.

PHAEDRIA: Now perhaps you'll satisfy *my* curiosity
On this. Where did you get these clothes? Well, you monstrosity?
Are you struck dumb? Have you got nothing to say?

DORUS: Chaerea came—

PHAEDRIA: My brother?

DORUS: Yes.

PHAEDRIA: When?

DORUS: Today.

PHAEDRIA: How long ago?

DORUS: Not long.

PHAEDRIA: Who with? Well, answer!

DORUS: With Parmeno.

PHAEDRIA: Did you know him?

DORUS: The young man, sir?
I'd never even heard of him till today.

PHAEDRIA: Then how did you know he was my brother, eh?

DORUS: Well, Parmeno said so. And the young man gave me
These clothes.

PHAEDRIA: *(aside)*   Oh, no! Some lucky star come and save me!

DORUS: He put on mine, and then they both went out.

PYTHIAS: *Now* are you satisfied, beyond all doubt,
That I'm not drunk or lying? Is it clear
That that girl's been assaulted?

PHAEDRIA: Now, look here,
         You don't take this thing's word?
PYTHIAS: Do I need to take it?
         Isn't the truth as clear as facts can make it?
PHAEDRIA: *(aside to Dorus)*
         Come over here a minute. Do you hear?
         A little further. Right. Let's get this clear.
         Chaerea took your clothes off you?
DORUS: *(aside)*   That's right, sir.
PHAEDRIA: *(aside)*
         And put them on himself? You're sure?
DORUS: *(aside)*   Oh, quite, sir.
PHAEDRIA: *(aside)*
         And then he was brought over in your place?
DORUS: *(aside)*
         Yes, sir.
PHAEDRIA: *(aloud)* Good God! How you can have the face—
         You lying devil!
PYTHIAS: Lord, Phaedria, give us some credit!
         This tale, this cruel trick's true.
PHAEDRIA: Because *he* said it?
         Oh, no! *(aside)* but what's to be done? *(aloud)* Beast, take it back!
         Every word! Or will we need to wrench and rack
         Truth from you? Did you, or didn't you see my brother?
DORUS: N-no, sir.
PHAEDRIA: The whip's the *one* way—there's no other—
         To force confession. Come! Now 'yes', now 'no'!
         (aside)
         Beg mercy.
DORUS: Mercy, please!
PHAEDRIA: Get in!
DORUS: Oh, oh! *(Exit)*
PHAEDRIA: *(aside)*
         I can't see any other decent escape.
         (aloud)
         It's the limit if even something in *that* shape
         Can make a fool of me! *(Follows Dorus)*
PYTHIAS: One thing I know
         As sure as I stand here. It's Parmeno
         Who played this damned trick.
DORIAS: Little doubt of that.
PYTHIAS: I'll get my own back on him, tit for tat.
         But meanwhile—what on earth am I to do?
DORIAS: About the girl, you mean?

PYTHIAS: Yes, what's my cue?
Do I speak out, or not?

DORIAS: By holy Juno,
If you've any sense, you won't know what you *do* know,
About the girl or the eunuch. The innocent attitude
Will be your safest—and it should earn gratitude
From Phaedria. Simply say, which is quite true,
That Dorus cleared off.

PYTHIAS: Yes, that's what I'll do.

DORIAS: Look, is that Chremes? Then Thais, too, no doubt,
Will soon be here.

PYTHIAS: Why so?

DORIAS: A row broke out
Before I left.

PYTHIAS: Take the jewels in. A row? *(Exit Dorias)*
I'll find from Chremes what's been happening.

CHREMES: *(entering tipsy)*   Wow!
I was certainly tricked. That wine has bowled me over.
Though while at table I felt fine and sober,
Since rising foot and head are most undutiful.

PYTHIAS: Chremes!

CHREMES: Who—? Pythias! You're much more beautiful
Than at first sight.

PYTHIAS: You're certainly much more merry.

CHREMES: I reckon it's a very true proverb, very,
That 'without wine and bread, our lady Love', as they say, 'is
Cold and dead'. Am I a long time after Thais?

PYTHIAS: Why, has she left the captain?

CHREMES: Left? And how!
Ages ago. They had a first-rate row.

PYTHIAS: Didn't she *tell* you to come home with her?

CHREMES: No.
She just gave me a nod as she turned to go.

PYTHIAS: Well, wasn't that enough?

CHREMES: I hadn't an inkling
She meant *that*. But the captain, in a twinkling,
Cured my slow wits by slinging me out. Hallo!
How did I get home first, I'd like to know?

THAIS: *(entering)*
He'll soon be here to get that girl away
By force. Well, let him come. But, should he lay
One little finger on her, sure as sure,
I'll scratch his eyes out. Oh, I can endure

His dullness and his big-mouthed talk, providing
It stays talk. Turned to acts—it'll earn a hiding.

CHREMES: Thais, I'm back already.

THAIS: Chremes! Oh,
Dear boy, the man I wanted. Do you know
It was all because of *you* I had that row?
The whole thing's very much your business.

CHREMES: How?

THAIS: Why, if it hadn't been my constant endeavour
To get your sister safely back, I'd never
Have stood for this, and lots more like it.

CHREMES: I say!
Where is my sister?

THAIS: In my house here.

CHREMES: Eh?

THAIS: Brought up to bring no shame on herself or you.
Don't worry.

CHREMES: You really mean that?

THAIS: Yes, I do.
She's yours, a gift. I've nothing to gain or get
By way of reward.

CHREMES: Oh, but I'm in your debt,
Of course, and hope to prove a grateful debtor.

THAIS: Mind you don't lose the girl before you get her.
It's her that horrible captain means to wrest
From us by force. Quick, Pythias, fetch the chest
Out here—you know, the one with the trinkets in it
Proving her parentage.

CHREMES: Eh, but wait a minute!
How many—?

PYTHIAS: Where is it?

THAIS: Quick, damn you, in the trunk!

CHREMES: How many followers has he?

THAIS: Not in a funk
By any chance, are you, Chremes?

CHREMES: Funk? Not me!
I'm the coolest man alive.

THAIS: You'd better be.

CHREMES: You've got a low opinion of me, I fear.

THAIS: Look, Chremes. What you've got to think of here
Again and again is this. You're a well-known figure
In Athens, with lots of acquaintances, a bigger
Circle of friends, more influence, he's a mere stranger.

CHREMES: I know that. But why court uncalled for danger?
          I say stop violence being used in time,
          Don't wait to suffer and then punish crime.
          So in you go, and bolt and bar your quarters,
          While I run down to the forum and find supporters
          For this encounter.
THAIS: Wait!
CHREMES: It's the wiser course.
THAIS: Don't bother.
CHREMES: I'll be straight back.
THAIS: Your rescuing force
          Is not required. State firmly she's your sister,
          That one day, in her childhood, you suddenly missed her,
          And now have recognized her.
          (Enter Pythias with a casket)
                                  Show her brother
          The tokens.
PYTHIAS: There!
THAIS: Take them. And if that other
          Tries violence, treat him to a prosecution.
          Right?
CHREMES: Sure.
THAIS: Speak up with spirit and resolution!
CHREMES: Sure.
THAIS: *(arranging Chremes' dress)*
                  Cloak up! *(aside)* Lord, the champion I've got
          Needs a defender for himself!
          *(Enter marching Thraso, Gnatho and various slaves armed
          with household implements)*
THRASO: What? What?
          So gross an insult, great gods, shall I swallow?
          I'd sooner die. Follow me, Donax, follow,
          Simalio, Syriscus. What we'll do
          Is this, chaps—*one* storm the house.
GNATHO: Good show, sir!
THRASO: *Two,*
          Secure possession of the girl.
GNATHO: Jolly good, sir.
THRASO: *Three,*
          Deal severe blow to Thais. So, let's see,
          Donax, with crowbar, centre of front rank—
          Simalio, Syriscus, left and right flank
          Respectively—the rest proceed—but where

Is Sergeant Sanga with his thief-force?

SANGA: Sir!

THRASO: What, coward! You come here with a sponge-stick, do you,
Expecting to fight with *that*?

SANGA: Oh, sir, I knew you
So stout a leader, such brave troops—who'd stop 'em?
There must be blows, blood, wounds. And that's to mop 'em.

THRASO: And our remaining forces?

SANGA: Remaining? Hell!
There's only Sannio, our home-guard, sir.

THRASO: Well,
Take up positions. I'm here, in the rear of the van.
Each unit will take orders from *me*.

GNATHO: *(aside)*   Wise man!
With plans so soundly based on self-preservation!

THRASO: King Pyrrhus often used this same formation.

CHREMES: Well, Thais, you see how the fellow's setting about it.
I was right about bolting and barring. Can you doubt it?

THAIS: You may think him a hero now, but he's a big booby.
Don't worry.

THRASO: What would *your* tactical point of view be?

GNATHO: It's a pity we haven't a sling for surprise attack—
Long-range, I mean, from here. They'd soon draw back.

THRASO: Ah, look, there's Thais.

GNATHO: How soon do we get cracking?

THRASO: Wait, wait. A wise commander, before attacking,
Considers carefully every other course.
Who knows? She may be ready, without force,
To accept our terms.

GNATHO: Oh, heavens, when I hear you,
I see what wit's worth. Every time I'm near you
I come away feeling a much wiser man, sir.

THRASO: Madam, I'll put one question first. Please answer.
On receipt of the girl, did you or did you not
Promise me three days' sole possession?

THAIS: So what?

THRASO: So what? Right under my nose you went and brought
That fancy-boy along— !

THAIS: I shouldn't have thought
He concerned *you*.

THRASO: You stole off home with him.
Might I ask why?

THAIS: Let's say it was my whim.

THRASO: All right. Give Pamphila back—unless, of course,
You'd rather have her taken back by force.

CHREMES: What? Thais give her up to you? Thais allow you
Of all men, to lay a finger on her?

GNATHO: Now, now, you!
Keep out of this.

THRASO: What the hell do you mean? Not lay
A finger on what's mine?

CHREMES: Yours, rogue?

GNATHO: I say!
Look out, you little know the man you're slanging.

CHREMES: Get out! I warn you. Mind your step. Start banging
And battering here, and, by high heaven, I'll see
You don't forget this day, this place, or me.

GNATHO: Poor lad! A pity to see you coming to grief.
Making an enemy of a big man like our chief!

CHREMES: Clear off, or else I'll cleave your skull in two.

GNATHO: Would you, young dog! You dare!

THRASO: And anyway *who*
The hell are *you*? What do you want? What's *she*
To do with you?

CHREMES: I'll tell you. First, she's free
By birth—

THRASO: By Pollux!

CHREMES: A citizen of this city.

THRASO: Good God!

CHREMES: My sister, in fact.

THRASO: Oh, very pretty!

CHREMES: If you manhandle her, so much the worse for you.
Thais, I'm going to fetch Sophrona, the old nurse, for you.
Then we'll produce these proofs.

THRASO: Now, look here, damn that!
Are *you* telling *me* not to touch *my* girl?

CHREMES: I am that.
I'll stop you.

GNATHO: Hear that? Robbery, those words make it,
Self-confessed robbery.

THRASO: Thais, am I to take it
These are your views?

THAIS: Find someone else to answer.

(Exit Chremes and Thais into her house)

THRASO: Well, what do we do now?

GNATHO: Our wisest plan, sir,

Is strategic withdrawal. She'll be back in no time, pleading
Of her own accord.

THRASO: You reckon so?

GNATHO: Trust my reading
Of women's ways—all icy, when we're burning;
As soon as we cool off, then they start yearning.

THRASO: By God, you're right!

GNATHO: Shall I dismiss these blighters?

THRASO: Whenever you like.

GNATHO: Sanga, like all good fighters,
The time has come to turn your martial ardour
To hearth and home.

SANGA: My heart's been in the larder
For ages already.

GNATHO: Your heart's in the right place.
Squad, behind me! Fall in. Quick march! Keep pace. *(Exeunt)*

ACT V

(Thais comes out of her house with Pythias)

THAIS: Stop stalling, girl, and give me one straight word!
You know, you don't know, he went off, you've heard,
But you weren't there—whatever it is, stop trying
To hide the truth. She sits there, speechless, crying,
Her dress torn, and the eunuch's gone. Why? How?
Speak, woman!

PYTHIAS: What can I say? They reckon now
He was no eunuch.

THAIS: Who was he?

PYTHIAS: That Chaerea.

THAIS: Which,
Which Chaerea?

PYTHIAS: Phaedria's kid brother.

THAIS: You bitch!
What are you trying to tell me?

PYTHIAS: It's true. I've proof.

THAIS: What errand brought Phaedria's brother under our roof?
What business had he here?

PYTHIAS: That I can't tell
For sure. I think it's possible he just fell
Madly in love with her.

THAIS: God help me if that's true.

Is *that* why she's crying?

PYTHIAS: I suppose so.

THAIS: You—
You wretch! Were those the orders I left you under?

PYTHIAS: I followed orders blindly—was that my blunder?
'Put her in his sole charge', you said.

THAIS: Oh, damn you!
You set the wolf in sole charge of the lamb, you—!
But I'm ashamed to have been so hoodwinked. Hell,
What sort of a fellow is this?

PYTHIAS: Hush! All's well.
We've got the man himself!

THAIS: Where?

PYTHIAS: Look left—see?

THAIS: I see.

PYTHIAS: Quick! Have him seized!

THAIS: And what should *we*
You fool, do with him?

PYTHIAS: Do with him? What do you mean?
Just take a look! Was ever such cheek seen,
So cheerfully defying the beholder?

THAIS: I see what you mean.

PYTHIAS: As bold as brass, and bolder.

CHAEREA: *(entering)*
Both parents being at home at Antipho's
I couldn't get in unnoticed. You'd suppose
They'd done it on purpose. While I stood outside
Up came an acquaintance. I made haste to hide
In a lonely alley. Soon after, I was slinking
Into a second, and then a third, heart sinking
For fear I might be recognized. And so
I've been on the run like a wretched fugitive. Oh!
That isn't Thais standing right across
My path? It is, though. Now I'm at a loss.
I'm really up the creek. But—what the hell?
What can she do to *me*?

THAIS: Let's tackle him. Well,
Dorus, my good man. So you tried to run?

CHAEREA: Yes, ma'am.

THAIS: And are you pleased with what you've done?

CHAEREA: No, ma'am.

THAIS: Do you think I'll overlook it?

CHAEREA: Pardon me,

It's a first offence—if I fall again be as hard on me
As you like. Yes, kill me!

THAIS: Did you, poor fugitive, fear
My cruelty?

CHAEREA: No.

THAIS: Then what?

CHAEREA: This woman here,
With her tale-telling tongue.

PYTHIAS: This tale was true!

CHAEREA: I know, but such a trifle!

PYTHIAS: Trifle! You—
You think it nothing to do *that* to the daughter
Of a free-born Athenian!

CHAEREA: But I thought her
Simply a fellow-slave.

PYTHIAS: Monster! You dare—!
I can hardly keep my hands out of his hair.
He's mocking us.

THAIS: No need to run wild.

PYTHIAS: Well,
I like that! If I ran as wild as hell
With *him*, I'd still be owing him quite a bit,
Especially as he's ready to admit
He *is* your slave.

THAIS: Do stop it! What you've done,
Chaerea, scarcely fits your father's son.
For such goings-on you might think *me* fair game;
It should have been beneath you all the same.
I simply don't know now what steps to take
About the girl, since you contrived to make
Such a fine mess of all my calculations.
She can't be handed over to her relations,
As right demands, and as I planned to do,
Hoping for their firm friendship as my due.

CHAEREA: But, Thais, I'd like to think that *we* can be friends.
Often a bad beginning in these things ends
By bringing people happily together
In perfect harmony. Why, who knows whether
This wasn't the will of heaven?

THAIS: I'd willingly take it so
With all my heart, I'm sure, and try to make it so.

CHAEREA: Please do. And please believe me, I didn't do it
In brutal sport—real passion drove me to it.

THAIS: I know. That's why you find me so forgiving.
I'm human enough. I've learned enough by living
To know the strength of passion.

CHAEREA: God help me, Thais,
But now I love you too!

PYTHIAS: All I can say is,
In that case, madam, watch out.

CHAEREA: I wouldn't dare—!

PYTHIAS: I wouldn't trust you as far as *that*!

THAIS: There, there!
We're friends.

CHAEREA: Oh, Thais, please be mine—you must.
In your good will and word lies all my trust.
You've got to be my champion and stand by me.
I mean to marry that girl—they can't deny me—
It'd kill me, if they did.

THAIS: Your father *might*—

CHAEREA: If she's an Athenian citizen, that's all right.
He might make that condition, but no other.

THAIS: Just stay around a bit and you'll meet her brother.
He's gone to fetch the nurse by whom she was reared
Right up to the very day she disappeared.
Her identity will be made as clear as day.
You'll see for yourself.

CHAEREA: For *that* I'll certainly stay.

THAIS: But, meanwhile, till he does arrive, no doubt
You'd rather wait inside the house than out.

CHAEREA: Much rather.

PYTHIAS: Madam, you must be off your head!

THAIS: Why so?

PYTHIAS: You're letting *him* in again, you said?

THAIS: Why not?

PYTHIAS: Why not? Because he'll start running riot
Again, you'll see.

THAIS: Oh, Pythias, do be quiet!

PYTHIAS: He's got such a nerve. You don't seem to perceive that.

CHAEREA: Pythias, I wouldn't dare—

PYTHIAS: And I'll believe that
As soon as I see you haven't dared.

CHAEREA: Look here.
You can take charge of me yourself.

PYTHIAS: No fear!
Be off with you! That's something I'd beware of

As much as giving you anything to take care of.

THAIS: Look! Here's her brother in person. Good!

CHAEREA: Oh, blimey!
Let's get inside. I don't want *him* to spy me
Wearing this sort of get-up in the street.

PYTHIAS: Embarrassed?

CHAEREA: Yes, I am.

PYTHIAS: You are? How sweet!
The modest maiden!

THAIS: In then! After you,
You, Pythias, wait to admit the other two.
(Exit with Chaerea into the house)

PYTHIAS: Oh, God in heaven, please send me some good plan
To pay that rogue out—planting this young man
In place of the eunuch on us!
(Chremes enters with the nurse Sophrona)

CHREMES: Faster, faster!
Oh, do get moving, nurse!

NURSE: I'm moving, master!

CHREMES: Yes, but not forwards.

PYTHIAS: *(to Chremes)*   Those tokens—did you show them?

CHREMES: Yes, all of them.

PYTHIAS: And the nurse here, did she know them?
What did she say?

CHREMES: Knew them by heart.

PYTHIAS: She did?
That's fine! I took a fancy to that kid
Right from the start. Madam's all agog, you know,
To see you. In you get!
(They go into Thais' house. Enter Parmeno)
                        Ah, Parmeno!
Our good old honest Parmeno, if you please,
Strolling along, so utterly at ease.
I reckon I've ways to put him to the rack
As long as I like. Just wait till I get back!
I'll see that child's identity made clear,
Then watch me drive this monster mad with fear! *(Exit)*

PARMENO: Well, back I've come to see how Chaerea's thriving.
If he played well this plot of my contriving
And matched my cunning, heavens, how unbounded
Will Parmeno's praises be—and how well-founded!
For, not to mention how I managed to wrench

Past hope, past purse, right out of reach, that wench
From that gold-digging trollop's grasp, no trouble
Or cost incurred, what makes my merit double,
My trick worth two, is—he's been taught home-truths
At home about these women. To learn in youth's
To loathe for ever. Nothing so nice, so neat,
So stately when they step into the street,
So delicate when they're dining with a lover,
Picking and licking. Ah, but to discover
The life they live at home, so seedy-needy,
So utterly sordid, grasping, grimy, greedy,
Swilling down last night's broth with black bread—oh,
Salvation's in that sight, could youth but know.
(Pythias returns in time to hear the second half of the speech)

PYTHIAS: *(aside)*
I'll pay you well for all you've said and done
Against us, gallows-bird! You shan't make fun
Of us for nothing. *(aloud)* Oh, God, what a shame!
It's shocking, wicked! Poor lad! The one to blame
Is Parmeno, for bringing him.

PARMENO: *(aside)*   Eh?

PYTHIAS: Oh, dear,
I pity him, I do. I dashed out here
So as not to see the horribly cruel way
They mean to punish the poor boy.

PARMENO: *(aside)*   I say!
What's all the fuss for? Is anything amiss?
I must find out. Say, Pythias, what's all this?
Who's going to be punished? What do you mean?

PYTHIAS: Oh, you!
You dare to ask! Why, that poor lad—that's who—
The one you brought instead of the eunuch. Oh,
You've wrecked him, trying to trick *us*.

PARMENO: How so?
What's happened? Come on. Out with it.

PYTHIAS: Oh, I'll out.
That girl we got as a gift today, no doubt
You're aware she's freeborn, from this town, no other,
With a real Athenian aristocrat for her brother?

PARMENO: I wasn't aware.

PYTHIAS: Well, now it's been proved. And that—
That is the girl he goes and rapes. Whereat
Her brother, being the high-spirited type, went mad—

PARMENO: What did he do?
PYTHIAS: He savagely seized the lad
And trussed him.
PARMENO: Trussed him?
PYTHIAS: Despite pleas from Thais.
PARMENO: Oh, no!
PYTHIAS: And now he'll fix him, as the way is
With adulterers—so he threatens. I've never seen that
And I don't want to.
PARMENO: Never! He can't mean that!
It's absolutely monstrous!
PYTHIAS: Is it?
PARMENO: Well!
I like that! Taken in adultery—hell!
Who ever heard of anyone having to undergo that
In your sort of establishment?
PYTHIAS: I wouldn't know that.
PARMENO: But this you'd better know, yes, Pythias, you,
And all of them in there—trust me, it's true,
The lad you're keeping there's my master's son.
PYTHIAS: Oh, no!
PARMENO: Oh, yes! Let Thais take care what's done
To him. But why aren't I in there already,
Instead of wasting time on the doorstep?
PYTHIAS: Steady!
You mightn't save him, and you'll bring down ruin
Upon yourself. They reckon it's all your doing.
PARMENO: Oh, what am I to do to avert disaster?
How can I start? . . . But who's that there? My master
Returning from the country. To tell or not to tell,
That is the question. Oh, God, I've got to tell.
Of course I'm calling down doom on my own head,
But I must save that poor young man.
PYTHIAS: Well said.
I'm going inside. But see that, without fail,
You tell him every bit of this sad tale. *(Exit)*
LACHES: *(entering)*
It's very handy having our estate
So near. It means I never come to hate
Country or town life. If one starts to pall,
I simply change my environment, that's all.
Hallo! Our Parmeno! Yes. Well, Parmeno,
What are you standing at that door for?

PARMENO: Oh,
     Who's that? O, you, sir, safe and sound. What luck
     I—
LACHES: What are you waiting for?
PARMENO: My tongue—it's stuck,
     Scared stiff, confound it!
LACHES: What's the matter, eh?
     What made you shake so? Sick? Come, can't you say?
PARMENO: Sir, let me assure you first—it's a solemn fact—
     I'm not to blame for any actual act
     Of his.
LACHES: Act? What act?
PARMENO: Oh, of course—I ought, sir,
     To have told you that first of all. Well, Phaedria bought, sir,
     A eunuch as a gift for—her *(pointing)*.
LACHES: For whom?
PARMENO: For Thais.
LACHES: Bought a eunuch? Death and doom!
     What for?
PARMENO: For twenty minae.
LACHES: This is the end!
PARMENO: No, sir, it's not. There's Chaerea's little friend,
     Who plays the harp. She lives here.
LACHES: What, him too?
     With a little friend! I didn't think he knew
     A whore from a horse. And so *he*'s in the city now?
     One damned curse dogs another!
PARMENO: Don't, sir, for pity, now
     Sco—scowl at me so. I didn't tell him to do it.
LACHES: Don't worry about yourself. You're going to rue it
     In any case. But *what* has Chaerea done?
PARMENO: He got sent over instead of the eunuch.
LACHES: My son?
     Instead of a eunuch?
PARMENO: But he's proved he isn't—
     Caught in the act, he was, tied up, imprisoned.
     And now—
LACHES: No!
PARMENO: Yes, sir. Aren't those bitches bold?
LACHES: Look, are you sure there's nothing left untold,
     No shock or shame to come?
PARMENO: No, that's the lot.
LACHES: Just let me get in there! *(Exit into Thais' house)*

PARMENO: That's that! Now what?
        Trouble I must expect, in ample measure.
        But as it had to be done, I get some pleasure
        At being the means of bringing down disaster
        On *that* establishment. For my dear old master
        Has long been looking for some chance, some ground
        Of drastic action against them. Now it's found.
PYTHIAS: *(entering)*
Oh, Lord, I've never in years known such delight
        At anything that's happened as at the sight
        Of that old buffer suddenly appearing,
        Blown right off course. I knew what he was fearing
        And had the joke to myself.
PARMENO: *(aside)*   What *does* she mean?
PYTHIAS: So now I've come out for a little scene
        With Parmeno. Where's he got to?
PARMENO: *(aside)*   It's me she's after.
PYTHIAS: Ah, there! Here goes!
PARMENO: Well? Why the girlish laughter?
        Half-wit, what's happened? Oh, for God's sake, stop!
PYTHIAS: You'll be the death of me! Oh, I could drop!
        You make me laugh so much I'm worn out.
PARMENO: Me?
        Why so?
PYTHIAS: I've never seen, nor never hope to see
        A sillier sight. I can't—I can't begin to—
        Describe what fits of laughter you've sent us into.
        At first I took you for a shrewd, hard head—
        But fancy swallowing every word I said!
        What? Weren't you satisfied with what the son,
        With you to prompt him, had so proudly done?
        Did you feel bound to betray the wretched lad
        To his father? Imagine his feelings when his dad
        Saw him in *that* gear! Well, now you know at least
        You've cooked your goose with both of them.
PARMENO: You beast!
        You bitch! You mean that tale was mere pretence, eh?
        Ha, ha! A jolly joke at our expense, eh?
        You think it's very funny—
PYTHIAS: Very.
PARMENO: Hell!
        You think you'll get away with this, but—
PYTHIAS: Well?

PARMENO: I'll make you pay for it.

PYTHIAS: Ah, but your threat
Will leave us unharmed for a long time yet.
You'll pay without delay, and you'll pay twice—
Inveigling that poor innocent into vice
And then informing on him. Father and son
Will both give you your due for what you've done.

PARMENO: I'm sunk!

PYTHIAS: We felt somehow we ought to convey to you
Our thanks for the gift you sent us. Well, good-day to you.
(Exit)

PARMENO: Oh, God! Oh, God! Why did I have to speak?
I've betrayed myself like a rat with my own squeak.
(Enter Thraso and Gnatho)

GNATHO: What now? What aim or plan are we pursuing
On this campaign? In other words, what are we doing?

THRASO: I'll tell you. We're surrendering to Thais,
Accepting, that is, her terms.

GNATHO: Oh!

THRASO: What I say is,
In fact, why not? Didn't Hercules fall at the feet
Of Omphale?[2]

GNATHO: A good precedent! What a treat
To see our Thais combing with her sandal
This hero's head! What's that? Her front door-handle!
(Chaerea rushes out of Thais' house in great delight)

THRASO: Good Lord, what's this? A fellow I've never seen!
The devil! What's his sudden sally mean?

CHAEREA: Friends and neighbours, I'm the luckiest man now living,
No doubt of that. The good gods have been giving
Full proof of all their might on me today,
Judged by the shower of blessings blown my way.

PARMENO:
(aside)   What's he so pleased with?

CHAEREA: Parmeno, my boy,
You founding father and perfector of joy,
Do *you* know just how full my store's been stacked?
Do *you* know my Pamphila's been found, in fact,
To be my fellow-citizen?

---

2 A legendary queen of Lydia. While her slave, Hercules fell in love with her. She
dressed him in women's garments and made him carry out women's tasks such as
weaving.

PARMENO: That I knew.
CHAEREA: And we're betrothed.
PARMENO: That's too good to be true.
GNATHO: *(aside)*
         Do *you* hear what he says?
CHAEREA: There's more besides.
         My brother's storm-tossed love-affair now rides
         In calm seas. We're one family, as it were.
         Thais has put herself under our care,
         Become the legal dependant of my father.
PARMENO: So Phaedria has her all to himself?
CHAEREA: Yes, rather!
PARMENO: Then to your count of blessings add one other—
         The captain's been kicked out.
CHAEREA: Quick, find my brother,
         Wherever he is, and tell him.
PARMENO: Straightaway.
         I'll see if he's at home. *(Exit)*
THRASO: *(aside)*   Well, would you say
         There's any doubt I'm dished completely?
GNATHO: *(aside)*   No.
         I'm afraid there is no doubt.
CHAEREA: Oh, I don't know
         Who first and most earns honourable mention!
         My man for sound advice and apt invention?
         Myself for boldness in the actual act?
         Or favouring Fortune, who's so neatly packed
         So much good in one day? Or shall I rather
         Bless my so reasonable and obliging father?
         O God, please make my good luck last for ever!
PHAEDRIA: *(entering)*
         This news of Parmeno's is wonderful! I'd never
         Have thought it possible! Where's my brother?
CHAEREA: Here!
PHAEDRIA: I'm clean beside myself with joy.
CHAEREA: That's clear.
         Ah, but your Thais—there's not a woman on earth
         So worthy of your love. She's proved that worth
         To every one of us.
PHAEDRIA: Need you sing her praises
         To me of all men?
THRASO: *(aside)*   Hell! My passion blazes
         The hotter, the less chance there seems. On you,

	Gnatho, I hang my hopes.
GNATHO:	What can I do?
THRASO:	Contrive at any cost, of price or prayer,
	That I may keep some little corner there
	With Thais.
GNATHO:	That's a mighty difficult task.
THRASO:	Not if you want—I know you. Whatever you ask
	By way of reward is yours if you achieve that.
GNATHO:	Honest?
THRASO:	You have my word, you can believe that.
GNATHO:	If I achieve this for you, I demand
	That, whether you're home or not, your door shall stand
	Wide open for me, with a place prepared,
	No invitation needed.
THRASO:	You've my word.
GNATHO:	Upon these terms, then, forward to the fray!
PHAEDRIA:	Who's that I hear? Ah, Thraso!
THRASO:	Yes. Nice day!
PHAEDRIA:	Perhaps you're unaware of what's occurred
	Round here today?
THRASO:	No, no, I've heard.
PHAEDRIA:	You've heard?
	Then how do we come to find you in this quarter?
THRASO:	Relying on your support—
PHAEDRIA:	Me, your supporter?
	Captain, I warn you. If ever, after this day,
	I meet you in this street, if ever you say
	You were looking for someone else and we lay en route—
	You're a dead man.
GNATHO:	Really, does this language suit—?
PHAEDRIA:	You heard.
GNATHO:	But this high tone, it isn't clear—
PHAEDRIA:	Take it or leave it.
GNATHO:	Will you first, please, hear
	A word or two from *me*? Then, if approving
	Or not, proceed.
CHAEREA:	Let's hear.
GNATHO:	*(to Thraso)* Do you mind moving
	That way a little, sir? *(To Chaerea)* First, there's one fact here
	I hope you'll take my word for—that I act here
	Mainly for my own good. Should you, however,
	Be fellow-gainers, it wouldn't be very clever
	To refuse what I propose.

PHAEDRIA: Your proposition
          Being what, exactly?
  GNATHO: Simply the admission
          Of Thraso as a rival.
PHAEDRIA: What?! In there?
  GNATHO: Please think now. You've a pleasant life with her—
          Yes, very pleasant. But her style of living
          Costs rather more than you've the means of giving.
          To smooth love's path, find free financial aid for it,
          What handier source than *that*? The man's just made for it.
          He's rich, he's a most lavish giver—and boring
          Beyond belief, dull, dumb, by day and night snoring
          His head off, not the man to gain her love.
          Whenever you've had enough, he'll get the shove.
 CHAEREA: *(to Phaedria)*
          Well, what about it?
  GNATHO: Last—but, for me, not least—
          Who gives a finer, more expensive feast?
 CHAEREA: I shouldn't wonder if, one way or another,
          We'll have to put up with him.
PHAEDRIA: I suppose so, brother.
  GNATHO: It's sound sense. And I've one more thing to ask—
          Admit me to your set. It's such a tough task
          Pushing that Sisyphus-rock around the way I've had to
          So long.
PHAEDRIA: Yes, we'll admit you.
 CHAEREA: We'll be glad to.
  GNATHO: *(pointing to Thraso)*
          And in return I promise you hereafter
          Drink for a dry hour, meat for mirth and laughter.
 CHAEREA: Done.
PHAEDRIA: Yes, he's worth it.
  GNATHO: *(to Thraso)*   You're welcome over here, sir,
          Whenever you please.
  THRASO: *(to Gnatho)*   How are we doing?
  GNATHO: It's clear, sir,
          They don't know you. I told them a few facts
          About your character, praised you as your acts
          And true worth warrant, and won them over.
  THRASO: *(to Gnatho)*   Oh!
          Good, thank you! Isn't it odd? Wherever I go
          I'm irresistible.
  GNATHO: *(to others)*   Didn't I tell you? There!

Such Attic elegance, such savoir-faire!
PHAEDRIA: He's all you promised. Follow me—this way.
   (Exeunt)
PRODUCER: And farewell all, and please applaud our play.

Phormio

Phormio

CHARACTERS

DAVUS: a slave
GETA: a slave of Demipho
ANTIPHO: a young man, son of Demipho
PHAEDRIA: a young man, son of Chremes
DEMIPHO: an old man, brother of Chremes, father of Antipho
PHORMIO: a trickster
HEGIO, CRATINUS, CRITO: friends of Demipho
DORIO: a pimp
CHREMES: an old man, brother of Demipho, father of Phaedria
SOPHRONA: a nurse of Chremes' family
NAUSISTRATA: wife of Chremes, mother of Phaedria

PROLOGUE

Rome's bad old bard, [1] finding he couldn't bridle
Our poet's fancy and force him to stay idle,
Tries with rough words to make him loath to write,
Dubbing his previous plays thin, trivial, light—
Apparently because he failed to include
A mad lad seeing a doe by hounds pursued
And in her flight pleading, imploring aid.
If he'd but grasped that what *that* piece, first played,
Achieved was more the manager's work than his,
He'd be less fiercely offensive than he is.
Should someone say or think, 'Your man would lack
Prologues with no such previous attack,
No one to carp at,' then what he replies is,
'To all who try the comic art its prizes
Are open. He'd have hurled me from the stage
To starve. My aim's to answer, not enrage.
I'd speak him fair if with fair words he'd fought us.

1 Luscius of Lanuvium.

Now let him ponder—we pay back as he taught us.'
But of discussing him I'll make an end,
Though he makes none nor ceases to offend.
To my main point. I bring you a new piece,
Once called *The Plaintiff*[2] as first played in Greece,
But *Phormio* is our poet's Latin title,
Since Phormio, a sort of parasite, will
Play the chief part. He's the king-pin, you'll find,
If your goodwill stays with our poet. Be kind,
Attentive, quiet, and spare us such a fate,
Such storms as drove us from this stage of late,
To which our manager's courage has restored us,
Helped by the fair kind hearing you now accord us.

Scene: A meeting place of streets, in Athens. The houses of the two old men, Demipho and Chremes, and of the pimp and slave-dealer, Dorio, are to be seen.

ACT I

(Enter the slave Davus, purse in hand)
DAVUS: My good friend and compatriot Geta came
To see me yesterday, apropos of a claim
Against me for a piddling little amount
Outstanding from a fiddling little account.
Would I please make it up? Well, that I've done.
I have it here. I'm told his master's son
Has taken a wife. No doubt a present for *her*
Is being scraped together. How unfair
The whole thing is, that folk with so much less
Must add their mite to wealthier men's excess!
What he, poor soul, saved up by penny-stages,
Stinting his pleasures, from his scanty wages,
She'll gobble at one gulp, nor even in passing
Think what vast labour went to its amassing.
Then, when she has a child, the child'll sting him
For another present. Then he'll have to bring him
Another on his birthday, and another
On his initiation day.[3] The mother

2 A comedy by the Greek author Apollodorus.
3 i.e. the day on which the child will be initiated into the Mysteries. A common
   feature of Athenian religious experience.

Will net the lot. The child will simply be
A gift-source . . . Is that Geta himself I see?
(The slave Geta comes out of Demipho's house)
GETA: *(to someone inside)*
    If a chap with red hair comes—
DAVUS: He's right behind you.
GETA: Oh, Davus, I was just going off to find you.
DAVUS: There, catch! You'll find that covers my little debt,
And no dud coins.
GETA: Nice of you not to forget,
And I'm most grateful.
DAVUS: Sure, with the modern attitude,
Anyone paying a debt deserves great gratitude.
That's what we've come to. But what's making *you*
The picture of misery?
GETA: Me! If you but knew
The risks and worry of my present position!
DAVUS: How come? What's up?
GETA: I'll tell you—on condition
You keep it dark.
DAVUS: Oh, now, you're just being funny!
You find a man reliable with money,
And daren't entrust him with a tale! What profit
Could I get from betraying your trust? Come off it!
GETA: Well, listen.
DAVUS: I'm all ears.
GETA: Well, now, you know
The elder brother of old Demipho
In there, old Chremes, don't you?
DAVUS: Sure I do.
GETA: And his son Phaedria?
DAVUS: As I know *you*.
GETA: The old men went abroad together, one brother
To Lemnos, to Cilicia the other—
Our boss, that is. An old friend wrote and sketched him
Landscapes with mountains of money there. That fetched him.
DAVUS: With his enough-and-to-spare? He could do without it!
GETA: It's how he's made. Don't let's go on about it.
DAVUS: Made! Oh, if I were made king—!
GETA: Well, they went,
And left me here with their two sons. I'm meant
To be a sort of tutor and take care of them.
DAVUS: You've landed a tough assignment with the pair of them!

GETA: Experience has taught me that all right.
　　　　My guardian-spirit did this out of spite.
　　　　I tried to stand firm at the earlier stage.
　　　　Need I say more? My loyalty to age
　　　　Has played my hinder parts some shabby tricks.
DAVUS: Well, yes, I thought—kicking against *those* pricks—
　　　　It's a mug's game.
GETA:　　　　　　　　　So what did I do then?
　　　　Just what they wished. I humoured my young men.
DAVUS: You knew your market.
GETA:　　　　　　　　　　　Well, my master's lad
　　　　At first got up to nothing very bad.
　　　　But Phaedria—he took no time at all
　　　　To find some little bit of a girl and fall
　　　　Madly in love with her. She plays the lute.
　　　　Her master's a pimp, of course, a perfect brute.
　　　　Funds there were none to buy her off the beast.
　　　　Their fathers had seen to that. He could only feast
　　　　His eyes on her, follow her around, escort her
　　　　Between the place she lived and where they taught her.
　　　　Well, we were at his service, being quite free,
　　　　And, where she learned her music, vis-à-vis
　　　　There was a barber's shop. So as a rule
　　　　We waited there for her coming home from school.
　　　　Well, one day, while we're waiting, there appears
　　　　A young man on the scene, his eyes all tears.
　　　　'What's up?' we ask, surprised. 'Till now', says he,
　　　　'I never knew what poverty can be,
　　　　How hard and bitter. But just round the corner
　　　　I've seen a girl—poor creature!—the sole mourner
　　　　For her dead mother, laid out in the hall.
　　　　No friend, acquaintance, relative, no one at all
　　　　To help her with the funeral, apart
　　　　From one old woman. Oh, it wrung my heart!
　　　　And she herself's a beauty!' Need I say
　　　　His story moved us all? And straightaway
　　　　Antipho cries, 'Let's go to her!' 'I'm game,'
　　　　Another says, 'Lead on!' We went, we came,
　　　　We saw. The girl *was* lovely. And what made
　　　　You feel that more, she had no sort of aid
　　　　To beauty, all unkempt, with long, loose hair,
　　　　Tears in her eyes, mean, wretched clothes, feet bare,
　　　　And if one hadn't seen a sort of power

Of goodness in her face, her beauty's flower
Would have been crushed to nothing. The other lad,
The lute girl's lover, simply said, 'Not bad.'
But ours—

DAVUS: I know. He fell head over ears.

GETA: But how!
You've no idea. And note what follows now.
Direct to that old dame he goes next day,
And asks to see the girl. But she won't play,
Says it's no way for him or her to act,
The girl being of Athenian birth, in fact,
Honest, of honest parents. 'If, young man,'
She says, 'You want to marry her, you can,
The lawful way. If not, the answer's no, sir.'
Well, that, of course, set our young man a poser,
What with his wish to marry her and his fear
Of absent Father.

DAVUS: You mean, if he were here,
He wouldn't let him?

GETA: Let him wed a wife
With neither birth nor wealth? Not on your life!

DAVUS: What happens next?

GETA: What happens? Do you know
A professional hanger-on, called Phormio?
You never met such nerve—God damn the man!

DAVUS: What did *he* do?

GETA: Thought up this little plan.
'There is a law which lays it down', he said,[4]
'That any girl left fatherless must wed
Her next-of-kin. Not only does it make her
Do this, it says the next-of-kin must take her.
I'll claim you're hers, and sue you. I'll pretend
I'm acting for her as her father's friend.
We'll come to court. Details of father, mother,
Exact degree of kinship with each other,
All that I'll dream up. Anything it may suit me
To allege I'll prove, since your side won't refute me.
I face a fine row on your dad's return,
But, well, that doesn't cause me much concern,
She's ours, by then.'

DAVUS: He's playing a bold game.

4 The law cited is that operative in classical Athens. See Diodorus Siculus 12.18.3.

GETA: The lad agreed. The thing was done. He came,
He sued, he conquered. Antipho got wed.

DAVUS: What? You don't mean—?

GETA: I mean just what I said.

DAVUS: But, Geta, what'll happen to *you*?

GETA: God knows.
I only know—I'll face all fortune's blows
Philosophically.

DAVUS: Fine! There's courage!

GETA: I rely
On no one but myself.

DAVUS: Well spoken!

GETA: Why,
Do you suppose I want anyone interceding
On my behalf with my master? You know—pleading
My cause like this—'For this once don't be hard on him.
If he does it again, I'll not ask you to pardon him.'
And practically adding, 'Once my back is turned,
Beat him to death as far as I'm concerned.'

DAVUS: And the other? The in-and-out-of-school-escorter
To the lute girl? Any progress in that quarter?

GETA: Scarcely.

DAVUS: No doubt he hasn't got much scope
Financially?

GETA: All he's got to offer is hope.

DAVUS: Is his father back?

GETA: Not yet.

DAVUS: And you're expecting
The old man—when?

GETA: I'm not sure. I'm collecting
A letter from him now, which I've just heard
Is at the harbour office—they sent word.

DAVUS: Well, if there's nothing else you want me for—

GETA: Take—my best wishes.
(Exit Davus. Geta turns back to knock at Demipho's door)
Hi there, boy! The door!
Is no one opening up? Upon my life—!
(A slave appears)
Ah, there, take that, and give it to my wife.
*(He hands over the purse and goes off towards the
harbour. Enter from the other side Antipho and Phaedria.)*

ANTIPHO: A fine state, mine! Afraid of the return

Of the one man, my father, whose main concern
Must be my good, when, with one moment's thought,
I'd be awaiting him the way I ought!
PHAEDRIA: What are you making such a fuss for?
ANTIPHO: What?
You, my accomplice in this crazy plot,
Can stand there, asking such a stupid question!
If only he'd never hit on that suggestion,
Nor pushed my over-eager, passionate heart
To that false step from which my troubles start!
I'd have lost her, which might have made me languish
A week, but I'd have had no hourly anguish
To haunt me—
PHAEDRIA: No?
ANTIPHO: Waiting and wondering when,
When will he come to part us?
PHAEDRIA: Other men
Suffer in love from lacking. To have double
The normal luck appears to be *your* trouble.
You've had a flood of it, an overflow.
Your life is one to envy, Antipho,
To pray for! Why, by all the powers above,
Just to enjoy that long the fruits of love
I'd mortgage my remaining days on earth.
Compare, now, your abundance with my dearth,
And ask yourself, whose the more favoured state is,
Not mentioning that you've managed, free and gratis,
To find a decent, free-born girl, and take her
Openly, honourably, your own wish, and make her
Your wife. Pure happiness, with one omission—
A decently contented disposition.
If you'd my pimp to deal with, you'd discover
Just what it means to be a luckless lover.
But that's the way we're all made, more or less,
Each very sorry for himself, I guess.
ANTIPHO: No, Phaedria. I find the luck's with *you*.
You're free to work out what you'd rather do,
Keep or not keep your girl. I've come the cropper,
I'm cornered. I can neither keep nor drop her.
Hey! Is that Geta flying here, flat out?
It is. Oh, God, I'm scared! Bad news, no doubt.
(Geta rushes in, and paces up and down, not seeing the others)

GETA: *(to himself)*
                  Think, Geta, think! Or you're as good as dead!
                  Caught napping! What a storm hangs over your head!
                  What port can you run for? How can you wriggle out of it?
                  Our bold stroke will be laid bare, not a doubt of it.
ANTIPHO: *(aside to Phaedria)*
                  What's upset him?
GETA: *(to himself)*   He's here! One moment's grace
                  Is all I've got!
ANTIPHO: *(aside)*   What's up?
GETA: *(to himself)*   How shall I face
                  His fury when he hears? Speak, and let loose
                  His rage? Keep mum and madden him? Try some excuse?
                  Try washing a blackamoor white! Oh, dear! Oh, dear!
                  It isn't only for myself I fear.
                  It's Antipho I'm sorry and afraid for.
                  It's him that worries me, it's him I've stayed for.
                  Else I'd have saved my own skin, paused to pack
                  A few stray things, to pay the old man back
                  For his foul temper, and abruptly left.
ANTIPHO: *(aside)*
                  What is he planning? Disappearance? Theft?
GETA: *(to himself)*
                  How to find Antipho, which way direct
                  The search?
PHAEDRIA: *(aside)*   You're wanted!
ANTIPHO: *(aside)*   Which means *I* can expect
                  Trouble for sure.
GETA: I'll try the homeward track.
                  *(He moves towards Demipho's door. The others are
                  standing away from it)*
                  He's nearly always there.
PHAEDRIA: *(aside)*   Quick! Call him back!
ANTIPHO: *(aloud)*
                  Halt there!
GETA: *(not turning round)*
                          Whoever you are, you're pretty ready
                  With orders, aren't you?
ANTIPHO: Steady on, Geta, steady!
GETA: *(turning)*
                  Ah, just the man I wanted!
ANTIPHO: What have you heard?
                  Let's have it quick—if possible in one word.

GETA: Okay.
ANTIPHO: Well?
GETA: At the docks.
ANTIPHO: My—?
GETA: Yes.
ANTIPHO: Doomed, dead!
PHAEDRIA: Eh?
ANTIPHO: What'll I do?
PHAEDRIA: What's Geta supposed to have said?
GETA: I've seen his father—yes, your uncle.
ANTIPHO: Oh!
God help me, how'll I face this sudden blow?
Oh, if it comes to this, my darling wife
That we'll be torn apart, I've done with life!
GETA: All the more reason to look lively now,
Fortune favours the brave, my boy.
ANTIPHO: Somehow
I'm all at sea.
GETA: That's just where you shouldn't be,
Now of all times. Just let your father see
You're scared, and he'll deduce bad conscience.
PHAEDRIA: True.
ANTIPHO: I can't change my own nature.
GETA: What'd you do,
If you were in an even bigger mess?
ANTIPHO: Being no use now, I'd be even worse, I guess.
GETA: Hopeless! Sheer waste of effort! I'm off.
PHAEDRIA: Me too.
ANTIPHO: No, please! I could *try* a . . . bold front. Will this do?
GETA: You're kidding.
ANTIPHO: Wait, watch my face. Will *that* do?
GETA: No.
ANTIPHO: Well—so?
GETA: That's something like it.
ANTIPHO: Maybe *so*?
GETA: Yes, that'll do. That's it. Just stay like that,
And give back word for word and tit for tat,
Mind, or he'll blast you to blazes with blind fury.
ANTIPHO: Yes.
GETA: *(prompting)*
               You'd no choice, forced, driven—
PHAEDRIA: *(likewise)*   By law, judge, jury.
GETA: Got it? Who's that old man I can just make out

At the end of the street? Himself, beyond a doubt!
ANTIPHO: Oh, I can't stay.
GETA: What's this? Hi, Antipho!
Where are you off to? Stop, I say!
ANTIPHO: No, no!
Knowing myself and what I've done—Oh, hell!
I leave my wife, my life, in *your* hands!
(Exit in the direction he came from)
PHAEDRIA: Well!
Geta, what next? What's going to happen now?
GETA: *You're* in for an immediate first-rate row.
I'll be uplifted, and lashed hard, unless
I'm very much mistaken in my guess.
But what we preached just now to Antipho
Is what we ought to practise ourselves, you know.
PHAEDRIA: Oh, give me orders, Geta! Leave the 'ought' out!
GETA: Do you remember, then, the speech we thought out,
As our defensive line at the beginning—
Their case being just, sound, perfect, sure of winning?
PHAEDRIA: Yes.
GETA: Well, we need that speech now, to the letter,
Or, if we can, one cleverer and better.
PHAEDRIA: I'll have a shot.
GETA: You open the attack
I'll be the hidden reserves, in case you crack.
PHAEDRIA: Right.

ACT II

*(No pause in action. Demipho enters, as from a journey,
with slaves carrying luggage)*
DEMIPHO: *(to himself)*
                    So my bold son, without my leave, gets wed!
A fig for my authority! Ha, who said
Authority? My rage! Gall unsurpassed!
And Geta—a fine mentor!
GETA: *(aside)*   Me at last!
DEMIPHO: I wonder just what words, what pleas they'll find.
GETA: *(aside)*
I'll hit on something or other. Never you mind.
DEMIPHO: Will my son say, 'This wasn't my wish but force
Of law'? All right. That plea I might endorse.

GETA: *(aside)*
      Oh thanks.

DEMIPHO: But then to let your case fall flat,
      Consciously dumb. Did force of law do *that*?

PHAEDRIA: *(aside)*
      He's got us there.

GETA: *(aside)*   I'll get us out. You leave it
      To Geta.

DEMIPHO: I never dreamt. I can't believe it,
      This sudden blow, it's got me so unsettled,
      Uncertain how to act, so numbed and nettled,
      I can't begin to think. Which shows the bright time
      Of man's prosperity's in fact the right time
      For pondering how we'll bear our future crosses.
      Homecoming should bring thoughts of dangers, losses,
      Delinquency of son, decease of wife,
      Sickness of daughter. They're all part of life,
      All possible. And so no visitation
      Should seem strange, while what betters expectation
      Should count as clear gain.

GETA: *(aside)*   Blimey, it's surprising
      How far I've passed *him* in philosophizing!
      Already I've imagined every ill
      His coming home could bring—work at the mill,
      Work on the farm, being beaten, put in fetters.
      Nothing will seem strange. And whatever betters
      My expectation, I'll count gain indeed.
      But why don't you accost him with all speed
      And start the honied speeches?

DEMIPHO: Who comes here?
      Ah, Phaedria, my nephew.

PHAEDRIA: Uncle dear,
      How are you?

DEMIPHO: How are *you*? Where's Antipho?

PHAEDRIA: I'm glad to see you in such—

DEMIPHO: Yes, I know.
      I asked you—

PHAEDRIA: Oh, he's fine. He's—somewhere there.
      Is everything all right?

DEMIPHO: I wish it were!

PHAEDRIA: What's up?

DEMIPHO: What's up? A marvellous match you've made

                    Behind my back!
PHAEDRIA: *(innocently)*   Are you displeased?
GETA: *(aside)*   Well played!
DEMIPHO: Displeased? I'm mad! Just get me that young rake
                    Here, face to face. I'll teach him, and no mistake,
                    How tough he's made his easy-going old dad.
PHAEDRIA: But, uncle, he's done nothing to make you mad.
DEMIPHO: Birds of a feather, singing the same song!
                    Know one and know the lot!
PHAEDRIA: But you're quite wrong.
DEMIPHO: If one plays tricks, the other's there to plead.
                    If he's at fault, the first's his friend in need.
                    The mutual benefit boys!
GETA: *(aside)*   If he but knew!
                    He's sketched him to the life.
DEMIPHO: If this weren't true
                    You'd not stick up for him.
PHAEDRIA: Uncle, if what you're saying
                    Is true, that Antipho's done anything betraying
                    Gross recklessness with property or repute,
                    Your right to punish him I don't dispute.
                    But if some rogue, some stranger to all truth,
                    And strong in that, laid traps for untried youth,
                    And triumphed, is that our fault, or the jury's,
                    Whose common practice between rich and poor is
                    To bleed the first for spite, and feed the latter,
                    Because they feel so sorry for him, fatter?
GETA: *(aside)*
                    Did I not know, I'd swear all this was true!
DEMIPHO: How can a jury judge your case, if you
                    As he did, never say one word in answer?
PHAEDRIA: He acted like a well-brought-up young man, sir,
                    Got up his case, but once in court, dumb-founded
                    By inborn bashfulness, stuck, gravelled, grounded.
GETA: *(aside)*
                    He's marvellous! But I mustn't miss my cue
                    For welcoming home. *(aloud)* Well, sir, how's things with you?
                    It's grand to see you back, all safe and sound.
DEMIPHO: And how are things with you, you faithful hound,
                    You mainstay of my household, in whose care
                    I left my son on my departure?
GETA: Sir,
                    I've listened to you charging us all this time,

None guilty, and I least, of any crime.
What could I do, seeing a slave's unfitness
In law to act as counsel or as witness?[5]

DEMIPHO: Okay. My son's a shy and callow youth,
You're a poor slave. Let this be ten times truth,
And her ten times related, was he bound
To marry her himself? You should have found
The sort of dowry laid down by our laws
And made another match for her. What cause
Had he to wed a pauper?

GETA: Cause enough,
But what he hadn't got was—cash, sir.

DEMIPHO: Stuff!
Borrow from someone!

GETA: Anyone can say
'Someone'.

DEMIPHO: At worst, if he'd no other way,
At interest.

GETA: Now you've really gone and said it.
As if, with you alive, they'd give him credit.[6]

DEMIPHO: It can't, it shan't be! Let *her* stay his wife
One single, damnable day? Not on your life!
This isn't a trick one easily forgives.
Show me that fellow's face, or where he lives!

GETA: Do you mean Phormio?

DEMIPHO: I mean the wretch
Who took her case up.

GETA: Him, sir, I'll soon fetch.

DEMIPHO: Where's Antipho?

GETA: Out.

DEMIPHO: Then, Phaedria, off you go.
Find him and fetch him.

PHAEDRIA: I'll go straight—

GETA: *(aside)*   We know.
To your girl friend.
(Exeunt Geta and Phaedria in different directions)

---

5 Both Athenian and Roman law forbade slaves to speak in court or give voluntary evidence.
6 This may refer either to actual legal restrictions on young men borrowing money or to the simple likelihood that a father would refuse to acknowledge such debts and refuse to pay the creditors.

DEMIPHO: I owe my family gods a greeting.
Then for the market-place in hope of meeting
A few friends to support my case. And so
I'll be prepared for master Phormio.
(Exit into his own house, followed by slaves)

(A short pause. Then Demipho comes out and goes off down town. Geta and Phormio enter from the opposite side)

PHORMIO: Daren't face his father, and beat it—just like that?
GETA: Just as I say.
PHORMIO: And left the poor girl flat?
GETA: Yes.
PHORMIO: And the old man hopping mad?
GETA: And how!
PHORMIO: So, Phormio, it's all in your hands now.
You cooked this scheme up, so you've got to cope.
Gird up your loins, my lad.
GETA: You're our one hope.
PHORMIO: *(to himself)*
Suppose he asks—
GETA: For God's sake, help!
PHORMIO: *(as before)*   Ah, yes,
And then he says—
GETA: You got us in this mess.
PHORMIO: *(as before)*
That's it.
GETA: So get us out.
PHORMIO: Fetch your old man.
I've got it here—a thoroughly worked-out plan.
GETA: What are you going to do?
PHORMIO: What would you say
To having Phanium allowed to stay,
Antipho cleared from blame in this connection,
The old man's full fire turned in my direction?
GETA: I'd say you're a stout fellow and firm friend.
And yet I'm often worried that the end
Of your audacity, Phormio, may be
To land you in the lock-up.
PHORMIO: No, not me.
I've tried the ground. I've found where one can tread.
How many bodies have I bashed half-dead,

Do you reckon? Well, has any sued me yet
For assault?

GETA: Then what's your secret?

PHORMIO: This. No net
Is spread for birds that hurt, like kite or hawk,
But for the harmless sort. Bad birds will baulk
Your effort, good reward it. Sheep you *can* shear
Have scissors sharpened on all sides to fear.
They know I've nothing. My person, you will say,
They'll take as forfeit. But what wish have *they*
To feed a hearty eater and requite
Bad deeds with benefits? And, by God, they're right!

GETA: My boss can never properly pay you back.

PHORMIO: Rot! It's the boss that never gets his whack.
Scot-free, care-free, with soap and scent well-groomed
You come. With bills he's plagued, with cares consumed.
You take your pleasure. While he growls, you grin.
You drink first, sit first, see a feast brought in,
A doughty do.

GETA: A what?

PHORMIO: That's when you doubt
Which of the fine fare first to single out.[7]
And reckoning up how sweet, how dear each dainty is,
'Our host's a god on earth,' you say, 'A saint he is!'

GETA: Look out! The old man's here. The first shock's sharpest.
Hold that, and you can play him like a harpist.
*(Enter Demipho with three friends—Hegio, Cratinus and
Crito—from the town)*

DEMIPHO: Did you ever hear of a racket more outrageous?
I'm counting on your aid, mind.

GETA: *(aside)*   He's rampageous.

PHORMIO: *(aside)*
Well, now to start and hound our quarry. Stand by.
(He and Geta begin to act for the benefit of Demipho)
(aloud)
Good God in Heaven, does Demipho deny
Her kinship?

GETA: *(acting up)*   He does indeed.

PHORMIO: And does he claim
He doesn't even know her father's name?

---

7 The *cena dubia* was a meal featuring so many dishes or ingredients that the diner
   could not know where to start.

GETA: He does indeed.

DEMIPHO: *(to his friends)*   I reckon this must be
The very man in question. Follow me.

PHORMIO: Because the poor girl has been left in need
No one will know her father, none take heed
Of her. How mean can men get!

GETA: If you throw
Mud at my boss, I'll make your name mud.

DEMIPHO: *(aside)*   Oh!
The impudence! Making up mud-lies for throwing
At *me*!

PHORMIO: Against the young man for not knowing
His relative I've no grievance. After all
My friend was no longer young, his means were small,
He lived by farming, and his days were spent
Down in the country. My father let him rent
Some land of ours. He often said the clan
In Athens had ignored him. Ignored that man!
Never saw his like!

GETA: I wish you a good view
Of yourself, in his present state.

PHORMIO: Be damned to *you*!
If I'd rated him less, I'd never have started this quarrel
For her sake with your family. Mean, immoral
Old man, disowning her!

GETA: You drop that line,
Calling my master names, you dirty swine,
Behind his back!

PHORMIO: Names given with good cause.

GETA: What's that, you jail-bird?

DEMIPHO: *(intervening)*   Geta!

GETA: *(pretending not to hear)*   Distorting laws,
Extorting money!

DEMIPHO: Geta!

PHORMIO: *(aside)*   Go on. Answer.

GETA: Who's that? Oh, sir, this—!

DEMIPHO: Pipe down.

GETA: But this man, sir,
Behind your back was piling on such abuse, sir,
Fit for his sort, but so unfit for you, sir.

DEMIPHO: Pipe down! Young man, could you p'raps condescend
To tell me who exactly *was* your friend,
If you don't mind—merely for information!

And *how* he made out he was my relation?
PHORMIO: Fishing, as if you didn't know him!
DEMIPHO: Know him? I?
PHORMIO: That's what I said.
DEMIPHO: And that's what I deny.
PHORMIO: Not know your cousin? You make me laugh.
DEMIPHO: His name?
I'm losing patience with your little game.
PHORMIO: Ah, so you'd like his name?
DEMIPHO: Precisely. Well?
Why don't you answer?
PHORMIO: *(aside)*   I've forgotten it. Hell!
DEMIPHO: What's that you said?
PHORMIO: *(aside)*   Geta, can you recall
The name we used? *(aloud)* I'm telling you nothing at all.
As if you'd never known the poor chap,
Trying to lay this trap for me!
DEMIPHO: What trap?
GETA: *(aside)*
Stilpho.
PHORMIO: But what do *I* care? Stilpho.
DEMIPHO: Who?
PHORMIO: Stilpho's the name. You knew him.
DEMIPHO: I never knew
Nor ever had a cousin of that name.
PHORMIO: Come now, in front of our honest friends! For shame!
I'm sure, though, if he'd left a tidy sum,
Ten talents—
DEMIPHO: Scoundrel!
PHORMIO: You'd be the first to come
Armed with a detailed pedigree—yes, rather—
Right down from grand—and great, great, great grandfather.
DEMIPHO: Yes, sir, you're right. I would. I would have stated,
When I'd come forward, how we were related.
How we're related you should likewise show.
GETA: *(aside)*
One for the boss! Be careful, Phormio!
PHORMIO: I gave a clear account, where it was due,
In court. On that occasion, if untrue,
Why did your son not prove it so?
DEMIPHO: My son!
Words fail me. He's a fool!
PHORMIO: But you are none.

        Go, get the courts to grant you a re-trial.
        You're Lord Muck here, you'll meet with no denial.

DEMIPHO: Though grossly wronged, sooner than drag this matter
        Through courts of law and listen to your chatter,
        I'll act as though she were in fact related,
        Which she is *not*, and pay the dowry stated
        By law. And you can take her, with the money,
        Ten minae.

PHORMIO: Ha, ha! Very, very funny!

DEMIPHO: What? Do you find what I propose unfair?
        Can't I get common justice?

PHORMIO: Really, sir,
        You can't suppose the law means you to treat
        Your cousin like a woman off the street,
        Paid and sent packing. Nonsense! It's decreed,
        To save a free-born girl being driven by need
        To a life of shame, she should become the wife
        Of her male next-of-kin, for good, for life.
        That's what you're trying to stop.

DEMIPHO: Her next-of-kin
        Of course. But why, how, where do we come in?

PHORMIO: Oh drop it! That's an egg you can't unscramble.

DEMIPHO: Can't I? You'll see.

PHORMIO: You're rambling.

DEMIPHO: Let me ramble.

PHORMIO: Look, Demipho, when all is said and done,
        We're not concerned with you. It was your son
        They found against. *You're* a bit old to wed.

DEMIPHO: You can take *him* as saying what I've said.
        Or else I'll shut the door on him and her.

GETA: *(aside)*
        He's furious.

PHORMIO: You'd better shut it, sir,
        On your good self.

DEMIPHO: I see you've come prepared
        To thwart me at all points?

PHORMIO: *(aside)*   We've got him scared.
        He's bluffing for all he's worth, though.

GETA: *(aside)*   A good start!

PHORMIO: Come, sir, what can't be cured take in good part.
        We know your character. To yourself be true,
        And let's be friends, eh?

DEMIPHO: Me be friends with you?

I never want to see or smell or hear you.

PHORMIO: If you hit it off with her she'll help to cheer you
In your decline. Take thought for your old age, sir.

DEMIPHO: You keep her to cheer *you*!

PHORMIO: Don't get in a rage, sir.

DEMIPHO: Listen. We've talked enough. Take her away
Quick, or I'll throw her out. I've said my say.

PHORMIO: Touch her in any way not fitting her birth,
And I'll touch you, in court, for all you're worth.
I've said *my* say. I'll be at home, you know,
Geta, if I should be required.

GETA: Quite so.

(Exit Phormio)

DEMIPHO: What care and trouble my son's flung me in,
With this damned nuptial noose he's hung me in,
Along with himself! He's keeping out of my way.
I'd like at least to know what he has to say,
What he thinks about it all. You, Geta, go,
And see if he's back yet.

GETA: As you say, sir. *(Exit)*

DEMIPHO: So!
My friends, I think you see how matters lie.
What's to be done? You tell me, Hegio.

HEGIO: I!
Well, Demipho, I suggest, if you'll agree,
You—ask Cratinus first.

DEMIPHO: *(to Cratinus)* Cratinus?

CRATINUS: Me?

DEMIPHO: Yes, you!

CRATINUS: Well, I advise you to do what's best
In your own interest. And I would suggest
It's right and fair that any act of your son done
While you were absent should be legally undone.
The court'll agree. That's that.

DEMIPHO: Now, Hegio.

HEGIO: My learned friend spoke forcefully. But, you know,
Two men, two minds. I'm convinced you can't undo
What has been legally done, and even to try to
Would be discreditable.

DEMIPHO: Your turn, Crito.

CRITO: Well, Demipho, it's a difficult situation,
Which calls, I think, for further deliberation.

HEGIO: Well, if there's nothing else that we can do now—

DEMIPHO: Thanks. You've done fine. I've got *no* point of view now.
            *(Exeunt Hegio, Cratinus, and Crito. Enter Geta from
            Demipho's house)*
GETA: They say he's not back.
DEMIPHO: Then I must await
            My brother's arrival, and let *him* dictate
            My course of action. I'll go down to the quay
            And find out when his boat's due. *(Exit)*
GETA: As for me
            I'll go and track down Antipho. He needs priming
            With the latest news. But here he comes. Good timing!

ACT III

            (Enter Antipho, from the opposite direction to Demipho)
ANTIPHO: *(to himself)*
            Oh, Antipho, for that display of funk
            You could be called some fine names! Doing a bunk
            Like that, and leaving others to defend
            Your very life! Did you think they'd attend
            To your concerns better than you? You ought
            At least to have spared a little bit of thought
            For that sweet creature at home, who through belief
            In her strong lover could have come to grief.
            All hope, all help, poor thing, she looks to you for!
GETA: *(coming forward)*
            Some fine abuse indeed you gave us the cue for
            Behind your back. Of all the base desertions—
ANTIPHO: The very man I wanted—
GETA: But our exertions
            In your cause never flagged.
ANTIPHO: Oh, tell me straight,
            For God's sake where I stand. What sort of state
            Are things in? Has my father smelt a rat yet?
GETA: Not the right one.
ANTIPHO: Any hope?
GETA: I can't say that yet.   .
            Phaedria's fought a stout fight, all for you.
ANTIPHO: There's nothing new in that.
GETA: And Phormio too,
            Tireless as always, showed his sterling mettle.
ANTIPHO: How?

GETA: With well-frozen words poured on the kettle
Of your dad's boiling rage.

ANTIPHO: Oh, jolly good
For Phormio!

GETA: And I did what I could.

ANTIPHO: I love you all, dear Geta.

GETA: That, my lad,
Was the first phase. Now it's 'all quiet'. Your dad
Intends to wait until your uncle's returned.

ANTIPHO: Why that?

GETA: As far as this affair's concerned
He said he'd follow *his* lead.

ANTIPHO: Now I start fearing
To see my uncle safe and sound, on hearing
My life hangs on *his* verdict.

GETA: There's your cousin.

ANTIPHO: Where?

GETA: There, sir—coming from his daily dozen.
(Enter Phaedria and Dorio from Dorio's house)

PHAEDRIA: Please, Dorio, won't you listen to me?

DORIO: No.

PHAEDRIA: But just a moment, Dorio.

DORIO: Let go!

PHAEDRIA: Hear what I have to say.

DORIO: I've heard enough.
Over and over again the same stale stuff.

PHAEDRIA: But this'll interest you.

DORIO: I'm all ears. Speak.

PHAEDRIA: Can I persuade you to wait half a week?
Where are you off to?

DORIO: I thought it slightly odd
You should come up with anything new.

ANTIPHO: *(to Geta)* My God,
I can see this pimp soon sewing up mouth, eyes, ears
And every hole in his head.

GETA: I share your fears.

PHAEDRIA: So you still aren't going to trust me?

DORIO: You're a prophet.

PHAEDRIA: But if I give you my solemn word?

DORIO: Come off it!

PHAEDRIA: You'll find obliging me's paid off.

DORIO: Forget it.

PHAEDRIA: Trust me, it's true. I swear you won't regret it.

DORIO: Moonshine!
PHAEDRIA: Look here! It isn't very long.
          Try the thing out.
DORIO: You try out some new song.
PHAEDRIA: I've come to feel you're a sort of relative rather
          Than mere acquaintance, a friend, a second father—
DORIO: Drivel away.
PHAEDRIA: Are you so hard and heartless?
          No pity, no plea can move you?
DORIO: Are you so artless
          And impudent as to try and flannel *me*
          With your flapdoodle and get *my* girl buckshee?
ANTIPHO: Poor lad!
PHAEDRIA: I'm licked, licked by the simple truth.
GETA: *(aside)*
          How utterly like himself is either youth!
PHAEDRIA: So just when Antipho's got his different trouble,
          This blow must hit me, making a nice double!
ANTIPHO: Phaedria, what's the matter?
PHAEDRIA: Antipho,
          You lucky fellow!
ANTIPHO: Lucky? Me? How so?
PHAEDRIA: You've got the girl you love safe home, in port.
          You've never had storms to cope with of this sort.
ANTIPHO: Safe home, you say? I'm like the chap in the fable
          With a wolf by the ears, and equally unable
          To hold on or let go.
DORIO: That's how I'm stuck
          With him.
ANTIPHO: You're a pimp and a half. What blow's he struck,
          Phaedria, now?
PHAEDRIA: What blow? The callous cad
          Has sold my Pamphila.
ANTIPHO: Sold her?
GETA: Sold?
DORIO: *(ironically)*   Too bad!
          To sell what I'd paid cash for!
PHAEDRIA: I can't persuade him
          To go back on the other offer made him
          And wait for me. It's only while I raise
          Money my friends have promised, just three days.
          If I don't give it you, you needn't wait
          One hour more.

DORIO: You're deafening me!
ANTIPHO: The date
      Is not far distant. If he could persuade you,
      You'll find, in the end, this service will have paid you
      Twice over.
DORIO: Words, words.
ANTIPHO: Will you have the heart
      To see her forced to leave, love torn apart?
DORIO: I shan't be responsible, any more than you.
GETA: May all the gods in heaven give you your due!
DORIO: Although it went against the grain, I've borne
      With you for several months. You've promised, sworn,
      Then produced—tears. Now it's a different tale,
      I've found a man who'll pay, not weep and wail.
      So make way for your betters.
ANTIPHO: But I say!
      If I remember right, you had a day,
      Phaedria, fixed already. On it, or by it,
      You were to pay.
PHAEDRIA: That's right.
DORIO: Do I deny it?
ANTIPHO: Has the day passed, then?
DORIO: No, but this day came
      Before it, see?
ANTIPHO: Have you no sense of shame
      To be so downright shifty?
DORIO: Not a bit,
      Provided that it pays.
GETA: You pile of—!
PHAEDRIA: Is this a way to behave?
DORIO: It's *my* way. So—
      Like it or lump it.
ANTIPHO: Such deception!
DORIO: No!
      No, Antipho, it's me that was deceived.
      He knew what I was like, but I believed
      He was a different type. He took me in.
      I'm being to him just what I've always been.
      However that may be, though, here's what I'll do.
      My captain[8] said he'd pay tomorrow. You

_____

8 As often in comedy, the rival for possession of the prostitute is a wealthy mercenary soldier.

Bring the sum first. 'First sum, first served', I say.
That's *my* rule, and I'll stick to it. Good day. *(Exit)*

PHAEDRIA: What can I do? Where can I go, poor wretch,
With less than nothing, and at one blow fetch
That sort of money? If only I'd succeeded
In getting out of him the three days needed,
I had it promised.

ANTIPHO: Geta, we can't allow
My cousin, who helped me all he could just now,
You said, to suffer like this. Now *he* needs aid,
And we must make sure that his help's repaid.

GETA: That's fair, no doubt.

ANTIPHO: Come on, then. Only *you*
Can save him.

GETA: What am I supposed to do?

ANTIPHO: Get him the cash.

GETA: Fine. Where's it to be got?

ANTIPHO: My father's back, you know.

GETA: I know. So what?

ANTIPHO: A hint's enough for a wise head.

GETA: You don't say!

ANTIPHO: I do.

GETA: And fine hints *you* give. Run away!
It's triumph enough for me, if for your wedding
I'm left unwhipped. And now you'd have me heading,
For *his* sake, from the whip into worse danger.

ANTIPHO: He's right.

PHAEDRIA: But damn it, Geta, I'm no stranger,
From anywhere.

GETA: Sure. But, damn it, our hands are full.
We've got the old man raging like a bull
At all of us. Do we want to goad and bait him
Beyond the point where we could ever placate him?

PHAEDRIA: Am I to let someone else go off with *her*,
Under my very eyes, to God knows where?
All right. While I'm still here, while you still can,
Look at me, talk to me.

ANTIPHO: Good gracious, man,
Whatever for? What are you going to do?

PHAEDRIA: Wherever on this earth she's taken to,
I am resolved to follow her or perish.

GETA: God prosper any fine project you may cherish,
But don't rush things.

ANTIPHO: Geta, you've really got
          To find him some way out.
GETA: Some way? But what?
ANTIPHO: For God's sake think of something. Or he'll be doing
          Something or other that we'll both be rueing.
GETA: I'm trying . . . I've got it. Yes, I think he's clear.
          But it means trouble for myself, I fear.
ANTIPHO: Don't worry about that. Whatever may come,
          Good, bad, we'll bear it with you.
GETA: What's the sum?
PHAEDRIA: Just thirty minae.
GETA: Thirty? Phew! She's dear!
PHAEDRIA: She's damned cheap!
GETA: Well, I'll have the money here.
PHAEDRIA: Good man!
GETA: Now, off with you.
PHAEDRIA: I need it *now*.
GETA: And you shall have it. But you must allow
          My getting Phormio's aid in this affair.
ANTIPHO: He's at your service. Whatever task you care
          To assign him, have no fear. You may depend
          He'll do it. He's our only faithful friend.
GETA: Let's go and find him with all possible speed.
ANTIPHO: I suppose there's nothing at the moment that you need
          My help for?
GETA: Nothing. So off home you go
          And comfort that poor wife of yours. I know
          She's there, half dead with fear. What's keeping you?
ANTIPHO: Nothing. There's nothing I'd more gladly do.
          (Exit into Demipho's house)
PHAEDRIA: How will you manage it?
GETA: *That* I'll make clear
          As we proceed. Let's get away from here. *(Exeunt)*

ACT IV

*(A short pause. Enter from the harbour Chremes with
slaves carrying luggage, and Demipho. The slaves go into
his house)*
DEMIPHO: About the matter, then, that made you go
          To Lemnos—did you fetch your daughter?
CHREMES: No.

DEMIPHO: Why not?
CHREMES: Her mother, finding at this stage,
My absence too prolonged, and the girl's age
Demanding more active steps from me, set sail,
I'm told, with her whole household, on my trail.
DEMIPHO: Did she indeed? But, why, then, did you choose
To stay so long there, when you'd had that news?
CHREMES: Illness detained me.
DEMIPHO: Illness? How caught? What kind?
CHREMES: Old age itself is illness, don't you find?
But from the captain of their ship I've found
They did arrive in Athens, safe and sound.
DEMIPHO: I see. You've heard what happened to my son
During my absence?
CHREMES: Yes, and what he's done
Unsettles all my plans. To marry her now
To any stranger means explaining how
And where I got her—the whole story. *You*
I could rely on utterly, I well knew,
As much as on myself. With any stranger
Marrying into the family, we face danger.
He'll keep quiet while relationships are good.
If they cool off he'll know more than he should.
And then my wife'll soon find out, I fear,
And all that's left for me, if she should hear,
Is to clear out, to quit. All I possess
At home is my own carcase, more or less.
DEMIPHO: I know. I'm worried too. And I shall strive
My utmost, tirelessly; somehow I'll contrive
To keep my word to you.
(They stroll to one end of the stage. Enter Geta)
GETA: *(to himself)*   I've never set
My eyes upon a sharper fellow yet
Than Phormio. I went to him just now
To say we wanted money, and why, and how.
When he'd heard barely half what I had to tell,
He cried, 'I get it! Lovely! You've done well,
Geta. Now get me your old man. Praise Heaven,
An opportunity has now been given
To demonstrate I'm Phaedria's friend as much
As Antipho's.' I said I'd put him in touch
With our old man. 'Wait in the market-square,'
I told him. But—would you believe it—there!

The man himself. And who's that just behind him?
Phew! Phaedria's father! . . . Fool, why should you mind him?
I've two instead of one to be bamboozled.
Two shots are much less likely to be foozled.
I'll tackle first the source I'd already reckoned on.
If that works, fine. If not, I'll try the second one.
(Enter Antipho from Demipho's house)

ANTIPHO: *(to himself)*
I'm wondering how long Geta's going to be
On that little errand. But what's this I see? *(Draws back)*
My uncle right here with my father? Oh dear,
I dread what kind of step his coming here
Will drive my father into.

GETA: Well, I'll go
And tackle them. Hallo, sir!

CHREMES: Ah, hallo!

GETA: It's nice to see you back, all safe and sound.

CHREMES: No doubt.

GETA: How's things? As usual, you'll have found
Many changes since you left, eh?

CHREMES: Lots.

GETA: Quite so.
You've heard what happened to our Antipho?

CHREMES: Yes, the whole story.

GETA: *(to Demipho)*   Ah, sir, you'll have told him?
It's scandalous. They simply bought and sold him.
Poor boy!

CHREMES: We were discussing it all just now.

GETA: I've thought and thought, and I've discovered how—
I think—we can solve this little problem.

CHREMES: Eh!

DEMIPHO: How, Geta?

GETA: Well, I happened, going away
From you, to meet with Phormio.

CHREMES: Who's he?

DEMIPHO: The man who put her up to this.

CHREMES: I see.

GETA: I thought I'd better sound his feelings. So
I got him on one side. 'Now, Phormio,
Why not seek means to settle this', said I,
'As friends, not enemies? My master's shy
Of law-suits. Being a gentleman, he'll think twice
Of *that*. His friends' unanimous advice

Was simply to sling her out.'

ANTIPHO: *(aside)*   Eh, what's he driving at?
What fine conclusion is all this arriving at?

GETA: 'You'll say there are legal penalties to beware of',
Said I, 'If he slings her out. That's taken care of.
My boss can talk your head off. He's really clever,
Try tricks with him, and you'll sweat for it. However,
Suppose you did win. It's no life and death matter.
It's only money at stake.' My little patter,
I could perceive, was now beginning to tell.
'Look here,' I said, 'We're by ourselves here. Well,
What'll you take, cash down, for him to drop
His case, the girl to quit, and you to stop
Making a nuisance of yourself?'

ANTIPHO: *(aside)*   What's bitten him?
With what stark lunacy have the planets smitten him?

GETA: 'He's a man of honour,' I added. 'If there's a jot
Of right and justice in your terms, you'll not,
I'm sure, need three words' talk with one another.'

DEMIPHO: Who told you to go saying that?

CHREMES: But, brother,
It's the best way to obtain our object!

ANTIPHO: *(aside)*   Hell!
Damnation!

DEMIPHO: Go on.

GETA: After raving a little—

CHREMES: Well,
What is he asking?

GETA: Oh, a hell of a lot.

CHREMES: How much?

GETA: Well, if you gave him sixty—

DEMIPHO: What?
Sixty good stripes! The nerve!

GETA: That's what I said.
'If he'd an only daughter getting wed,
How much', I asked, 'would you want him to be giving?
He's not gained much by having no daughter living,
Since one's been found to claim a dowry.' Well,
To cut the story short, and not to dwell
On all his silly tricks, at last he said,
'My wish at the beginning was to wed
My old friend's daughter myself, and do what's right.
My mind's been haunted by her present plight.

Poor girls aren't *married* to rich men, they're *bought*.
But, frankly, I needed another type, that brought
A bit to pay my debts; but even yet
If Demipho will give what I'm due to get
From this girl I'm now engaged to, why,' he said,
'The other's the one girl in the world I'd wed.'

ANTIPHO: *(aside)*
Is he up to some mischief now, or merely blundering,
Wittingly or unwittingly, I'm wondering?

DEMIPHO: Suppose he owes the earth?

GETA: One item there is—
Ten minae mortgage on some land of his.

DEMIPHO: Well, well, I'll pay it, to see him marry her.

GETA: Then
A small house mortgaged for another ten.

DEMIPHO: No, it's too much!

CHREMES: Hush! Get it back from me.

GETA: 'And then my wife must get a maid,' says he.
'We'll want a few sticks of furniture. The wedding's
Got to be paid for. Under all these headings
Put down another ten.'

DEMIPHO: No! Let him bring
Actions galore! I'll not put down a thing,
To have that rogue just laughing!

CHREMES: Don't get so nettled,
Please, now. I'll pay. *You* get your son's mind settled
To marry as we both wish.

ANTIPHO: *(aside)*   A fine fix
You've got me into, Geta, with your tricks!

CHREMES: It's for my sake the girl has got to go.
It's right I should stand the loss.

GETA: 'Well, let me know,'
Says he, 'as soon as you can about all this,
That, if they're offering her, I can dismiss
The other offer, and not be left in doubt.
The other side had settled to pay out
The dowry at once.'

CHREMES: Oh, let him have it, brother,
At once, and let him break it off with that other
And marry this one.

DEMIPHO: And God mar the marrying!

CHREMES: It's lucky that I happen to be carrying
Some money with me now—the rents, in fact,

From my wife's farms in Lemnos. I'll subtract
This money from that total, and tell her *you*
Had urgent need of it, that's what I'll do.
(Chremes and Demipho go into Demipho's house)

ANTIPHO: Geta!

GETA: Hi!

ANTIPHO: What have you done?

GETA: I've done *them*.

ANTIPHO: So?
And I'm supposed to be satisfied?

GETA: I don't know.
I got the sum demanded.

ANTIPHO: Don't be funny,
You rogue. You know I didn't mean the money!

GETA: What *are* you driving at, exactly?

ANTIPHO: Driving?
To ruin, it's quite clear, by your contriving!
May all the gods of heaven and hell pursue you
And make an example of you. Trust *him* to do you
Whatever you've set your heart on—he'll soon steer you
Out of a calm on to the rocks. Look here, you!
What could be worse than touching that sore spot
Of mentioning my wife like that? Now what?
You've filled my father with fine hopes of shedding her.
If Phormio takes the dowry, he's driven to wedding her.
What follows?

GETA: He'll never marry her.

ANTIPHO: Oh no?
And doubtless, all for us, he'll opt to go
To prison when they claim the money back.

GETA: There's no blue sky a pessimist can't paint black.
You cut the good side out and stress the bad.
Now hear the other side. Once Phormio's had
The money, he must marry, as you say.
I grant you that. But then some small delay
Will be allowed for wedding preparations,
Religious ceremonies, invitations.
Meanwhile what those friends promised they'll produce.
He'll pay them back from that.

ANTIPHO: With what excuse,
What grounds for crying off?

GETA: Easy. He'll allege
Most ominous warnings since he gave this pledge.

'A strange black dog strayed in; a serpent fell
Plop from the roof', he'll say, 'into my well.
A hen crowed, a wise sorcerer forbade it.
A seer said if I did it, I'd have had it.
Before the shortest day is a bad season
For any new venture'—that's a very good reason.
That's what'll happen.

ANTIPHO: I hope so.
GETA: Beyond doubt.
Trust me. Hallo! Your father's coming out.
Run and tell Phaedria that the money's there.
(*Exit Antipho. Enter from Chremes' house Demipho and Chremes*)

DEMIPHO: Don't worry, Chremes, I tell you. I'll take care
He doesn't cheat. I'll not part with the cash
Till I have witnesses. I'm not so rash.
I'll state to whom, from whom, and why and wherefore.

GETA: (*aside*)
What does he think he's taking all this care for?

CHREMES: That's right. And quick! If the other side starts pushing him,
He may go back on us yet. It's a question of rushing him
And making use of this mood while he's still in it.

GETA: (*aloud*)
You're right there.

DEMIPHO: Lead me to him, then.
GETA: This minute.
CHREMES: Wait! When that's fixed, just step across the street
To see my wife. I'd like her to go and meet
This girl before she leaves, and tell her this—
That we're marrying her, which she mustn't take amiss,
To Phormio, who, since she knows him better,
Will be a more suitable husband, and we've let her
Have the full dowry that he claimed from us.
We've not failed in our duty.

DEMIPHO: But why fuss?
What does it matter to *you*?

CHREMES: Lots, Demipho.
To do your duty's not enough, you know,
Unless report confirms it. I'm intent
On having everything done with her consent,
So that she doesn't later say it was *we*
Who threw her out.

DEMIPHO: You could leave that to *me*

To make clear.
CHREMES: But I think it's wiser, brother,
To have one woman dealing with another.
DEMIPHO: All right. I'll see your wife later. *(Exit with Geta)*
CHREMES: *(to himself)*   Where to find
My other women—that's what's on my mind.

ACT V

(No pause in action. Enter Sophrona from Demipho's house)
SOPHRONA: What shall I do? What friend here can I fly to
In my distress? What counsellor apply to
To sort this out? Where can I ask for aid?
My mistress, thanks to my advice, I'm afraid,
May suffer cruel wrong. The young man's dad,
I'm told, doesn't like it at all. He's hopping mad.
CHREMES: *(aside)*
Who's this old woman, rushing like one distracted,
Out of my brother's house?
SOPHRONA: I simply acted
Out of sheer naked need, although I knew
The marriage was shaky. All I wanted to do
Was to get her some means of living, to secure
At least the immediate future.
CHREMES: *(aside)*   Heavens! I'm sure
Unless my eyesight's failing, or my mind,
That woman's my daughter's nurse.
SOPHRONA: And we can't find—
CHREMES: *(aside)*
What now?
SOPHRONA: — any traces of the poor child's father.
CHREMES: *(aside)*
Shall I accost her now, or hang back rather,
Until I'm a little clearer what she's saying?
SOPHRONA: If only I could find out where he's staying.
I'd surely have no further cause to fear.
CHREMES: *(aside)*
It *is*. I'll speak to her.
SOPHRONA: Who's that I hear?
CHREMES: Sophrona!
SOPHRONA: What! My name?

CHREMES: Look—this way.
SOPHRONA: Oh!
Heavens, it's not, or can it be, Stilpho?
CHREMES: No!
SOPHRONA: Do you deny it?
CHREMES: Come here. Move away,
Please, from that door. Now, Sophrona, never say
That name to me again.
SOPHRONA: Aren't you the person
You always said?
CHREMES: *(glancing at his own door)*
                        Hush!
SOPHRONA: What's the terrible curse on
That door?
CHREMES: The curse is, that behind that same
I have a wife, a terror. That false name
I used in case your lips leaked unawares
And let her know too much of my affairs.
SOPHRONA: And that's the reason we poor fools couldn't find you!
CHREMES: But what's your business in *that* house behind you?
And where's your mistress and my daughter, eh?
SOPHRONA: Oh dear! Oh dear!
CHREMES: What's the matter? Can't you say?
Are they alive at least?
SOPHRONA: The girl's alive,
But her poor mother didn't long survive
Her sorrows.
CHREMES: Oh, that's sad.
SOPHRONA: Then, as things stood,
Stranded, old, poor, a stranger, I did what I could.
I got her married to this lad, you know,
The owner of this house.
CHREMES: To Antipho?
SOPHRONA: Yes, him, sir.
CHREMES: How, has he two wives, or what?
SOPHRONA: Lord, no, sir! This one's all the wives *he's* got.
CHREMES: But what about that other girl they claim
To be related to him?
SOPHRONA: It's the same.
They worked it so he could marry, out of pure love,
Our girl, she having no dowry.
CHREMES: Gods above!
How often mere coincidence will contrive

What you'd not dare to pray for. I arrive
To find my daughter settled as and where
I wished. What we both strove for, with such care,
She, without troubling us, has brought about,
Though she had trouble enough herself, no doubt.

SOPHRONA: Well, now what's to be done? The young man's dad
Has turned up, and they say he's raging mad.

CHREMES: There's no risk there. But mind, by heaven and earth,
That no one learns the truth about her birth.

SOPHRONA: No one shall know from me, sir.

CHREMES: Very well.
Come in. Let's hear what else you have to tell.
*(Exeunt into Demipho's house. A short pause. Enter
Demipho with Geta)*

DEMIPHO: It's our own fault—so fond of hearing men say
We're just and generous that we make crime pay.
There's an old proverb tells us, 'Don't rush past
Your own house door by running away too fast.'
As if it wasn't enough to let that brute
Get away with murder, we've gone and thrown him loot
To live on while he thinks up further crimes.

GETA: I'm afraid that's only too obvious.

DEMIPHO: Our times
Reward this type who don't care what they do,
Crooked or straight.

GETA: I'm afraid that's only too true.

DEMIPHO: Only too witless, therefore, is the way
We've managed this affair.

GETA: I only pray
That this does prove a possible way out,
And that he marries this other.

DEMIPHO: Is that in doubt?

GETA: Lord knows, sir. I can't say. He *is* that kind,
So he might change his mind, sir.

DEMIPHO: Change his mind!

GETA: I don't know, sir. I only say he *might*.

DEMIPHO: I'll take my brother's tip, anyway, and invite
His wife across to talk with her. Geta, go
And tell the girl to expect this visit.
(Exit into Chremes' house)

GETA: So!
Cash found for Phaedria, talk of law-suits dropped,
The girl's removal for the moment stopped—

What'll be happening now? Ah, yes, what will?
Geta, you're sticking in the old mud still.
You've paid by borrowing, which means more to pay,
Solved present troubles for the present day,
But if you don't look out, the lashings mount.
Well, I'll pop in and give a full account
To Phanium, so she won't fear having to wed
Phormio, or be scared by anything said.
*(Exit into Demipho's house. Enter Demipho with
Nausistrata from Chremes' house)*

DEMIPHO: You'll talk her round then, with your usual tact,
So that she does what she's got to as an act
Of her own will?

NAUSISTRATA: Very well.

DEMIPHO: You really double
My obligation, giving this time and trouble
As well as that help with money.

NAUSISTRATA: It's a pleasure.
Compared with what I should do, it's short measure.
But that's my husband's fault.

DEMIPHO: How do you mean?

NAUSISTRATA: God knows how slack and negligent he's been
With Father's honest savings. Why, every year
Those farms brought him a hundred minae clear.
How different men can be!

DEMIPHO: A hundred, eh?

NAUSISTRATA: *And* with a lower cost of living.

DEMIPHO: I say!

NAUSISTRATA: Quite so. What *do* you say?

DEMIPHO: What *can* be said?

NAUSISTRATA: If only I'd been born a man instead,
I'd show—

DEMIPHO: I'm sure—

NAUSISTRATA: —just how—

DEMIPHO: Do save your strength,
She's so much younger. Talking to her at length
May really tire you out.

NAUSISTRATA: I'll say no more.
Ah, there's my husband coming from your door.
*(Enter Chremes from Demipho's house. He does not see his
wife at first)*

CHREMES: Hey, Demipho, have you paid that fellow already?

DEMIPHO: Sure—saw to it at once.

CHREMES: Too bad. *(aside)* Whoa! Steady!
My wife! I nearly said too much then.
DEMIPHO: How?
How too bad?
CHREMES: Oh, it doesn't matter now.
DEMIPHO: And *your* job? Did you have your little chat
And tell her why we're bringing your wife?
CHREMES: Oh, that!
That's fixed.
DEMIPHO: Her answer?
CHREMES: She—can't be moved.
DEMIPHO: Why not?
CHREMES: Well, they're in love.
DEMIPHO: What's that to us?
CHREMES: A lot.
Besides I've found she really is connected.
DEMIPHO: Rubbish!
CHREMES: You'll find it's true. I've recollected.
I know what I'm talking about.
DEMIPHO: You must be raving!
NAUSISTRATA: Good Lord, you'd better mind how you're behaving
To a real relation!
DEMIPHO: But she's not related!
CHREMES: No use denying it. They just mis-stated
The parent's name, and that misled you rather.
DEMIPHO: You mean to say she doesn't know her father?
CHREMES: Of course she knew him!
DEMIPHO: Then why name another?
CHREMES: Oh, won't you understand or trust me, brother?
DEMIPHO: When you talk rubbish?
CHREMES: Oh, you'll be my ruin!
NAUSISTRATA: I wish I knew what everyone is doing.
DEMIPHO: Search me!
CHREMES: Look here. I swear I am no liar.
No man is closer to her than you and I are.
DEMIPHO: For God's sake then, let's all establish whether
It's true or not by going to her all together.
CHREMES: Oh, God!
DEMIPHO: What's up?
CHREMES: You really are absurd,
Being so mistrustful.
DEMIPHO: I'm to take your word
And ask no questions, eh? All right, then, brother,

But look here,—what's to happen to that other,
The daughter of *our friend*?

CHREMES: Oh, that's all right.

DEMIPHO: We drop her?

CHREMES: Yes.

DEMIPHO: And keep this other?

CHREMES: Quite.

DEMIPHO: Well, then, Nausistrata, you needn't stay.

NAUSISTRATA: I think it's nicer for everyone this way
Than what you'd planned—getting rid of her. Much better.
She made a well-bred impression when I met her.
(Exit into Chremes' house)

DEMIPHO: What's all this?

CHREMES: Is the door shut?

DEMIPHO: Yes.

CHREMES: Fate's kind
To us, by God it is! What do I find?
My daughter's got herself married to your son!

DEMIPHO: But how, in heaven's name, could she have done?

CHREMES: It isn't safe to tell you here.

DEMIPHO: Let's go
Inside then.

CHREMES: This not even our sons must know.
(Exeunt into Demipho's house. Enter Antipho)

ANTIPHO: Well, seeing how things are going with me, I'm glad
My cousin at least has got his wish. Wise lad
To pick such passions that you can be sure,
If things go wrong, to find a ready cure.
Soon as he got the cash, he'd cut his noose.
But I can see no means of wriggling loose
From *my* dilemma. If my deed's concealed,
I live in terror, while, if it's revealed,
I'm in disgrace. I'd not have come home *now*
But for the hope held out—I don't know how—
Of keeping her after all. But where the hell
Has Geta got to in the meantime?
(Enter Phormio)

PHORMIO: *(to himself)*   Well,
I've got the money, paid off master pander,
Carted the girl off, and contrived to hand her
To Phaedria for keeps. For she's been freed now
Quite legally. A rest is all I need now,
From rude old men, time for some good hard drinking.

I'll take a few days off for that, I'm thinking.

ANTIPHO: Ah, there comes Phormio. What now?

PHORMIO: 'What now?'

ANTIPHO: I mean, what's Phaedria going to do, where, how
Does he propose to satisfy his passion?

PHORMIO: Oh, he'll be following, for a change, your fashion.

ANTIPHO: What fashion?

PHORMIO: Keeping out of father's way.
He asks you to assume his role, and say
A word for him. He'll be at my place, drinking.
In case the old men miss me and start thinking
I'm blueing their cash, I'll say I'm off to the fair
At Sunium, to buy the slave girl there
That Geta's told them the bride needs. Hallo!
Your door creaked.

ANTIPHO: See who's coming.

PHORMIO: Geta.

GETA: Oh,
Fortune most fair, most fortunate, what a load
Of blessings in one heap have you bestowed
On my young master Antipho!—

ANTIPHO: (aside)   What's he mean?

GETA: And freed his friends, like me, from fear most keen.
But now to find him, and, before it's colder,
Feed him his good luck. So, cloak over shoulder,
Quick march!

ANTIPHO: (aside)   Do you get his drift at all?

PHORMIO: (aside)   Do you?

ANTIPHO: (aside)
Not in the least.

PHORMIO: (aside)   I certainly haven't a clue.

GETA: Off to the pimp's house. They'll be there.

ANTIPHO: Hi! Whoa,
Geta!

GETA: (not turning)
                There now. As soon as you've said 'go',
You're called back to the mark. It would be strange
If one could get away unchecked for a change.

ANTIPHO: Geta!

GETA: Still at it? Drag at me till you drop.
I'll not be brought down.

ANTIPHO: Oh, for God's sake, stop!

GETA: Beat it, or I'll beat *you*.
ANTIPHO: That's just the fate,
      You rogue, in store for you, if you don't wait.
GETA: He must be close to the family to dare
      To threaten me with beating. But who's there?
      (Turning round)
      Is it the very man I want, or not?
      It is! A meeting most well-timed!
ANTIPHO: For what?
GETA: Oh, Antipho, of all men living, who
      Has been more fortune-favoured? Surely you,
      And you alone must be the belov'd of Heaven.
ANTIPHO: I wish I were. I wish I might be given
      Some cause to think so.
GETA: If I stuff and cram you
      With joy, will you be satisfied?
ANTIPHO: Oh, damn you,
      Stop torturing!
PHORMIO: Yes, stop talking fine and tell
      Your news.
GETA: Ah, Phormio, you're there as well?
PHORMIO: I'm here. Get talking.
GETA: Listen then. We'd paid
      Your money out in the market-square, then made
      For home at once. And then the old man gave me
      A message for your wife.
ANTIPHO: What message?
GETA: Save me
      Irrelevant details. The reason I was sent
      Isn't important, really. Off I went
      To the women's quarters. Out flashed, like a stroke
      Of lightning, Mida, the page-boy, caught my cloak
      And hauled me back. I looked round, saw the lad,
      And asked him what the devil reason he had
      For stopping me. 'I've orders not to allow
      Anyone into my mistress', he said, 'just now.
      Sophrona brought in Chremes, the master's brother.
      They're all in there, conferring with one another.'
      On hearing this, tiptoe to the door I crept.
      I came, I stood, I held my breath. I kept
      My ear to the door, intent. This seemed the way
      Not to miss anything anyone might say.
PHORMIO: Full marks for Geta!

GETA: And at once I heard
          The loveliest bit of news. Upon my word,
          It nearly made me yell out loud for joy.
ANTIPHO: What was it?
GETA: What do you think it was, my boy?
ANTIPHO: How should I know?
GETA: The wonder of your life.
          I find your uncle's—the father of your wife.
ANTIPHO: What?
GETA: Yes, he knew her mother years ago
          In Lemnos.
PHORMIO: Rot! As if she wouldn't know
          Her father!
GETA: Oh, there'll be some explanation
          Of that. You mustn't suppose that from my station
          Outside the door, I could hear every word
          They said inside.
ANTIPHO: By heaven, you know, I've heard
          Some rumour that might fit this tale before.
GETA: I'll give you reason to believe it more.
          Your uncle sallies forth, comes back again
          Straight with your father. They go in, and then
          They both declare at once that they don't mind
          Phanium staying, and I'm sent to find
          And bring you.
ANTIPHO: Bring me? Wing me! Why so slow?
GETA: At once, sir.
ANTIPHO: Oh, so long, dearest Phormio!
          (Exeunt Antipho and Geta into Demipho's house)
PHORMIO: Dear Antipho, so long! By God, those two
          Have had a lucky bolt out of the blue!
          Lovely! Delightful! Now I've got the chance
          Of leading those old dotards a fine dance,
          With Phaedria's money troubles at an end,
          So that he needn't beg from any friend.
          The cash those two coughed up he'll keep intact,
          However little they like it. Force of fact
          Has given me the power to make them bow.
          A change of face, a change of bearing—now
          I'm ready for them. Into this next alley
          I'll slip, and when they come along out I sally.
          As for that fair at Sunium I've been saying
          I'd pay a visit to, that's off. I'm staying.

(Enter from Demipho's house Demipho and Chremes.
They do not see Phormio at first)

DEMIPHO: Thank Heaven, for Heaven's earned it, Heaven knows,
A thousand times. Why, Chremes, everything goes
The way we want. Let's get on Phormio's track
At once, and have our thirty minae back
Before he's squandered them.

PHORMIO: *(pretending not to see them)* Well, I'll just see
If Demipho's at home.

DEMIPHO: Just fancy! *We*
Were setting off to see you, Phormio.

PHORMIO: About the same old business, eh?

DEMIPHO: Quite so.

PHORMIO: I thought so. But why should you? It's absurd!
Were you afraid I wouldn't keep my word?
Poor I may be, but one thing's undeniable—
No one has ever found me unreliable.

CHREMES: Didn't I say he was honourable?

DEMIPHO: Quite so.

PHORMIO: And so I've come along to let you know
I'm ready. Whenever you wish, bring out your bride.
For seeing you so keen, I've put aside
All other business, as in duty bound.

DEMIPHO: Quite, but my brother here has talked me round.
For what, he pointed out, will people say?
Once, when this young girl could have been given away
Without any sort of disgrace, she wasn't given.
Now, when it must discredit us, out she's driven.
In fact, his points are very much the same
As you first made.

PHORMIO: A fine high-handed game
You're playing with me!

DEMIPHO: How do you mean?

PHORMIO: How? How?
Why, I can't wed the other girl either now.
How, having rejected her once, can I return?
How can I have the face?

CHREMES: *(aside)* Say you now learn
That Antipho's averse to losing her.
Go on, now!

DEMIPHO: I now learn, moreover, sir,
My son has a strong aversion to the loss
Of this young lady. So let's step across

To the bank, if you don't mind, and we'll have that sum
Transferred to my account, eh? Come.

PHORMIO: You mean that money which went on cheques I drew
To pay my debts?

DEMIPHO: Oh, now, what shall we do?

PHORMIO: If you're prepared to bring the bride I stand
Engaged to, I'll marry her. If you demand
That she should stay with you, then I'll agree,
Provided that the dowry stays with me.
It isn't fair that for your family's sake
I should be cheated, since I chose to break,
Out of regard for you and your good name,
My pledge to the other girl, who'd got the same
Amount of dowry.

DEMIPHO: Oh, the hangman fetch you,
With your fine airs, you runaway slave, you wretch, you!
Do you still think we don't know what you are
Or what you're up to?

PHORMIO: Sir, you go too far.

DEMIPHO: Bah! If this girl were given you, would you take her?

PHORMIO: Try me and see.

DEMIPHO: So that my son could make her
His mistress, living at your house! That's been
Your little plan all along.

PHORMIO: What *do* you mean?

DEMIPHO: My money, sir!

PHORMIO: My wife, sir!

DEMIPHO: Come to court.

PHORMIO: If I have more annoyance of this sort—

DEMIPHO: You'll what?

PHORMIO: No doubt you think I only act
For dowerless girls. But I defend, in fact,
Women with dowries as well.

CHREMES: What's that to do
With us, pray?

PHORMIO: Nothing. Nothing. I once knew
A woman here whose husband had another —

CHREMES: Oh!

DEMIPHO: Eh?

PHORMIO: Another wife in Lemnos.

CHREMES: Brother,
I'm sunk.

PHORMIO: By her he had a daughter whom

He brought up secretly.

CHREMES: Oh, seal my tomb!

PHORMIO: I'm going to tell the lady everything.

CHREMES: No!

For God's sake, don't go doing that!

PHORMIO: Oho!

Were *you* the man?

DEMIPHO: Oh, how he mocks us, brother!

CHREMES: All right, we'll call it quits.

PHORMIO: Tell me another.

CHREMES: What do you want? We leave you with the money.

PHORMIO: No doubt you do. No doubt you think it funny,
This childish dilly-dallying. I don't.
'I won't. I will. I will. Oh, no, I won't.
Take. Give back.' Said's unsaid, and what just now
Was settled is unsettled.

CHREMES: Where and how
Did he discover this?

DEMIPHO: Oh, I can't say.
I'm sure I never gave anything away.

CHREMES: There's something supernatural at the bottom
Of this. God help me if there isn't.

PHORMIO: *(aside)*   I've got 'em
On tenterhooks with *that* announcement!

DEMIPHO: Oh!
Is he to rob *and* ridicule us so
Before the world? I'd sooner die. Get ready,
With presence of mind and courage firm and steady,
To face this. Look. This dark spot in your life
Is out, you can't conceal it from your wife.
She'll be more easily appeased if, brother,
We tell the tale she'll soon hear from another.
Then we can pay in our own coin this lout,
This swine, this scum.

PHORMIO: Hey, if I don't look out,
They'll do a gladiators' march on *me*!

CHREMES: She may be past appeasing.

DEMIPHO: No. Not she.
What's sure to reconcile you with each other
Is the providential removal of this girl's mother.

PHORMIO: So that's it? A sly onslaught! Demipho,
You've done him no good to provoke me so,
What, sir? You go abroad, enjoying the life,

Checked by no feelings for your excellent wife,
You find a fine new way to insult her in,
And now you come and beg to purge your sin.
But I'll send such a fire through those pure ears,
You'll never drown it, though you drip with tears.

DEMIPHO: You'd think that such incredible audacity
Would be beyond a single man's capacity!
The rogue should be conveyed at public cost
To an uninhabited island.

CHREMES: I'm quite lost.
I can't think what to do with him.

DEMIPHO: I can.
To court!

PHORMIO: *(moving to Chremes' door)*
                    This court, please!

CHREMES: After him! Hold him, man!
I'll summon the slaves.

DEMIPHO: *(struggling with Phormio)*
                    I can't alone. Quick, brother!

PHORMIO: That's one assault, sir!

DEMIPHO: *(hitting him again)*   Sue me.

PHORMIO: That's another!

CHREMES: Off with him!

PHORMIO: Now I'll really have to shout,
If that's your game. Nausistrata, come on out!

CHREMES: Shut his foul mouth. Oh, but he's strong!

PHORMIO: *(loudly)*   Hallo!
Nausistrata!

DEMIPHO: Won't you come quietly?

PHORMIO: No!

DEMIPHO: Just punch his belly, if he gives you trouble.

PHORMIO: Or knock an eye out. I can pay back double.
(Nausistrata comes out of Chremes' house)

NAUSISTRATA: Who called my name? Lord, what's this rumpus? Come, now,
My dear, what is it?

PHORMIO: Well, what's up? Struck dumb, now?

NAUSISTRATA: Who's this? . . . I'm waiting for your answer.

PHORMIO: His?
He doesn't know, God help him, where he is.

CHREMES: I warn you. Don't believe a word you're told
By *him*.

PHORMIO: Look at him! If he's not stone-cold
All over, I'll be hanged.

CHREMES: It's nothing, dear.
NAUSISTRATA: What is? What has he got to say?
PHORMIO: *That* you shall hear
At once. Just listen.
CHREMES: Do you mean to credit
What *he* says?
NAUSISTRATA: I don't know. He hasn't said it.
PHORMIO: Look! The poor fellow's paralysed with fear.
NAUSISTRATA: It's not for nothing you're so scared, that's clear.
CHREMES: Me scared? Why, what do you mean?
PHORMIO: Oh, very well, then,
You're not. What I'd to tell is nothing. *You* tell, then.
DEMIPHO: What, tell your tale, you twister!
PHORMIO: Don't *you* start.
We've seen you staunchly taking your brother's part.
NAUSISTRATA: Husband dear, aren't you going to tell me?
CHREMES: Well—
NAUSISTRATA: Well what?
CHREMES: I don't see any need to tell.
PHORMIO: There's none, for you. The need's for her to hear.
In Lemnos—
NAUSISTRATA: Ah!
CHREMES: Stop!
PHORMIO: —hidden from you—
CHREMES: Oh, dear!
PHORMIO: He took a wife.
NAUSISTRATA: Oh, no, no! Heaven forbid!
What are you saying?
PHORMIO: What your husband did.
NAUSISTRATA: Oh, no, this is the end!
PHORMIO: He had, and kept,
One daughter by her, while you happily slept.
CHREMES: *(to Demipho)*
What shall we do?
NAUSISTRATA: Good God, how base and mean!
PHORMIO: Your doing's been done, sir.
NAUSISTRATA: Was there ever seen
More monstrous conduct! Oh, no wonder, then,
They come back to their wives such tired old men.
Oh, Demipho, it's to *you* that I appeal.
For talking with this creature himself I feel
Too much distaste. *This* is the background, is it,
Of that so frequent need to pay a visit

To Lemnos, those long stays, that dwindling rent
'Due to low prices'? This is what it meant!

DEMIPHO: My dear, he did you wrong, I do admit,
But can't we let his sins rest?

PHORMIO: Fine words, fit
For funeral speeches. And he's dead.

DEMIPHO: No slight
Was meant to you. It wasn't done for spite.
But fifteen years ago, in drink, my brother
Got hold of a wench who became that young girl's mother.
It was only once, and that one stumbling-block,
Now that she's dead, is gone. It's been a shock,
I know, but one that I would beg you bear
As you've borne other blows. Be calm. Be fair.

NAUSISTRATA: Why should I? Oh, I wish this was the end!
But why should I hope *that*, or think he'll mend
His ways with years? He was no youngster then,
If age has sobering effects on men.
Or am I now a more attractive wife
Than then, with these looks, at this time of life?
What reasons can you give, what expectation
Or hope of any future reformation?

PHORMIO: Re. Chremes' funeral, for any friend
Who wishes and is able to attend,
The time and place is here and now . . . And so
Let anyone who will, dare Phormio.
I'll deal with him. I'll crush him flat. I'll leave him
Like Chremes here. But now—shall we reprieve him?
His sentence satisfies me. I've given his wife
A theme to nag on all his natural life.

NAUSISTRATA: And that's my due? The sort of wife I've been
Need I recall in detail?

DEMIPHO: That I've seen,
Of course. I know all that as well as you.

NAUSISTRATA: Well, can you say that I've received my due?

DEMIPHO: No, not at all. But blame won't cure this case
Or make what's done undone, so grant him grace.
He pleads, admits, begs pardon. Well, what more
Do you demand of him?

PHORMIO: Oh, no! Before
She grants the grace he asks for, I'll take care
Of Phaedria and myself. Madam, beware!
Before you answer rashly, hear me.

NAUSISTRATA:	What?
PHORMIO:	There's a sum of thirty minae which I got
	By guile out of your husband. I gave your son that
	To buy a girl from a dealer.
CHREMES:	And he's *done* that?
	Damn him!
NAUSISTRATA:	So shocked, if younger blood contrives
	To keep one mistress, when you've kept two wives?
	Have you no shame? How will you have the cheek
	To check him for it? Well, why don't you speak?
DEMIPHO:	He'll take your terms.
NAUSISTRATA:	No. Wait. He shall receive
	My verdict now. No pardon, no reprieve,
	No pledge, no answer, till I've seen my son.
	He shall decide. What he says shall be done.
PHORMIO:	Madam, you're wise.
NAUSISTRATA:	Is that agreed?
DEMIPHO:	Agreed.
CHREMES:	*(aside)*
	I come off well—beyond all hope indeed.
NAUSISTRATA:	What do they call you?
PHORMIO:	Phormio's the name,
	Madam,—a friend of the family, I might claim,
	And very close to your son.
NAUSISTRATA:	Well, from today,
	Whatever, Phormio, I can do or say
	To help you at all, I will.
PHORMIO:	You're very kind.
NAUSISTRATA:	No more than you deserve.
PHORMIO:	Have you a mind,
	Madam, this very day to make a start
	With something that would both rejoice my heart
	And be one in the eye for your husband?
NAUSISTRATA:	I'd be delighted.
PHORMIO:	Invite me, then, to dinner.
NAUSISTRATA:	You're invited.
DEMIPHO:	Well, let's go in, then.
NAUSISTRATA:	Certainly. But wait.
	Where's Phaedria, our judge?
PHORMIO:	I'll fetch him straight.
PRODUCER:	*(to audience)*
	Goodbye to you. If pleased, please indicate.

The Mother-in-Law

The Mother-in-Law

CHARACTERS

PHILOTIS: a young courtesan
SYRA: an old courtesan
PARMENO: a slave of Laches
LACHES: an old man, father of Pamphilus
SOSTRATA: wife of Laches
PHIDIPPUS: an old man, father of Philumena
PAMPHILUS: a young man, son of Laches and Sostrata
SOSIA: a slave of Laches
MYRRINA: wife of Phidippus, mother of Philumena
BACCHIS: a courtesan

FIRST PROLOGUE TO *THE MOTHER-IN-LAW*

We present our *Mother-in-Law*, whose first appearance
Left her, by strange, disastrous interference,
Unshown, unknown. So utterly entrancing
To the great Roman public was tight-rope dancing.
Welcome this new face, then. The writer's reason,
For not reviving his *Mother-in-Law* that season,
Was to revive that fresh feel of first showing.
You know his plays—in part. This, too's worth knowing

SECOND PROLOGUE TO *THE MOTHER-IN-LAW*
Spoken by the actor-manager Lucius Ambivius Turpio

With pleas I come to you in prologue dress.
Grant these; grant me in age my old success,
When for new pieces, here hissed off the stage,
I in my youth procured a ripe old age,
And rescued from extinction piece and poet.
The history of Caecilius' plays will show it.[1]

---

1 Caecilius was the pre-eminent comic poet of the generation between Plautus and Terence. His works survive only in fragments.

For of those early works I first came out with
Some held their ground—just; some I suffered real rout with.
But knowing the fickle fortune of the boards,
I risked sure trouble for unsure rewards.
To coax new plays from him, I steadily played
The old, and kept him steadily at his trade.
I got them shown. Once known they were approved;
Their author, well-nigh from our ranks removed,
From care and effort in the comic art,
By unfair opposition on the part
Of certain persons, to his rightful place
I thus restored. Had I, too, set my face
Against his efforts at the very start
And gone right out to rob him of all heart,
Made leisure and not labour more inviting,
I'd soon have sickened him for further writing.
Now for my sake attend to my intent
With fair and open minds. I here present
My *Mother-in-Law*, who, more than once appearing,
Has never once obtained a silent hearing.
Doom's dogged her. But we've done *our* best. If *you* do,
Our toil and your good taste will beat this voodoo.
Our first time round the boxer's big-mouthed boast,
The bedlam gathering of the fans, but most
The unfair sex, so clamorous, made certain,
Our premature retirement and prompt curtain.
What did I do? With new play follow old practice—
'Try, try again'—I revive her. The first act is
This second time well-received. Then comes the cry
'Swordfighters up next!' From all sides they fly,
And, while they shout and shove and fight like mad
To get a place, bang goes the place I had.
Today we have no rivals, no boxer riot,
No super-bloody swordsmen. In peace and quiet
I'm free to act and you to play your part
In adding honour to the comic art.
Don't let a small clique make it their monopoly.
Back my prestige with yours. If I can properly
Claim that in my producer's books most gain meant
Most given always for your entertainment—
Service, not surplus—let me be supported
In this request. Let nobody be thwarted
And mocked by unfair means of unfair men
When he entrusts the travails of his pen

To my protection and to your fair dealing.
Pray silence then. It's Ambivius appealing
For Terence, but hoping to make *you* make writing
Offer to others prospects more inviting.
Prove to my purse that to present new plays,
Not by poor poets presented but purchased, pays.

Scene: A street in Athens, showing the neighbouring houses of Laches and Phidippus, with that of Bacchis somewhat further off.

ACT I

(Enter Philotis, a young courtesan, and Syra, an older woman of the same class)

PHILOTIS: Oh, Syra, how few men one seems to find
Faithful in love to women of our kind!
There's Pamphilus now—what woman wouldn't readily
Have taken *his* word, so stoutly and so steadily
He swore to Bacchis, while one breath of life
Was in her body, never to take a wife?
And now—he's married.

SYRA: That's why I say so often,
So emphatically—with the male sex never soften!
Cling—where your claws light, let them rip, rob, rend!

PHILOTIS: Make no exception of *any* gentleman friend,
You mean to say?

SYRA: I do. There's not a man
But acts according to a worked-out plan.
Along they come, so pleasant and so nice,
And all they want's—the lot at the lowest price.
Well, you just show them, two can play that game.

PHILOTIS: I'm sure it's wrong to treat them all the same.

SYRA: Wrong to pay out the enemy, tit for tat?
To catch him as he'd catch *you*? I like that!
Lord, you should let *me* have your looks and youth,
My girl, or take my tips—and that's the truth.
(Parmeno comes out of Laches' house, talking to someone inside)

PARMENO: Scirtus, if our old man should ask for me,
I've gone to make inquiries at the quay
About his son's arrival. Now note well
My exact words. *If* he should ask, you tell;

If not, you don't, and I've one sound excuse
For absence left intact for later use.
But say—is that Philotis that I spy there?
Now where on earth has she turned up from? Hi there,
Philotis honey, may an old friend greet you?

PHILOTIS: Why if it isn't Parmeno! Pleased to meet you.

SYRA: How are you, Parmeno?

PARMENO: Fine. And you? But say,
Where's my Philotis been this many a day?
Living it up?

PHILOTIS: Are you kidding? I went out
To Corinth with a captain. Such a lout
You never saw. I tolerated him
For two eternal years—and were they grim!

PARMENO: You often yearned for good old Athens, eh,
And cursed your own judgement?

PHILOTIS: Words won't say
Just how I longed to quit, come back, and see
My friends, and live the old life, open, free,
With all you lot. I tell you, in that town,
All talk, except as previously laid down
In orders by *his* high command, was barred.

PARMENO: A military censor, eh? Bit hard.

PHILOTIS: But what's all this we've heard from Bacchis here?
I never thought your master, Parmeno dear,
Would bring himself, while she'd one breath of life,
To take a wife like this.

PARMENO: H'm. Take a wife?

PHILOTIS: Well, hasn't he?

PARMENO: He got as far as marrying,
But I'm afraid that match *may* be miscarrying.

PHILOTIS: If that helps Bacchis, then God send it *is* so.
But what are the grounds for hope? What's up?

PARMENO: Don't quiz so.
The grounds are private, not to be let out.

PHILOTIS: Lest all should be let into them, no doubt.
But honestly, as I hope for heaven's blessing,
It's not for publication I'm so pressing,
But purely private pleasure.

PARMENO: I'll not confide
To your sealed lips the safety of my hide,
However hard you coax.

PHILOTIS: Come, Parmeno,

        You're keener to confide than I to know.

PARMENO: *(aside)*
        She's right. It's my worst fault. *(aloud)* Well, if you'll swear
        Not to let it go any further, I'll tell you.

PHILOTIS: There!
        That's more like *you*. Okay. I swear. Now tell.
        Out with it.

PARMENO: Listen then.

PHILOTIS: I'm with you.

PARMENO: Well,
        Young Pamphilus was dead keen on Bacchis still,
        As much as ever, when, as fathers will,
        His old man started urging him to wed
        With all the usual arguments. He said,
        'I'm getting on. You're my only son. Your dad
        Will soon be needing your support, my lad.'
        At first the boy wouldn't hear of it, then under
        Fiercer paternal pressure got to wonder
        If his own feelings or the family rather
        Should have first claim. Well, in the end his father
        By dint of nagging him ad nauseam won,
        And—guess what—to the girl next door got his son
        Engaged. Still Pamphilus didn't seem to think
        Things were so black till on the very brink
        Of marriage, when he saw where he was heading,
        With nothing that could now avert a wedding.
        And then he really did begin to fret.
        Bacchis herself would have been bound, I bet,
        To pity him, if she'd seen the pathetic state
        He was in. Whenever he got me tête-à-tête,
        'Oh, Parmeno,' he'd moan, 'what made me do it?
        Led to the altar, or halter—however you view it,
        The nuptial noose, at *his* bidding! Grabbed, tied, garotted!'

PHILOTIS: God grab the old tyrant soon and tell *him* to get knotted!

PARMENO: To make a short tale, he got spliced all right
        And brought his bride home. Now, on that first night—
        He didn't touch her, nor the next night either.

PHILOTIS: You mean a lad in his prime, in bed, in liquor, could lie there,
        A total abstainer, super-chaste non-achiever?
        That's a *tall* tale, and I'm an unbeliever.

PARMENO: I'll bet you are. All visitors to *your* bed
        Are volunteers. He was drafted, driven to wed.

PHILOTIS: What then?

PARMENO: A few days later here outside
He got me on my own, said how his bride
Was still 'in statu quo', how up till now,
Before the marriage, he'd still hoped somehow
To make a go of it. 'But since', he said,
'I've made my mind up that we can't stay wed,
She must be sent home—soon. I can't cheapen and cheat her
Out of all chance with some better man who might meet her.
I'm not some fickle deceiver. I'll have deceived her
Worse though, if I don't send her back as I received her.'

PHILOTIS: You make your master out a nice sensitive youth.

PARMENO: 'The tricky bit', he said, 'will be the plain truth
About Bacchis. But simply sending back a young bride
With no fault found—just can't be justified.
My hope is, being no fool, she herself'll admit
This marriage has no future and quietly quit.'

PHILOTIS: But meanwhile? Was he seeing Bacchis still?

PARMENO: Daily—or nightly. But she, as women will,
Feeling he wasn't hers quite in the old way,
Received him in a new, rough, tough, bold, cold way.

PHILOTIS: Can you wonder?

PARMENO: Well, on that rough rock they split.
She overdid it. And he began, bit by bit,
To see her and himself straight—and his wife.
Her station stamped her, not as trouble and strife,
But pure, sweet patience. All her husband did
To hurt, harm, vex, she put up with, pocketed, hid,
Till partly pity for her and in part
The other's harshness told on him. His heart
From Bacchis slowly slipped, all his affection
Ebbed, ever-deepening, in the other direction,
Where his true complement in character lies.
Then suddenly—some old cousin in Imbros dies,
As heirs we've got to see to things. And so
To Imbros Pamphilus, now most loath to go,
Having learned sincerely to love his wife, was sent
By his insistent father. Off he went,
Left his mother in charge of the now cherished bride,
The old man's rarely in town, prefers to hide
Down on the farm—

PHILOTIS: But how does it appear
This marriage is 'miscarrying'—

PARMENO: You shall hear.

The women got on well with one another
The first few days. Then suddenly his mother,
It seems, falls out of favour with his wife,
But very strangely. There's no open strife,
And no complaint from either.

PHILOTIS: Then what's the matter?

PARMENO: Each time the old lady goes for a little natter
To the girl's room, what does she do but flee her,
Run from the sight of her, refuse to see her!
Then, as though desperate, saying her mother'd sent
To have her at some family occasion, she went.
After she'd been at home some days, his mother
Sends for her. They make some excuse or other.
Once more we send. No luck. Once more. The same.
Again. They say she's sick. Then our old dame
Goes off sick-visiting, can't get past the gate.
Then our old man comes up to town, goes straight
To see *her* father—that was yesterday.
What passed between that pair I still can't say,
But I do wonder where all this will end.
Well, that's the lot. And now I must attend
To my own business and be off.

PHILOTIS: Me too.
I've got a foreign client to interview.

PARMENO: God speed the good work. Here's to your success!

PHILOTIS: Goodbye.

PARMENO: Goodbye, Philotis dear. God bless.
(Exeunt separately. The stage is empty for a minute)

ACT II

(Laches bursts out of his house, followed by his wife, Sostrata)

LACHES: God give me strength! What a species! Curst, conspiring—
Women! All one, detesting or desiring,
Not one a damn breadth's different from the others—
Mothers hate wives and wives hate husbands' mothers.
Each mad to thwart *us*, obstinate as a mule.
They could have learned pure cussedness in one school,
And, naming no names, we know who'd head *that* college.

SOSTRATA: Why I'm being picked on passes my poor knowledge.

LACHES: Ha!

SOSTRATA: Truly, as I hope we yet may share

                                 Many years with Heaven's grace.
LACHES: May Heaven's grace spare
That trial at least.
SOSTRATA: You'll soon discover, my dear,
That I've been blamed most unfairly.
LACHES: You? No fear!
What fit words can be found for what you've done,
Made our name mud, sown sorrow for your son,
Soured good relations, raised questionings from a quarter
Quite happy, well pleased to trust our son with their daughter,
But you, as usual, can't leave well alone!
SOSTRATA: Me, Laches?
LACHES: Yes, you, you! You think I'm stone
Not flesh and blood. Because I'm stuck down there
On the farm, you seem to suppose I'm unaware
What you're all up to. But I'm more in touch
With *this* than *that* end, though I'm there so much.
I'd heard our daughter-in-law didn't like you. That,
Indeed, is little to be wondered at.
If she *had* liked you, that'd be the wonder,
But that this cloud was one we all came under
I couldn't believe. If I'd known that before,
I'd have shown that girl her duty—and *you* the door.
But seriously, Sostrata, do you find it fair
To load my shoulders with this double share?
For your sake and the lad's I started living
Down on the farm, with the idea of giving
My whole time to our property, that my wife
And son might be supported in a life
Of leisure, not to say luxury. In season
And out I've slaved away, beyond all reason
And all regard for my own years. You might
At least have seen that things up here went right
And spared me from further trouble.
SOSTRATA: But this affair
Is not my doing, it's not my fault, I swear.
LACHES: Of course it is. The whole blame falls on you.
Left here alone the least that you could do
Was give some care to things here, since I'd freed you
From all cares else. Why now, at *your* age, need you
Pick quarrels with a girl? Aren't you ashamed?
Or will you blame her?
SOSTRATA: Her I never blamed.

LACHES: I'm glad to hear that—glad for our son's sake,
Finding more faults in *you* could scarcely make
Much difference to the score now.

SOSTRATA: I wonder whether
She feigned dislike of me to be together
With her own mother more?

LACHES: Not likely, is it,
Seeing that yesterday, when you paid a visit
You found yourself fobbed off with 'no admission'?

SOSTRATA: That was explained by a slight indisposition.

LACHES: She's sick all right—of you. And that's not so odd!
You all want your sons wed. And then, by God,
The wished-for match is made, and, having forced them
To marry, you can't wait till you've divorced them!
(Phidippus comes out of his house, talking back to his daughter inside)

PHIDIPPUS: Although I know by rights I could compel you,
Philumena, to do whatever I tell you,
Yet, as a naturally affectionate father,
My feelings, mistaken maybe, have led me rather
To yield this once and give way to your whim.

LACHES: Ah, there's Phidippus. Good! I'll get from *him*
What's going on here. Phidippus, though I know
I'm soft enough with my family, I don't go
So far child-spoiling that it spells child-ruin.
If you took a leaf out of *my* book, you'd be doing
More service to both sides. But you, it's clear, sir,
Are governed by your women-folks' whims—

PHIDIPPUS: Look here, sir—

LACHES: I came to see you yesterday concerning
Your daughter, only to find myself returning
No wiser. If you want a lasting link
Between us, then the right thing, if you think
We've wronged you, is to tell us how. We'll prove
Our innocence, or apologize, and remove
The grievance either way. You shall be judge.
But don't go harbouring some hidden grudge.
If it's because of illness that you've kept
The girl with you, I really can't accept
That you have grounds for any apprehension
That in our house she might have less attention.
You *are* her father, but I can't admit
That your anxiety to see her fit

Is greater than mine—for my son's sake. His wife
Means more to that young man than—yes, than life.
And I just hate to think how he'll react
If he finds what's happening here, and that's a fact.
And that's the reason why I'm most concerned
To have her back by the time my son's returned.

PHIDIPPUS: Laches, your kindness and concern I know,
And I'm convinced that what you say is so.
But please believe me—could I but contrive
The girl's return, I'd welcome it.

LACHES: Man alive!
What hinders you 'contriving' it? Eh? What?
Does she blame *him*?

PHIDIPPUS: Oh, definitely not.
Why, when I made the matter my concern
And tried, in fact, to force her to return,
She begged and prayed, protested she couldn't bear
Being left in your house with your—with your son not there.
We all have faults. I may be over-mild
But I *can't* rule with rod of iron wife or child.

LACHES: Well, Sostrata, you see the situation.

SOSTRATA: Oh, dear!
That's definite, is it?

PHIDIPPUS: So it would appear
For now. Is there anything else that I can do?
I've business in the town.

LACHES: I'm coming too. *(Exeunt)*

SOSTRATA: Oh, it's not fair! Equality of status
We women have—all husbands equally hate us,
Because of a few, who make us all appear
So ill-deserving. On these charges here
I have, as truly as I hope for grace,
An easy conscience —but no easy case.
They're so convinced that every mother-in-law's
A tyrant. Well, in my case they've no cause.
I've treated her like my own child, and how,
God help me, this has happened to me now
I've no idea. I only know I yearn
With all my heart for my dear boy's return.
(She goes back into the house)

ACT III

(Enter, after a short pause, Pamphilus and Parmeno from the harbour)

PAMPHILUS: Who, Parmeno, ever found the path of love
Strewn thicker with thorns? Was this, this—God above!—
This life that on board ship I dreaded losing,
Burned to get back to? *Now* I'd sooner chance choosing
Any hole on earth than rush home—home!—to hear
Your nice hot news. Oh, my conclusion's clear—
If one *must* meet half-troubles halfway, like this,
Each moment's ignorance of the whole's half-bliss.

PARMENO: Oh, no, sir. *Now* you'll sooner solve this trouble.
If you'd not come, the odds they're at would double.
Now they'll be cowed and calmed by your appearance,
You'll find the facts of the case, have a grand clearance
Of the air, a reconciliation scene, and all
The worries you've thought big will prove *so* small.

PAMPHILUS: Oh, keep your comfort! Who on God's earth carried
A bigger load of cares? Till I got married
My love lay elsewhere. But I daredn't refuse
The wife my father had seen fit to choose.
My sufferings then no man needs words to see.
And hardly have I wrenched my feelings free,
Torn one attachment, turned towards the other,
Than fresh pain comes to part us. For my mother
I now must find at fault, or else my wife.
And then what's left? A wrecked and wretched life!
My mother, however unjustified her attitude,
I'm bound in duty to bear with. But my gratitude
To my poor wife is also very strong,
So patiently putting up with all the wrong
I did her at first, and never saying a word.
It must be something big that has occurred
Between them, to blow up into a squall
That's lasted all this time.

PARMENO: Or something small,
You'll find, on putting facts in their true compass,
The biggest wrongs don't cause the biggest rumpus.
Issues that elsewhere wouldn't raise a flicker
Make bitter enmities where the temperature's quicker.
Take children now—what silly things they seize on
To row about, being so little ruled by reason!

And women are the same, all boil and bubble.
A trifle could have triggered off this trouble.
PAMPHILUS: Well, Parmeno, get inside, give them the word—
I've come.
(Cries are heard from Phidippus' house)
PARMENO: What's that?
PAMPHILUS: Shut up! I'd swear I heard
A hustling, bustling female to-ing and fro-ing.
PARMENO: Nearer their door we'd stand more chance of knowing—
Did you hear that?
PAMPHILUS: Stop chattering . . . God! That shriek!
PARMENO: Who's squawking now? I wasn't allowed one squeak!
MYRRINA: *(inside)*
Hush, hush, my child!
PAMPHILUS: That sounded like her mother.
My God!
PARMENO: What's up?
PAMPHILUS: Hell!
PARMENO: Eh?
PAMPHILUS: There's something or other
Really wrong being hidden!
PARMENO: Some sort of shivering fit
Was mentioned—I don't know. This might be it.
PAMPHILUS: Why didn't you say, you fool? This is slow death!
PARMENO: I couldn't say everything in a single breath.
PAMPHILUS: What ails her?
PARMENO: I don't know.
PAMPHILUS: Did no one go
To fetch a doctor for her?
PARMENO: I don't know.
PAMPHILUS: What am I waiting for? Inside! Let's see
The worst at once, whatever it may be!
How will I find you? One thing's sure, dear wife,
If you're in danger, then—I've done with life!
(He rushes into Phidippus' house)
PARMENO: *(phlegmatically)*
No use going after him. They hate us all.
When our old lady yesterday paid a call,
They shut her out. And if the sickness did—
Which heaven, for my master's sake, forbid—
Get worse, a slave of Sostrata's, they'll affirm,
Was here, and brought some fearful, fateful germ
Into their house—which means more blame will duly

Fall on my mistress, more hard blows on yours truly.
(Sostrata comes out of the house, not seeing Parmeno)

SOSTRATA: I've heard such noises from next door. Oh, dear,
My daughter-in-law must have got worse, I fear.
O powers of healing, grant I'm wrong! I'll go there
And see her.

PARMENO: Sostrata!

SOSTRATA: Who on earth . . . ?

PARMENO: Whoa there!
They'll shut you out again.

SOSTRATA: Oh, Parmeno, is it?
Why, goodness me, what *shall* I do? Not visit
My son's wife when she's ill so near me?

PARMENO: No.
Not even send, and certainly not go.
Love them that hate you, and your duncedom's double—
You take vain pains to give unwanted trouble.
Besides, your son himself went in to learn
Exactly how she was on his return.

SOSTRATA: Is my son back?

PARMENO: He is.

SOSTRATA: Oh, Heaven be praised!
Just hearing *that* I feel my spirits raised,
My troubles half blown away.

PARMENO: And that's the reason
I say a visit would be out of season.
As soon as the young lady's pains abate,
She'll tell him the whole business, tête-à-tête,
What came between you, how the quarrel started.
(Pamphilus, looking stunned, comes out of Phidippus' house)
But talk of angels! . . . Oh! Aren't we down-hearted?
Look at that face!

SOSTRATA: Oh, Pamphilus, dear boy!

PAMPHILUS: *(distractedly)*
Oh, mother—I hope you're well.

SOSTRATA: Oh, what a joy
To see you safe! But how's Philumena keeping?

PAMPHILUS: Better—a bit.

SOSTRATA: Let's hope so. But—you're weeping.
You look quite wretched. Why?

PAMPHILUS: No, I'm okay.

SOSTRATA: Then what was the commotion? . . . Won't you say?
A sudden attack, or what?

PAMPHILUS: Yes, yes, that's it.
  SOSTRATA: What's the trouble?
PAMPHILUS: Fever.
  SOSTRATA: What, a daily fit?
PAMPHILUS: Yes, so they say. Now, mother, in you go.
           I'll follow.
  SOSTRATA: Very well. *(She goes into her own house)*
PAMPHILUS: You, Parmeno,
           Go meet the boys, help them with what they're carrying.
  PARMENO: They know the way.
PAMPHILUS: Get on with it! Talking, tarrying—!
(Parmeno goes off hastily towards the harbour)
           The state I'm in I don't know where to start
           Describing this bolt from the blue that's struck me. Part
           I saw with my own eyes, part grasped by ear,
           And, half-dead, rushed outside. When, full of fear,
           A moment ago, I dashed in, I expected
           Quite different trouble from what I soon detected.
           When all her servants saw me, at first sight
           They cried 'He's come!'—a chorus of delight,
           And then their faces changed. They sighed that fate
           Should send me home on this ill-chosen date.
           One of them ran to say that I was there.
           On fire to see my wife I followed her,
           And once inside—oh, God, I saw her ailment!
           I'd been too quick. They'd no time for concealment,
           And she herself was in no state for speech
           Beyond such cries as her cruel pains might teach.
           In shock I called her 'shameless', burst into tears, then, crushed,
           By cruel, incredible fact, out, out I rushed.
           Her mother followed. I was half outside.
           She fell down at my feet, poor soul, and cried.
           I pitied her plight. But I suppose we all,
           As fortune calls the tune, sing big or small.
           And then she started to appeal to me.
           'Dear boy, dear Pamphilus,' she said, 'you see
           What made Philumena leave. It's not her fault.
           She was the victim of a vile, vicious assault,
           And the only help she could hope for was her mother's,
           In hiding the birth, when it came, from you and others.'
           I can't help weeping, when I call to mind
           The way she begged me. 'By whatever kind
           Of good angel it was that brought you home today,

Dear Pamphilus,' she said, 'we both of us pray,
As long as laws of God and man allow,
Keep her misfortune dark. She begs you now,
If ever you felt her kindness, not to grudge
This favour in return. But you must judge
About having her back, and let your own good guide you.
Nobody knows she's having a child besides you,
Or that it's not yours. That it was conceived
Just two months later is what'll be believed.
It's seven months since she and you got wed—
I needn't tell you that. But, oh,' she said,
'If it's possible, Pamphilus—I hope it may be—
I want to try and see she has the baby
Without her father or anyone finding out.
But if it simply can't be done without
Their knowing, I'll say the poor girl had a miscarriage.
The child *could* be the offspring of your marriage,
And who will ever suspect that isn't true?
We'll have it put out at once. No harm for you
Can come of that, and you'll have helped to hide
The shameful wrong done to your poor young bride.'
I gave my word then, and I'm sticking to it.
But having her back's not right, I just can't do it,
In spite of my affection and the link
Time's forged between us. Tears come when I think
What sort of life, what loneliness each of us faces—
One never stays long, it seems, in Luck's good graces.
But I've been schooled. I made myself dismiss love
By strength of will before. So now with *this* love
I'll try to do the same, as best I can.
Oh! Parmeno with the boys! The very man
I most could do without. What I didn't confide
To anyone else I told *him*—how my bride
Had never been touched by me when I left here,
Should he hear all this commotion, I very much fear
He'll guess about the birth. He must be sent
Out of harm's way till after the event.
(Parmeno enters with Sosia and the other slaves carrying baggage)

PARMENO: You say this wasn't exactly a pleasure-trip?
SOSIA: Pleasure! The hell of being on board a ship
Simply defies description, Parmeno.
PARMENO: You don't say!

SOSIA: Yes, I do. You little know
How lucky you are and what you've managed to miss
By staying on terra firma. Just take this—
Leaving aside the other types of torment—
That month or more I was on board each moment
I thought would be my last. Yes, that's how rough
We had it, right from start to finish.

PARMENO: Tough.

SOSIA: You're telling *me*. I'd run away, I swear,
If I thought coming back here meant going back there.

PARMENO: And you're the man to do just what you say.
You've run away from nothing before now . . . Hey!
What's Pamphilus up to? Standing like a sentry?
Go on in. What new little chore will delay *my* entry,
I wonder?
(Sosia and slaves go into house)
      Hallo! Still standing at the door, sir?

PAMPHILUS: Yes. I've been waiting for you.

PARMENO: For me? What for, sir?

PAMPHILUS: I've this trip to the Citadel—

PARMENO: *(sitting down)*   See you later, then.

PAMPHILUS: It's for *you.*

PARMENO: For me? To the Citadel? With what end in view?

PAMPHILUS: Callidemides—yes, that's the name. He's a friend
From Myconos. We met on the boat. He's the end,
As you put it, in view.

PARMENO: *(aside)*   He'll be *mine*. They've vowed, I see,
A sacrifice for safe landing—little me.
I'm to be run dead.

PAMPHILUS: What's keeping you?

PARMENO: What do I say?
Just 'Hi, there, Calli!'?

PAMPHILUS: Fool! I'd a date today
Up there with—What's-his-name—I nearly forgot—
Say I can't make it and not to wait. Now what?
Why are *you* waiting?

PARMENO: I'm quite unacquainted
With his appearance.

PAMPHILUS: You shall have it painted.
Big, burly, curly, ruddy, eyes grey-blue,
A little stiff, cold.

PARMENO: Dead-like? What do I do
If the corpse doesn't come? Sit there till set of sun?

PAMPHILUS: Yes, sit, sit. Not now! Run!

PARMENO: Me, with *my* wind, run!
(But he goes, after a threatening gesture from Pamphilus)

PAMPHILUS: Shut of *him*. What shall I do, though? This defeats me.
How *can* I, as my mother-in-law entreats me,
Keep dark her daughter's having had a baby?
I'm sorry for them. I'll help as far as may be.
I do love her. But family must come first.
Falsehood to family, of all sins, is the worst.
But there's my father, heading right this way,
And with Phidippus! God, what shall I say?
(Enter Laches and Phidippus)

LACHES: You said she said she's waiting for *him*?

PHIDIPPUS: That's so.

LACHES: Well, now, they say he's come. So let her go.

PAMPHILUS: *(aside)*
What reason can I give if I refuse?

LACHES: I heard a voice just then, I don't know whose.

PAMPHILUS: *(aside)*
My mind's made up. I *must* stick to my plan.
And make that clear to *them*.

LACHES: *(seeing him)*   Why, there's our man.

PAMPHILUS: How are you, father?

LACHES: Well, how's life, my lad?

PHIDIPPUS: Ah, Pamphilus! Believe me, I *am* glad
You're back and in good health—eh? That's what counts.

PAMPHILUS: Sure, sure.

LACHES: *(warily)*   Just come?

PAMPHILUS: Just.

LACHES: Well, what sort of amount's
Our cousin Phania left, my boy?

PAMPHILUS: Well, father,
Alive he was a good-time character rather,
And that sort doesn't do his heirs much good.
They leave—a name for living while they could.

LACHES: That bright thought's all you've brought?

PAMPHILUS: We can be glad
Of what he did leave.

LACHES: *(solemnly)*   No, no, Pamphilus— sad.
I wish he were alive and well as ever.

PAMPHILUS: *(aside)*
No harm in wishing. Dead men rise up never.
I know what news of our cousin he'd rather hear.

LACHES: Last night your wife was sent for by her father here.
(aside)
Hey! Say you sent.

PHIDIPPUS: *(aside)*   Don't nudge! *(aloud)* I sent—

LACHES: But now
She'll come back.

PHIDIPPUS: Quite.

PAMPHILUS: *(grimly)*   I know about the row.
I was told it all as soon as I had landed!

LACHES: Blast
Their spiteful tongues that spill black beans so fast!

PAMPHILUS: Phidippus, I've taken care to give no cause
For any deserved affront from my in-laws.
How loyal I've been to your daughter—caring and kind, too—
I could quite honestly say, if I'd a mind to.
But I'd much rather it was she that said it,
Since then you'll give my character more credit
If she does justice to it, despite these quarrels.
This rift's no question of *my* manners or morals.
She can't adapt with any ease or grace
To my mother's little ways. She can't help it. It's a case
Of mutual incompatability with each other.
They can't be reconciled. So wife or mother
I must be parted from. My mother's claim
Comes first. *Her* ease of mind must be my aim.

LACHES: I'm pleased to hear a parent's ease being reckoned
So prime a factor and all else put second.
But aren't you maybe letting angry feelings
Make you too harsh and hasty in your dealings
With your young wife?

PAMPHILUS: What angry feelings ever
Could make me harsh to that poor girl, who never
Did anything to displease *me*—looking always rather
For little ways to please? What I feel for her, father,
Is love, respect, deep sorrow at being parted.
She was so true to me, so tender-hearted!
And I sincerely wish her, as the wife
Of some more fortunate man, a happy life,
Since harsh necessity parts us perforce.

PHIDIPPUS: That's surely in your power to prevent.

LACHES: Of course,
With common sense. Just tell her to return.

PAMPHILUS: No, dad. My mind's made up. My main concern

Must be my mother's comfort from now on.
(He rushes off)
LACHES: Here! Where are you off to? Stop, I say! Where—Gone!
PHIDIPPUS: What kind of stupid stubbornness is this?
LACHES: Didn't I say he might take this amiss?
That's why I begged you so to send her back.
PHIDIPPUS: I never imagined him showing such a lack
Of sense for ordinary civilized behaviour.
Does he suppose I'll beg him as a favour
To take her back? If he finds on due reflection,
He wants her back, *we* shall raise no objection,
But if that doesn't commend itself to your son,
Let him pay back the dowry and be done.
LACHES: Now don't let anger make *you* hasty and foolish.
PHIDIPPUS: Fine manners he's brought home with him—sullen, mulish!
LACHES: My son won't harbour a grudge—however merited.
PHIDIPPUS: It's gone to your heads, the half-drachma you've inherited!
LACHES: Don't start on *me* now!
PHIDIPPUS: Let that young man weigh
The matter well and send me word today
One way or the other. I should like to make her
Somebody's wife at least, if *he* won't take her!
(Phidippus goes into his house)
LACHES: Phidippus, wait! One word! He's gone. So what?
Those two can just sort out this little lot,
However they like, between them. They couldn't care less
What *I* say. I'm ignored. Well, this ripe mess
My wife shall share—upon whose head, since from it
The whole thing sprang, my gall, by God, I'll vomit!
(Exit into his house)

ACT IV

(Myrrina comes out of house)
MYRRINA: What's to be done? Where can I turn? How, how
Explain to my husband? It's all over now.
The baby's cries I'm sure he must have heard—
He rushed so suddenly, and without a word,
To see her. If he does discover the birth,
God help me, I don't know what grounds on earth
To give for keeping it dark. There goes the door,
He's coming out after me, and I know what for!

(Phidippus enters from house)

PHIDIPPUS: When Myrrina saw me going to see our daughter,
She slipped outside. Ah, there we are! I've caught her!
Well, Myrrina? . . . Myrrina! I'm talking to you!

MYRRINA: To me, dear husband?

PHIDIPPUS: You acknowledge, do you,
That I'm your husband? By the way you act
I think you think I'm something else in fact:
A fool, a guy, a gormless gaga gaby!

MYRRINA: Act? How?

PHIDIPPUS: You ask? Our daughter's had a baby!
Well, dumb? Whose is it?

MYRRINA: *(with all the force of conscious guilt)*
                    Whose do you think it is, then, rather
Than her own husband's? Fine question for a father!

PHIDIPPUS: *(after a slight pause)*
I take your word. What father could do other
Than trust his child? But then—what makes her mother
So secretive? A fine boy, no miscarriage,
Legitimate, born just seven months after their marriage . . .
Are you so Pamphilophobe, so bigoted, that you think,
Since that child's bound to strengthen the marriage link
I'd striven to make, you'd sooner see him dead
Than have your daughter, despite your whims, stay wed?
I thought the fault theirs, and now find it's you.

MYRRINA: Oh, I'm so wretched!

PHIDIPPUS: Bah! I wish I knew
You were 'so wretched'! I remember now,
When first we men had settled this marriage, how—
Yes—how you raised your wretched objections. You said
One moral point worried you. No man she wed
Should keep his kept wench and stay out all night.

MYRRINA: *(aside)*
God, guide his guess, please, any road but the right!

PHIDIPPUS: I'd known about that kept wench quite some time,
But didn't reckon it, at that age, a crime,
It's natural, normal—though the time approaches,
I'm sure, when he'll be full of self-reproaches
For that infatuation. *You're* unchanging,
Unbendingly bent, now, as before, on estranging
A young man *made* for her, merely to make my aim miss.
Now, now, at last I see what your little game is.

MYRRINA: Am I so wicked as to feel that way
Towards our own child, if our interest lay

In this alliance then?

PHIDIPPUS: Are you so wise
To judge or to conjecture where it lies,
Or where it will lie? You had heard, no doubt,
That he was seen going in or coming out
From Bacchis. So what? If he's been doing it rarely
And with restraint, shan't we be doing more fairly
By him to ignore it, not be keen to uncover
Wrong that might rouse resentment? If a lover
Like him were to break every bond
At once with a woman of whom he'd been so fond
Over the years, I'd doubt if I was dealing
With a future son-in-law of true deep feeling.

MYRRINA: Forget his good character and my bad! Just go,
Talk to him man to man, ask whether or no
He wants her. Then, either you yourself can escort her
Home happy, or—I'll have done what was best for our daughter.

PHIDIPPUS: If he does say no, if your insight *was* so clear
Into his shocking shortcomings, well, wasn't I here,
On the spot, with a father's wise and watchful care?
Oh, this does make me mad, the way you dare
To ignore my very existence! You didn't, did you,
Mean to remove that infant? I forbid you—
The more fool I, expecting her to obey me.
I'll go and tell the slaves to see that baby
Is not put out of the house. *(He goes indoors)*

MYRRINA: Oh, I'll be sworn
No woman more miserable was ever born.
For how he'll take it, if he does find out
The true facts of the case, there's little doubt,
When this, that's so much less, upset him so.
And how to change his mind —I just don't know.
It only needed this to fill my cup,
His forcing us to take the infant up
Begot by God knows whom—for in the dark
She couldn't see her assailant. She's no mark
Or token of identity—not a thing.
It was the other way around. He took a ring
By force from off her finger when he went.
And Pamphilus, I fear, will never consent
To shield us then, on seeing how it is,
Another man's child being taken and reared as his.
*(She follows her husband just as Sostrata and Pamphilus come
out of the other house)*

SOSTRATA: It's no use hiding it, my boy, I know
You think she left because of me, although
I swear, by all my hopes of heaven, and you,
I never did a thing, as far as I knew,
To make her hate me so. Your love, my dear,
I never doubted, and you've made it clear
Once more by this decision, that your father
Was telling me about, to honour rather
My claim than young love's; a fine selfless attitude,
Which I'm resolved to match with proper gratitude.
You'll see I give a dutiful son his due.
My mind's made up. It's best for both of you
And my own good name. I'm going down to the farm
To join your father and undo what harm
My being here may have done. There's nothing then
To stop Philumena's coming home again.

PAMPHILUS: What an idea! Give in to *her* whims, go
And bury yourself down in the country? No!
I won't allow it. I'm not giving a handle
To anyone who wants a bit of scandal
About our family to misconstrue this
And say it wasn't your kindness made you do this
But my impossible conduct. I refuse
To let you just for my sake, mother, lose
Friends, neighbours, happy town-life, fairs, feasts, holidays—

SOSTRATA: I don't enjoy those now. I've had my jolly days
At the right time. But I've left all that behind me.
My one wish now's that nobody should find me
Too long-lived, waiting for my hour to strike.
And here, where I appear to arouse dislike,
Though undeserved, it's time I quit, so best
Putting for all concerned all strife at rest,
Clearing myself from this unfair suspicion,
Obliging your in-laws. My one petition
Is that you'll help *me* to escape being named for
The sort of thing so many women are blamed for.

PAMPHILUS: How happy, with a wife and mother like these,
I *could* be, but for one thing!

SOSTRATA: Well, Pamphilus, please
Try and accept that one fly in your ointment.
If you've no other cause of disappointment,
As I have every reason to believe,
Do me, dear boy, this favour—please receive

Your wife back.

PAMPHILUS: Oh, God help my wretchedness!

SOSTRATA: And mine! God knows my misery is no less!
(Laches, who has followed them out, comes forward)

LACHES: I've happily overheard your conversation.
Wise men adapt to a given situation.
This step, that later on he might be forced to,
Our son will now with good grace have recourse to.

SOSTRATA: God grant it.

LACHES: Come. It's us for the country, mother,
Where you and I'll—put up with one another.

SOSTRATA: I hope so.

LACHES: Well, go in, and pack what you need, dear,
And let's waste no more words. What?

SOSTRATA: Yes, indeed dear. *(Exit)*

PAMPHILUS: Father!

LACHES: Well, son?

PAMPHILUS: Look, father, this suggestion
Of mother's going away—it's out of the question!

LACHES: Why?

PAMPHILUS: Well, I'm still unsure about my wife,
What best to do with *her.*

LACHES: Upon my life!
Do with her? There aren't any doubts on that point, are there?
We take the poor girl back.

PAMPHILUS: I'd like to, father.
I find it hard to refuse. But, having judged
What's best, I'm standing firm. I won't be budged.
In any case I don't think it will make her
More friendly with my mother if I take her.

LACHES: You can't tell, and, good Lord, why worry whether
It makes them friendlier when they're not together?
Your mother's going. The young are bored by the old.
It's time to make room. We're a tale that's told.
Darby and Joan. Which door creaked? Fancy that!
Enter Phidippus from front-door left, just pat!
Let's greet him.
(Enter Phidippus, talking to Myrrina and Philumena inside)

PHIDIPPUS: Really, I resent this very strongly.
You, too, Philumena, acted very wrongly,
Though, as your mother made you, you'd some reason.
She'd none.

LACHES: Phidippus! You're a sight in season!

PHIDIPPUS: I'd like to know why.

PAMPHILUS: *(aside)*   I'd like some suggestions
How to hide births and parry parental questions!

LACHES: Your daughter can return. She's nothing to fear.
My wife's off to the farm, well away from here.

PHIDIPPUS: Ah, but your wife has never been to blame.
It was from mine that all the trouble came!

PAMPHILUS: *(aside)*
All change!

PHIDIPPUS: It's she that got us in this jam.

PAMPHILUS: *(aside)*
What they get into I don't give a damn,
As long as I can get out of agreeing
To take her back again.

PHIDIPPUS: Well, Pamphilus, seeing
We've got tied up together, that's the way
I for my part would much prefer to stay,
If it's still possible. You feel different maybe.
If that's the case you'll have to take the baby.

PAMPHILUS: *(aside)*
The brat's out of the bag! Hell!

LACHES: What baby?

PHIDIPPUS: Why,
We've got a grandson, Laches, you and I!
My daughter, when she left you, was expecting it
Without my ever till this day detecting it!

LACHES: My goodness, that's good news, eh what? A boy!
The mother doing well, too? This *is* a joy!
But say—what sort of woman is your wife,
Not telling us all this time? Upon my life,
My view of *that* I really can't express!

PHIDIPPUS: My anger at it, Laches, is no less.

PAMPHILUS: *(aside)*
If I had doubts before, now I have none,
Since she brings someone else's child.

LACHES: Well, son,
This ends your argument.

PAMPHILUS: *(aside)*   Oh, this ends *me*!

LACHES: We've often prayed for this moment. Prayed to see
Our son made a proper, proud, fond father. Well,
It's here, thank heaven, at last!

PAMPHILUS: *(aside)*   But where in hell
Am I?

LACHES: So take her back . . . Come. Don't defy me.
PAMPHILUS: If she had wanted to have children by me,
          Or be my wife still, tell me why she hid
          This infant's birth, as you've just heard she did.
          I know her heart's not mine. I doubt if we
          Are ever likely really to agree.
          Why should I have her back?
LACHES: She acted under
          Her mother's influence, and that's small wonder.
          She's young. Do *you* think you can find us, then,
          A woman without fault—or perfect men
          For that matter?
PHIDIPPUS: Well, I'll leave you two together
          To sort this matter out and settle whether
          She's to be kept with us or sent to you.
          I'll accept either. For what my wife may do
          Or say, I'll not go bail. What about the baby?
LACHES: That's a daft question! Be all else as it may be,
          The child goes to his father, Pamphilus here,
          To be brought up as ours. That's obvious.
PAMPHILUS: No fear!
          (aside)
          Bring up a brat abandoned by its father!
LACHES: What are you mumbling? Not rear him! Would you rather
          Expose him? I'll expose *you*, by God, and your game-playing!
          This is the moment of truth. I'll not shirk saying
          What I'd no wish to, in our neighbour's ears.
          I'm not fooled by your tantrums, tales, fake tears,
          Mysterical mummery. First of all you seize on
          Your mother as a motive—she's the reason
          Your wife won't stay. 'In that case', says your mother,
          'I'll go.' The reason's wrecked. You find another,
          Your child's birth being concealed. You don't think, do you,
          That I'm so dim and daft I can't see through you?
          How long I let your little affair continue,
          Hoping more easily in the end to win you
          To happy wedlock! How patiently I bore
          With your dear Bacchis—dear indeed, but more
          Our Bacchis than yours merely, by the score!—
          Till finally I was forced to plead, implore—
          'It's time you settled, son, high time,' I said,
          And those words seemed to work. At least you wed,
          Bowed to my will, your natural duty. Now,

Drifter, drab-driven, to *her* will you bow,
Backsliding, slithering into your bad old life.
Behaving abominably to that sweet young wife—

PAMPHILUS: Me?

LACHES: Treating her like dirt with trumped-up quarrels.
You want no wife. Wives chide and check our morals.
You want your wench—your wife could well perceive it.
What faults else in our family could make her leave it?

PHIDIPPUS: He's hit the nail on the head like a holy prophet,
Tracked truth down!

PAMPHILUS: *(aside)*   Truth! He couldn't be further off it!

LACHES: Take back your wife, or give us one good reason.

PAMPHILUS: I can't—not now.

LACHES: You mean later? Good. In due season.
Of course you'll take care and custody of the child on
Meantime—*he*'s done no harm.

PAMPHILUS: *(aside)*   Oh, this is misery piled on
By the minute, with no power in me to meet it!
He pins me down at every point. I'll beat it,
Go to ground. I'm hopeless here. There's no risk of my father
Rearing the child against my will, the rather
As there my mother-in-law'll support me. *(He rushes off)*

LACHES: Hi!
Just running away with no sort of reply?
D'you think he's out of his mind? I very much fear it.
Well, let him go. Bring that child over. We'll rear it.

PHIDIPPUS: Right. But no wonder my wife jibbed at this.
Women are sharp. They take these things amiss.
Here *was* the rub, but, even when she'd said it,
I couldn't, to his face—and didn't at first credit.
Now it's a clear case—allergy to wedlock.

LACHES: And what's your cure for this male mental deadlock?

PHIDIPPUS: Well, you *might* meet this Bacchis person. Once met,
She could be asked, tasked, served with—well, some threat,
Should she continue her contact with your son.

LACHES: Good thinking! I'll do it. Boy! Boy! Ah, there you are. Run
Over to Bacchis' house, just up the street.
Say I'd like to see her.
(To Phidippus)   One more trifle I must entreat.
It *is* a matter of vital support, though.

PHIDIPPUS: Sir,
Whole-hearted support of this marriage, without demur,
Has always been my attitude and is still,

If it proves viable, as I hope it will.
You'd welcome my presence at this meeting maybe?
LACHES: I *meant*—you might get us a wet-nurse for the baby.
(Exit Phidippus)

ACT V

(Bacchis enters, talking to two of her servants)

BACCHIS: It's not for nothing Laches wants to meet me,
And I know why, or all my instincts cheat me.
LACHES: *(aside)*
I'll have to watch my step. She might be ready
To see sense after all. So, temper, steady!
No overdoing and wanting to undo!
Let's tackle her. Well, Bacchis, how are *you*?
BACCHIS: Oh, Laches! How are you?
LACHES: Well, now, no doubt
You're pretty puzzled what it's all about,
My boy's being sent to fetch you?
BACCHIS: Yes, and scared,
A bit, being what I am—I mean, the word
Itself being apt to count in our disfavour.
My acts I'll answer for, my own behaviour.
LACHES: You needn't fear *me*, if you tell the truth.
I can't now claim the privilege of youth,
When our offences find an easier pardon,
And so my impulses I keep good guard on.
If you've been doing, I mean, or if you intend
To do the decent thing, who could defend
My offering insult, like a boorish lad,
To an unoffending female?
BACCHIS: Oh, I'm so glad
To hear you say that. Apology or excuse
After the insult isn't very much use.
Why did you send for me?
LACHES: You let my son
Visit you still.
BACCHIS: I—
LACHES: Wait, please, till I've done.
I winked at your little affair till he got wed.
Allow me—just one moment. I've not said
Quite all I wished. Well, *now* he's got a wife.

His present feelings for you won't last for life,
Nor will your looks. For your own sake, see reason
And find yourself a firmer friend in season.

BACCHIS: Who says I see him still?

LACHES: Who? His wife's mother.

BACCHIS: I do?

LACHES: Yes, you. For which cause and no other
She fetched her daughter home and sought to destroy
Without our knowing it, their new-born boy.

BACCHIS: By all the gods—and, if I knew what could,
With more conviction than all oaths, make good
My words with you, I'd give them all that backing,
Laches, to prove, once wed, I sent him packing.

LACHES: *(after a pause)*
That rings true. Good girl! I believe you. But—

BACCHIS: What is it?

LACHES: Well, could you pay those women in there a visit,
Give them the same sworn pledge, put them at ease
And clear yourself of this suspicion—please?

BACCHIS: All right. Not many in my way of life
Would go and face, in such a case, the wife.
But—I don't want unfair suspicion cast
On Pamphilus, with his family, the last
Who should suspect him, thinking him that sort
Of no-good, just because of some report
Without any truth in it. After all, I owe him
Enough to make me feel I ought to show him
What kindnesses I can.

LACHES: Well, *that* from you
Makes me feel friendly and obliging too.
His wife and mother-in-law were not alone
In what they thought. I shared their doubts, I own.
Now, since it seems I was mistaken in you,
Stay as I've found you, and you may continue
To find us friends in need. Or otherwise you—
Whoa! No harsh words! But this I will advise you
In your own interests, that you get to know
My ways and worth and weight as friend, not foe.
(Phidippus enters with the nurse)

PHIDIPPUS: *(to the nurse)*
You shall lack nothing, we'll find everything needful,
But, having fed yourself full—and drunk—see that you feed full
The child we've put in your charge. Now, don't forget, nurse.

LACHES: Ah, there's Philumena's father with the wet-nurse.
           Sir, Bacchis by all the gods all guilt denies.

PHIDIPPUS: Is that her?

LACHES: Yes.

PHIDIPPUS: Well, perjury's no surprise
           With *that* lot. One expects to find them appealing
           To gods and men. And gods don't show much feeling
           For truth. They don't trouble how that sort behaves.

BACCHIS: Try pulling truth out of *this* pair. Yes. They're slaves.
           With *them* you've a legal lie-detector—the rack,[2]
           My sole aim is to get that young girl back.
           I won't mind comments like 'Bacchis, is it true
           You did what no other in your trade would do?'

LACHES: Phidippus, facts have forced us to the admission
           That we'd held both our wives under false suspicion.
           Let's now try Bacchis. If she gives good proof
           That, since my son wed, she's held well aloof,
           Your wife'll drop charges. If *he*'s still sore at not knowing
           He was a father, that grievance must be growing
           Less every minute. He'll calm down in due course.
           We've no giant issue justifying divorce.

PHIDIPPUS: I hope you're right.

LACHES: She's here to be questioned by you,
           Prepared to give any proof that'll satisfy you.

PHIDIPPUS: Why address me? My views you've heard long since.
           It's the womenfolk you've got to try and convince.
           (He goes into his house with the nurse)

LACHES: Well, Bacchis, how about your promise?

BACCHIS: Oh!
           You want me to go in and—?

LACHES: Yes, please go.
           Convince them for us, set their minds at rest.

BACCHIS: I'll go, then, though I know how they'll detest
           The very sight of me. There's natural strife
           Between my sort and a separated wife.

LACHES: But they'll be friends on finding your intention.
           You'll clear your name and their misapprehension.

BACCHIS: Well, I don't like the prospect. All the same . . .
           Come on you two. She'll make me die of shame!
           (Exit with her maids into Phidippus' house)

---

2 In Athens evidence from slaves was deemed valid only if extracted by torture.

LACHES: Most satisfactory I would say this looks.
It costs her nothing. She gets in our good books
By one good turn. If her account's correct,
About her giving him up, she can expect
Honour and credit for it, and our gratitude
And friendship for her very sensible attitude.
(Exit into his own house. Parmeno enters indignantly, coming from the town)

PARMENO: Little my master rates my labour at!
For no sense was I sent, for no sense sat—
Dumb waiter in rock-seated Citadel,
For a myth from Myconos—or a corpse from hell!
I sat there, feeling daft and sore, all day,
Accosting all likely lads who came that way.
'Sir, sir, are you from Myconos?' 'I am not.'
'Sir, is your name Callidemides?' 'Calli-what?'
Try, try again. 'Sir, have you got a friend
Called Pamphilus here?' 'No.' Short and sharp. In the end
I gave the game up for sheer blushing shame.
There ain't no such a person—not with that name.
But—Bacchis leaving our in-laws? What reason
Had she to visit there?
(Bacchis comes out of Phidippus' house with her maids)

BACCHIS: God-sent in season!
Run, Parmeno, fetch Pamphilus!

PARMENO: Fetch Pamphilus? Why?

BACCHIS: Ask him from me to come at once. Fly, fly!

PARMENO: Come? To your house?

BACCHIS: No, his mother-in-law's.

PARMENO: What for?

BACCHIS: Mind your own. As the poet said, ask me no more.

PARMENO: And tell *him* no more either?

BACCHIS: Yes, one thing.
Say Myrrina has recognized the ring,
That gift, as being from her daughter.

PARMENO: Oh . . . I see.
Is that all?

BACCHIS: Yes, that's all. Take it from me
When he's told that, he'll be back here like a shot . . .
Is this an indefinite stay?

PARMENO: No, it is not.
I've stood no chance today of stopping or staying;
Tramping and trotting's what I've spent *my* day in.

(He goes off towards the town)

BACCHIS: What luck for Pamphilus my visit's proved!
What light I brought, what clouds of doubt removed!
Rescued a child that nearly lost its life
Between the lot of them, restored a wife
He'd given up for good—suspicions held
Of him by both the fathers I've dispelled.
From that one ring such happy findings flow!
One night-fall, it's still vivid, nine months ago,
Alone, the worse for liquor, pale, out of breath,
He rushed in with this ring. I, scared to death,
Cried, 'What's the panic? That ring—where did you get it?'
He acted deaf, his face, I'll never forget it.
Looked just not there. Alarmed, suspicious, I pressed
For explanation. Finally he confessed.
En route he'd met and assaulted some girl or other.
In the struggle he'd grabbed her ring, which his wife's mother
Myrrina, sees me wearing, as mine, just now
And recognizes it, and asks me how
I got it. I tell all, and all's made known—
His wife's that girl in the dark, the child's his own!
I'm glad he's had all this good luck through me,
Though others in my line may disagree,
Good husbands being bad business. But cash-keenness
Won't make me stoop to nastiness or meanness.
And Pamphilus I found, while fate permitted,
Nice, kind and generous. His marriage was, admitted,
A bit of a blow for me. But—well, I feel acquitted
Of having earned it, and to take some rough,
Where you've had lots of smooth, is fair enough.

(Pamphilus and Parmeno enter from the town)

PAMPHILUS: Now listen, Parmeno. Can you assure me
That this is firm fact? Take heed you don't just lure me
With false and short-lived hopes.

PARMENO: Heed taken. Proceed.

PAMPHILUS: You're sure?

PARMENO: Sure.

PAMPHILUS: I'm in heaven, if this indeed
Is really true.

PARMENO: It's true, you'll see.

PAMPHILUS: But wait now.
I'm so afraid that what you mean to state now
Is one thing, what you seem to state another.

PARMENO: Waiting.
PAMPHILUS: I *think* you said that my wife's mother
Said Bacchis had *her* ring.
PARMENO: That's right.
PAMPHILUS: The ring
I gave to Bacchis? And she told *you* to bring
This news to *me*? Right?
PARMENO: As I said.
PAMPHILUS: Hurray!
Lucky in love, that's me! You've made my day
Delivering that message—and me, Parmeno!
What am I going to to give you? Blest if I know
PARMENO: I do.
PAMPHILUS: What?
PARMENO: Nothing. Blest if I can see
What's marvellous in my message or in me.
PAMPHILUS: From death to life, from hell to heaven restored,
How could I let you go without reward?
Do I seem so ungrateful? Ah, but see!
Bacchis outside our house—waiting for *me*
I guess! Let's go.
BACCHIS: Why, Pamphilus! How's life?
PAMPHILUS: Saved, Bacchis dear, by you!
BACCHIS: Yes, with your wife
All's well. I'm glad.
PAMPHILUS: Well, *that* your actions prove.
But you've not changed. The way you talk, walk, move
To meet a chap—you're a charmer!
BACCHIS: How true, how true—
To yourself. The way you talk's unaltered too—
Most winning, wheedling wooer on this earth!
PAMPHILUS: Well, coming from you!
BACCHIS: Ah, but your wife was worth
Your whole heart. I'd not seen her, that I knew.
She's a nice good girl, a thoroughbred through and through.
Good luck!
PAMPHILUS: You mean that?
BACCHIS: Sure.
PAMPHILUS: Has my old man heard
Any part of this?
BACCHIS: Not a murmur.
PAMPHILUS: Then mum's the word.
This isn't made-up comedy, where the right end

            Is only reached by all parties being enlightened
            On every point. With us all know, who ought.
            Who needs no teaching shall remain untaught.

BACCHIS: You can be sure this secret will be kept.
            Myrrina told Phidippus she'd accept
            My oath as clearing you entirely.

PAMPHILUS: Splendid!
            So all, I hope, for all has happily ended.

PARMENO: Sir, is it possible for you to say
            Apropos of my apparent good deed for the day,
            What it was, what you're talking about?

PAMPHILUS: Ah, no can tell!

PARMENO: But I can guess, I think. 'From death, from hell
            Restored'—by me . . .

PAMPHILUS: It's no good. You don't know
            The service you have done me, Parmeno,
            The plight you plucked me from.

PARMENO: I know—and knew
            What I was at.

PAMPHILUS: *(ironically)*   Of course you did—and do.

PARMENO: Catch Parmeno failing to take all steps fitting!

PAMPHILUS: Take some inside, then.

PARMENO: Sure, sir. *(aside)* Yet unwitting
            I was today—and did more good than ever
            I did before today by being clever!

PRODUCER: Clap, please.

The Brothers

The Brothers

CHARACTERS

MICIO: an old man, adoptive father of Aeschinus
DEMEA: his brother, father of Aeschinus and Ctesipho
AESCHINUS: Demea's son, adopted by Micio
SANNIO: a pimp
SYRUS: a slave of Micio
CTESIPHO: Demea's son
SOSTRATA: a widow, mother of Pamphila
CANTHARA: her old nurse
GETA: her slave
HEGIO: her elderly relative
DROMO: a slave of Micio

PROLOGUE

Our poet, seeing Envy still waylay
His work, and enemies *tra*duce the play
We would *pro*duce, will call himself as witness,
And you as jurymen shall judge the fitness
Of his proceeding to be praised or blamed.
There is a comedy by Diphilus,[1] named
SYNAPOTHNESKONTES—*Joined in Death*—which Plautus
In his play, called COMMORIENTES, brought us.
In that Greek play boy gets girl at the start
From white-slave-peddling pimp, by force; this part
Plautus left out, but, word for word, our poet
Has put in his play, *The Brothers*. Now we shall show it
For the first time ever. First, then, get to know it,
And then consider if your verdict's 'Theft',
Or 'Salvage of a scene by laxness left'.
And as for envy's tale that famous men[2]

---

1 Distinguished poet of Greek New Comedy.
2 For possible candidates for this role, see Introduction.

Assist our poet, and often aid his pen,
What envy thinks a mighty condemnation
He thinks his highest praise, the approbation
Of men you all approve, as does the nation;
Men by whose aid in war, peace, work or play
Each without pride had profit in his day.
Now don't expect I'll tell the plot; for part
The words of these old men, with whom we start,
Will show, and part their acts. Now may your fairness
Fire this rare poet to write with much less rareness.

*Scene: a place in Athens where various roads meet. The neighbouring
houses of Micio and Sostrata are seen.*

ACT I

(It is early morning. Micio comes out of his house.)

MICIO: Storax! Hi, Storax!... Silence ... So that young sinner,
Aeschinus, isn't back from last night's dinner,
Nor any of the slave boys I sent out
To meet Young Master. The old crack's true, no doubt,
That if you're missing anywhere or late,
It's far, far better to have met the fate
A furious wife affirms and fancies rather
Than what is feared and fancied by fond father.
The wife, if you're stuck somewhere, will start thinking
'Wine, women, chased or chasing, deep-draught-drinking,'
But here I am, because that boy's out still,
A mass of nerves, imagining every ill
That he could possibly meet with, feverish chill,
Bad fall, involving maybe a broken limb ...
Why any man should indulge in this odd whim
Of having some object meaning more to him
Than himself, God knows. And this boy belongs to my brother,
Not me. From the womb we weren't much like one another.
I've led my easy, leisured, urban life,
And—luckily, sufferers say—I've had no wife.
His rustic existence could seem contrast carried
To extremes, so spartan and sparing. He, of course, married,
And had two sons; of whom this elder one
I adopted, yes, and as my own dear son
I've reared, regarded, loved him from a boy.
He's all I'm fond of, he's my one real joy.
To make it mutual's my firm endeavour.

Give and forgive, say I, don't feel for ever
Bound to stand on parental rights. In fact
Where others, unbeknown of fathers, act
According to the wilful wont of youth,
I've trained my boy to tell me the whole truth.
The rest of the world will certainly be had
By any child used to cheat and fool his dad.
Free reins, plus sense of shame, to me appear
The means to check a free-born child, not fear.
My brother differs, doesn't hold with *that*;
He's constantly coming and shouting, 'What *are* you at?
That lad of ours is on the road to ruin
With wine and women, and it's all your doing!
Why must you furnish him the means of payment
For this extravagance? Talk about soft raiment!
You're soft yourself!' He's hard, though, past what's right
And reasonable, I reckon. He just won't see the light.
He thinks the bonds of force more stout and stable
Than any alliance linked by friendship's cable.
What I think's this. My theory is, anyone made
To do what's right by force will be afraid
While he expects to be found out; but when
He thinks you'll not know, he's himself again.
But bonds of kindness make a boy sincere,
Anxious to pay you in *your* coin, and near
And far the same person still. Your ideal father
Trains children to do right by free choice rather
Than fear of others. That's what makes masters less
Than a parent. If you lack this art, confess
You can't manage children . . . Wait, though, is that him?
Talk of the devil! *And* he's looking grim
At something. I reckon, as usual, he'll raise hell.
(Demea enters, angry. Micio greets him cheerfully)
Ah, Demea! I'm glad to see you well.

DEMEA: It's well I see you. You're the man I've come for!

MICIO: Why, Demea, what *are* you looking so glum for?

DEMEA: You ask, when we've an Aeschinus for our son?

MICIO: *(aside)*
What did I tell you? *(aloud)* What's he done then?

MICIO: Done?

Ashamed of nothing and afraid of none,
Laughing at laws—oh I leave out all past time,
But what's he perpetrated now, this last time?

MICIO: What *has* he perpetrated?

DEMEA: *(with gestures)*

> Why, he's smashed in
> Somebody's door, that's what he's done, and dashed in
> And bashed them, man and master, nearly dead,
> To get some girl he's stuck on! Everyone said
> It was an outrage. How often, just now, coming,
> Have I been told of it! The whole town's humming.
> Ah, if he wants a pattern to compare,
> He's only got to look at his brother there,
> Down on the farm, giving his whole attention
> To business, sober, thrifty, never a mention
> Of acts like these—acts which I count your doing
> As much as Aeschinus'! You condone his ruin.

MICIO: *(calmly)*

> There's no worse bigotry beneath the sun
> Than thinking what you never did's not done.

DEMEA: The point of which being what?

MICIO:

> The point being this,
> That you, my dear man, judge these things amiss.
> Sure, it's no shame if lads go boozing, whoring—
> It's not, you know—or even bash a door in.
> *We* didn't, but our means would not allow.
> Necessity *then* will you make virtue *now*?
> That's most unfair. These deeds we should have done, too,
> If we'd had means, and you'd allow your son to,
> If you had sense, now, at the right time, rather
> Than wait to mourn his late, his too late father,
> Then sow his wild oats still, but out of season.

DEMEA: You and your sense—Good God!—will sap my reason!
> No shame for boys to act like this!!

MICIO:

> Now steady on!
> Don't stun me stiff with what you've harped already on
> A hundred times. Listen. You gave your son
> To me to be adopted. Well, it's done.
> He's mine now. And his faults are my affair.
> Whatever he may do, the biggest share
> Falls on my back. The bills for dinners, wine,
> And all that scent he stinks of, will be mine;
> For his kept wench—the cash will come from me,
> While it's not crippling. When it is, then she,
> No doubt, will shut him out. The smashed-in door
> Will be made good. The coat or shirt he tore
> Will be repaired. My means, thank God, allow;
> It's really been no trouble up to now.

So call a truce, please—or a referee.
I'll prove to him more faults in you than me.
DEMEA: Bah! Learn a father's job from one who knows it.
MICIO: By chance of birth—but I, with much thought, chose it.
DEMEA: Thought! You!
MICIO: Enough! I'm off.
DEMEA: The way I'm treated!
MICIO: The way I have to hear one song repeated!
DEMEA: I care—
MICIO: And I care too. But let us, brother,
Go shares in cares. Mind one, leave me the other.
To care for both's as bad as to reclaim
The boy you gave—
DEMEA: Oh, come!
MICIO: It seems the same
To me.
DEMEA: All right. Let him, if that's your line,
Spend, spoil, be spoiled—it's no affair of mine.
And if I say another word about it—
MICIO: You're off again.
DEMEA: I mean this, don't you doubt it.
When have I asked him back? It's hard, God knows,
He *is* my flesh and blood. If I oppose—
I'll say no more. You want my care all given
To one boy. Well, it is. And he, thank Heaven,
Is all I'd wish. That lad of yours some day
Will see—and worse against him I won't say. *(Exit)*
MICIO: He's got a point—not all the points, though. Still,
I am a bit put out. But I'd no will
To let him see I found his news disquieting.
You see, his disposition needs—well, dieting.
To bring his temper down, I contradict him,
Pouring cold water on his rage. My victim
Hardly shows patience proper to a man
Under *that* treatment. But, if I began
To feed his fever, reinforce his passion,
I'd soon be raving in the selfsame fashion.
However, I *do* feel *some* wrong's been done,
Some wrong to *me*, by my adopted son.
Of all kept women in Athens is there any one
He hasn't kept—and spent a pretty penny on?
Until at last, the other day, he said—
Sick of them all, no doubt—'I want to wed.'

'Thank God,' thought I, 'he's burned those fires of youth out.'
But here we go again! I must find the truth out,
Whatever it may be in this affair.
Maybe I'll catch him in the market-square. *(Exit)*

ACT II

*(Enter Aeschinus with his slave Parmeno and the music girl
whom he has taken from the slave-dealer and pander, Sannio.
Sannio pursues them, appealing to the populace at large)*

SANNIO: Help, citizens, for a hapless innocent, aid
    A poor wretch!

AESCHINUS: *(to girl)*   Stand just there. Don't be afraid.
    Why do you look around? You've got nothing to fear.
    He'll not lay hands on you as long as I'm here.

SANNIO: That wench, though all of you obstruct me, I—

AESCHINUS: *(to girl)*
    He's a beast, but, being once beaten , he's twice shy.

SANNIO: Now listen, Aeschinus, before you assert
    You didn't know the sort of man you hurt—
    I *am* a pimp—

AESCHINUS: You are.

SANNIO: Yes, but as fair
    And straight as any man was anywhere.
    And as for you're coming later with 'Do excuse me,'
    And saying you were sorry to misuse me,
    I'll not give *that* much. No, I'll take—I say,
    I'll take my case to court, and words won't pay
    For actions, your outrageous actions, there.
    I know your 'I'm so sorry. Oh, I'll swear
    To treat a man like you like that's a shame'—
    When I've been shamefully treated all the same.

AESCHINUS: Now, Parmeno, hurry up there, go ahead,
    And open the door for us.

SANNIO: So all I've said
    Just goes for nothing, does it?

AESCHINUS: *(to girl)*   In you go.

SANNIO: I won't put up with it.

AESCHINUS: Forward, Parmeno . . .
    Too far that way . . . Stand here, by him. That's fine.
    Now see you never take your eyes off mine,
    So, if I nod, at once your fist will fly
    Straight to his jaw.

SANNIO: I'd like to see him try.
            (He moves to seize the girl)
AESCHINUS: Look out, look out there! *(to Sannio)* Let the lady go.
            (Sannio does not. Aeschinus nods. Parmeno hits Sannio)
SANNIO: Ow! Hell! How dare you?
AESCHINUS: He'll repeat the blow
            If you're not careful.
            (Parmeno hits Sannio again)
SANNIO: Ow! Ow! Ow! My God!
AESCHINUS: Well, Parmeno, that time I didn't nod.
            A mistake on the right side though. Go on—in there.
            (Parmeno and the girl go into the house)
SANNIO: Are you the ruddy king here?
AESCHINUS: *(with hanging gesture)*   If I were
            You'd reach the heights for which your merits call.
SANNIO: What business have *you* with *me*?
AESCHINUS: Why none at all.
SANNIO: Do you even know me?
AESCHINUS: I don't want to, much.
SANNIO: And can you say you've ever seen me touch
            Anything of yours?
AESCHINUS: Well, if you did, you'd rue it.
SANNIO: And how have you a better right to do it?
            To take *my* girl, bought with *my* money? How?
AESCHINUS: You'll find it better not to make a row
            Outside the house. For, if you give more trouble,
            I'll have you marched inside there, at the double,
            And have the lash laid on till you're half-dead.
SANNIO: A free Athenian lashed!
AESCHINUS: That's what I said.
SANNIO: Oh, you young thug! And this is what they call
            The land of equal liberty for all!
AESCHINUS: *If* you've done running amuck and making a scene,
            Pimp, listen to me a minute.
SANNIO: What do you mean?
            You ran amuck with *me*.
AESCHINUS: Now chuck the chatter.
            Come back to the matter in hand.
SANNIO: Back where? What matter?
AESCHINUS: Well, would you like me, in your present state,
            To point out your best interest?
SANNIO: I can't wait.
            It had better be a fair deal, though.

AESCHINUS: That's new—
          A pimp who rules out unfair deals, eh?
SANNIO: True,
          I *am* a pimp, the bane of bawdy youth,
          A perjured pest. It's equally the truth
          That up to now I've never done you wrong.
AESCHINUS: Meaning, no doubt, that now it won't be long?
SANNIO: *(wearily)*
          Come back to the matter in hand.
AESCHINUS: That girl you got for—
          What? Twenty minae—which I hope you'll rot for.
          Well, I'm prepared to pay you—twenty.
SANNIO: Oh!
          And if I won't sell? Will you force me?
AESCHINUS: No.
SANNIO: I feared you might.
AESCHINUS: Oh, no . . . I claim she's free,
          And can't be sold.[3] Before the court that plea,
          Before yourself this choice I'll duly place,
          To get your cash down, or get up your case.
          So ponder that, pimp, till I get back. *(Goes into house)*
SANNIO: God!
          If men run mad with wrongs—well, is it odd?
          He's hauled me from my house, he's lammed and lashed me,
          He's grabbed my wench, defied my warnings, bashed me
          Five hundred blows or more—and now makes claim,
          For these misdeeds, to have her for the same
          As what I paid . . . Right, then. For services rendered
          Let's say the claim is good, and take what's tendered.
          I'm ready, eager, if he'd only pay.
          But—he'll have witnesses ready, when I say
          I'll take his price, to prove—that's my prediction—
          The fact of sale, the price will prove a fiction.
          'Soon . . . Come again tomorrow'—I could bear
          That, too, if he would pay, though it's unfair.
          But then, I tell myself, and it's the truth,
          My trade means taking raw deals from raw youth
          With never a murmur . . . But why bother weighing
          The pros and cons? There's no hope of his paying.

---

3 In both Athenian and Roman law, it was possible legally to assert the free status
   of a citizen wrongly enslaved.

(Syrus comes out of Micio's house, talking to Aeschinus inside as he does so)

SYRUS: Okay, I'll see him, and he'll take it—gladly,
You'll see—*and* own he's not been treated badly.
Why, Sannio, what's this they tell me? *You*
At odds with my young master?

SANNIO: Odds! That's true!
I never knew a more uneven bout
Since I was born. I took and he dished out
Until we both were tired.

SYRUS: You were to blame.

SANNIO: Me? What should *I* have done, in the devil's name?

SYRUS: Done? Let the young man have his head a bit.

SANNIO: I did my best. He had *my* head, to hit.

SYRUS: Do you know what *I* think? I think, sometimes profit
Thrives better through you taking one eye off it.
You've been too scared to waive one jot or tittle
Of your just rights, scared to oblige a little
And lose the odd per cent. Oh, you blind dope!

SANNIO: I don't pay hard cash down for pious hope.

SYRUS: You'll never make your fortune. You don't know
What's meat for baiting man-hooks, Sannio.

SANNIO: No doubt you're smarter. I was never yet
So cute as not to take what I could get.

SYRUS: Come on! I know your feelings. As if you cared
For twenty paltry minae, now, compared
With doing the lad a service . . . I heard tell
Moreover, that you're off to Cyprus.

SANNIO: *(aside)*   Hell!

SYRUS: And that you've bought a large consignment here
To take there, and the ship's hired. So it's clear
You're tied up rather, dangling on that rope.
But when you're back you'll settle with us, I hope.

SANNIO: I'll not budge. *(aside)* Damn! They banked on this from the start.

SYRUS: *(aside)*
Ah! Wind up! Sown the seeds of doubt.

SANNIO: *(aside)*   They're smart!
Bastards! By God, he's got me on the hip there.
I've bought some girls and other goods to ship there.
And if I miss the market, I lose a packet;
But, if I let this lie till I come back, it
Won't keep, the case'll be stone-cold. 'Come *now*?'
They'll say. 'Where were you? Why did you allow

The outrage *then*?' I'd sooner lose than wait
So long here now, or come to court so late.

SYRUS: Worked out yet what your net receipts should be?

SANNIO: Look, is this worthy of the lad? That he,
Your master, should have done this, I mean, taken
This girl from me by downright force!

SYRUS: *(aside)*   He's shaken!
(aloud)
I've a proposal. See if you'll admit it.
Sooner than stand to lose or keep all—split it.
He'll scrape *ten* minae up from somewhere.

SANNIO: Hell!
What *is* this? Is my outlay, then, as well
At stake? God help us! Has that promising youth
No conscience? Look! He's loosened every tooth
I've got and made my head one bulging bruise—
And now he'll cheat me? I'm staying.

SYRUS: As you choose.
If that's all I'll be off.

SANNIO: *(stopping him)*   No, Syrus, no.
However you treat me, I've no wish to go
To law about it. All I ask's my own,
Cost price, at least. I know, now, you've not known
My friendship up till now. But—well, you'll find
I'm grateful, Syrus, I bear things in mind.
(He slips him a bribe)

SYRUS: I'll try. But there comes Ctesipho, feeling great,
Now that we've grabbed the girl.

SANNIO: *(anxiously)*   You will, though?

SYRUS: Wait.
*(Ctesipho enters in high delight. He does not see Syrus and
Sannio at first)*

CTESIPHO: Good turns are always welcome. They delight one.
Doubly, however, when the doer's the right one.
Dear, dear old Aeschinus! I can't properly praise him.
I know my best superlatives can't raise him
To the right height. With such a brother to guide me
So good a teacher, who can stand beside me?

SYRUS: Well, sir?

CTESIPHO: Well, Syrus! Where's my brother, eh?

SYRUS: There, waiting for you in the house.

CTESIPHO: Hurray!

SYRUS: What's that for?

CTESIPHO: Why, he's saved my life, the beauty,
The wizard! Made my welfare his first duty!
The shame, the blame, for my girl, manfully battling,
He's shouldered. Can you beat it?
(A noise at the door makes him jump back)
                         What's that rattling
At our front door?

SYRUS: Wait, wait! He's coming out!

AESCHINUS: *(appearing)*
Where is he? Where's that lousy, low-down lout?

SANNIO: Aha! I'm wanted. I wonder if he's got—
No, damn it. As far as I can see, he's not.

AESCHINUS: Ah fine! The very man! Well, feeling more cheerful?
(to Ctesipho)
Come on! All's well. Stop looking so damned tearful!

CTESIPHO: I'll stop, I'll stop, having found that a brother in need,
Like you are, Aeschinus, is a brother indeed!
I'm shy of talking about your marvellous attitude
In front of you. *You* might think it's not real gratitude,
But a lot of blarney.

AESCHINUS: Oh, my silly kid-brother,
As if by now we didn't know each other!
I'm only sorry we found out so late,
When things had very nearly reached a state
Where, with the best will, no one could help you—

CTESIPHO: Shame
Had kept me dumb.

AESCHINUS: Yes, dumb's the word. You came,
For such a stupid reason, within inches
Of running off abroad! One honestly flinches
From mentioning such a thing, and God forbid
It should ever happen.

CTESIPHO: I *was* a silly kid.

AESCHINUS: Well, now, and what has Sannio to say?

SYRUS: He's mellowed.

AESCHINUS: Good! I'll go down town and pay.
Off with you, she's inside there, Ctesipho!
(Ctesipho goes into the house)

SANNIO: Hey, Syrus, press my claim!

SYRUS: Well, sir, let's go.
He's off to Cyprus. He's in a bit of a hurry. *(Exit Aeschinus)*

SANNIO: Less than you'd like. I'll stop. I've time.

SYRUS: *(to Sannio)*   Don't worry.

	He'll pay.
SANNIO:	The full amount?
SYRUS:	The total sum.
	Only shut up and come along.
SANNIO:	I'll come. *(Exit Sannio)*

(Ctesipho suddenly comes out of the house and calls Syrus back)

CTESIPHO:	Hey, Syrus!
SYRUS:	What?
CTESIPHO:	Look, for the love of mike,

Do settle at once with that vicious little tyke.
Don't goad him, or our craft'll spring a leak,
My dad'll hear and I'll be up the creek.

SYRUS: Oh, that'll never happen, don't you fret.
Go and have fun with your girl-friend—in you get!
And tell 'em to have the dinner-couches laid out,
And everything else got ready. When we've paid out,
I'll be back—with some provisions.

CTESIPHO: That's the way.
We've won! We'll make a day of it! Hurray!
(Syrus goes off to the town, Ctesipho disappears inside again. The stage is empty for a minute)

ACT III

(Sostrata comes out of her house, talking agitatedly to the nurse Canthara. Cries are heard within)

SOSTRATA: How will my daughter manage, nurse dear?

CANTHARA: How?
Why, well, I hope.

SOSTRATA: Poor child, what you feel *now*
Are just first pains!

CANTHARA: Lord, madam, what's amiss?
As if you'd never seen or been through this!

SOSTRATA: Oh dear, we're all alone. I haven't one friend.
Geta's not here. I've no one I can send
For the midwife, or for Aeschinus.

CANTHARA: My dear,
You can be sure that *he* will soon be here.
He always comes, he's never missed a day.
In our present trouble he's our one strength and stay.
All things considered, it couldn't have turned out better.

I mean, if she had to be wronged, at least heaven let her
Be wronged by the right young man. Oh, he's a beauty!
He's got such character, such sense of duty,
And such a good family.

SOSTRATA: Yes, he's all you say.
So Heaven preserve him for our sakes, I pray.
*(Geta rushes on in great excitement and indignation, not
seeing his mistress and the nurse at first)*

GETA: Should all mankind now put their heads together,
They'd find no shelter from this hurricane weather
That's hit us, no way out—in such deep water
We're sinking—myself, my mistress and her daughter.
God help us! We're shut in by every shape
Of bolts from the blue, a blank wall, no escape,
Force, poverty, wrong, desertion and disgrace.
What times! What crimes! Oh, what a rogue, a race
Of rogues, a monster!

SOSTRATA: Oh, now I'm really worried.
Why's Geta dashing about so flushed and flurried?

GETA: No loyalty held him back, no conscience pricked him,
No oaths he'd sworn, no pity for his victim,
And she so near her time!

SOSTRATA: I wish it were clearer
What the man's saying.

CANTHARA: Lord, madam, let's go nearer.

GETA: God help me, I'm scarcely sane, I'm so on fire
With rage. There's nothing I could more desire
Than to have that whole house here, where I might spew
My full spite at them, while the hurt is new.
The father first, who spawned this vice, this virus—
I'd squeeze the breath out of his guts. Then Syrus,
The setter-on, by Heaven, how I'd bash him!
I'd clutch his waist—so—whirl him up—so—then dash him
Down, hard, on his head, and leave his brains dispersed so
All round the road. The youth's eyes I'd have first—so—
Then—out with him on his neck. The rest I'd rush—so—
Hound, pound, tread, trample. But why beat about the bush so?
My mistress must be told this crushing blow.
(He rushes past the two women towards the house)

SOSTRATA: Let's call him back. Oh, Geta!

GETA: Aw, let me go,
Whoever you are.

SOSTRATA: I'm Sostrata.

GETA: *(spinning round)*   Oh, where?
I've waited, waited—oh, it's well you're there.
Oh, madam!
SOSTRATA: What's the matter? Why the flurry?
GETA: Oh, God! Oh Heaven!
SOSTRATA: Dear Geta, what's the hurry?
Get your breath back.
GETA: Oh, we're utterly—
SOSTRATA: Well?
Utterly what?
GETA: Down. Done for.
SOSTRATA: How? Speak! Tell!
What's wrong?
GETA: Now that—
SOSTRATA: Now what?
GETA: Now that he who
                              wronged her—
SOSTRATA: Aeschinus? What of him?
GETA: —is our friend no longer.
SOSTRATA: God help us, why?
GETA: He's found another flame.
SOSTRATA: No!
GETA: It's no secret. It was himself who came,
Saw, conquered, pinched her from a pimp—no disguise.
SOSTRATA: Are you quite sure?
GETA: Saw it with these two eyes.
SOSTRATA: What—whom—shall one trust now? Our Aeschinus—
God help us—the life of all and each of us,
In whom our whole hope, help, salvation lay,
Who swore without her he'd not live a day,
Who said he'd take the baby to his father
And beg his leave to wed!
GETA: Stop crying. Think rather
What action this blow calls for. Do you feel it
As something you must accept, or will you reveal it?
CANTHARA: Reveal it? Do you imagine for a minute
We'd do that? You must be mad!
GETA: I'm all agin it.
We know he's not our friend now. Facts belie it.
If we try to prove the truth, he'll simply deny it.
Your child's good name, her life, would be in danger;
And if he admitted the lot, he loves a stranger.
It's no good making him marry her. And so,
However you look at it—mum's the word.

SOSTRATA: Oh, no,
It's not.
GETA: What then?
SOSTRATA: I'll tell the world.
CANTHARA: Our ruin?
Oh, madam, for heaven's sake, think what you're doing.
SOSTRATA: We've nothing to lose. Look at the facts of the case.
First, she's no dowry. In the second place,
Her other asset's gone. Whoever she's given to,
It can't be as a virgin. So what we're driven to
Is what I said. I've got evidence I can bring,
If he denies it all—his own lost ring.
I've a clear conscience too. I'm not to blame.
No payment passed, or anything that could shame
My daughter or myself. I'll make it a court—a test case.
GETA: Right, I withdraw my objections. Yours is the best case.
SOSTRATA: Quick as you can, then, Geta, off you go,
Tell the whole tale to cousin Hegio.
My husband always held him in high regard,
And he's worried most about us.
GETA: That's not hard.
I never noticed one other acquaintance worry
The least little bit.
SOSTRATA: And you, dear nurse, now hurry
And fetch the midwife. Do be quick about it,
Or, when we most need her aid, we'll be left without it.
(Geta and Canthara go off, Sostrata returns to the house.
Demea enters in great agitation from the town)
DEMEA: Now I've been told my own, my younger lad,
Was in this girl-grab too. Oh, it's too bad!
That's all I needed to fill my cup to the brim,
That Aeschinus should manage to drag *him*,
Who was still some good, into the mire as well.
Where shall I start to look for him? In some hell
Of vice his brother's taken him to, I'll bet.
Led him astray, that ruffian has, Micio's pet.
Ah, there comes Syrus. I'll make *him* disclose
Their whereabouts. Wait! He's in the gang. If he *knows*
I'm fishing at all, the rogue will never tell.
I'll have to hide my line, finesse.
(Syrus enters, with another slave, carrying fish and other
provisions, who passes into the house. Syrus sees Demea but
pretends not to)

SYRUS: *(rubbing his hands)*   Well, well!
I told our gaffer the whole story, right
From start to finish. And such sheer delight
You never saw.

DEMEA: *(aside)*   God! Micio must be mad!

SYRUS: He heartily congratulated the lad,
And thanked me for my good advice.

DEMEA: *(aside)*   I'll burst!

SYRUS: He paid the twenty for the slave girl first,
Then gave me half a mina just for blueing—
Which I've succeeded admirably in doing.

DEMEA: *(aside ironically)*
By God, give *him* a job, he'll guarantee you
Good service!

SYRUS: *(pretending to see Demea for the first time)*
          You, sir? Why, I didn't see you.
How goes the world?

DEMEA: How goes the world, you say?
I can't help wondering at your house, the way
That's going.

SYRUS: Indeed, it's not as one would wish there,
To tell the truth, it's daft. *(calling inside the house)*
          Those other fish there,
Dromo, clean now, but let the largest conger
Play in the water just a little longer,
And when I'm back, but not before, we'll bone it.

DEMEA: Disgraceful conduct!

SYRUS: Oh, I don't condone it
Myself, sir. And I shout at them, sir, often. *(shouts inside)*
Stephanio, make sure you soak and soften
Those salt fish properly.

DEMEA: Gods! Is it his whim
Or will he feel he's done well if through him
That lad is lost? I see the dark day nearing
When he'll be ruined, reduced to volunteering!

SYRUS: Ah, you're long-sighted, sir, you don't just see
What is, here under your nose, but what's to be.

DEMEA: Just tell me this, now. Have you people got
That girl in the house?

SYRUS: Yes, sir, inside, sir.

DEMEA: What?
And will he keep her there?

SYRUS: Well, we're so mad

I think he will, sir.

DEMEA: Oh, it's all too bad!

SYRUS: Yes, sir, it's all his father's foolish, mild way,
His crazy spare-the-rod and spoil-the-child way.

DEMEA: It makes me ashamed, it makes me sick. My brother—

SYRUS: Ah, sir, you're poles apart from one another.
I don't say this just to your face, you know.
You're solid matter, sir, from top to toe;
He's empty air. I mean, would you allow
Your lad to act as that one's acting now?
(Demea gives Syrus a sharp glance, then decides to take the question as innocent)

DEMEA: Me? I'd have smelt each move before he could make one,
Six months ahead.

SYRUS: Ah, you're the wide-awake one!

DEMEA: I only pray he'll end as he's begun.

SYRUS: *(cryptic)*
Well, as each father wills, so is each son.

DEMEA: *(casual)*
By the way, have you seen him anywhere today?

SYRUS: Who, sir? Your son, sir? *(aside)* Now to get him away.
(aloud)
He's on the farm, as far as I'm aware, sir,
Since quite some time. He's got some business there, sir.

DEMEA: Are you quite sure?

SYRUS: Oh, yes, I took him down.

DEMEA: Good, good! I feared he might be stuck in town.

SYRUS: Oh, yes, he went, and was he furious!

DEMEA: Why?

SYRUS: About that lute-girl. Lord, how he let fly
In the market, threw the book at his brother's head!

DEMEA: Indeed?

SYRUS: Oh, yes, sir, he left nothing unsaid.
You see, the cash was just being counted out
When up he comes by chance and starts to shout
And rage, 'How, Aeschinus, can you have the face
To act like this, doing things that bring disgrace
On our whole family?'

DEMEA: I could weep for joy!

SYRUS: 'You're wasting your life, not money!'

DEMEA: Bless the boy!
A chip off the old block!

SYRUS: Sure—a regular preacher.

DEMEA: He's full of pearls like that.
SYRUS: He's had a good teacher.
DEMEA: That's true. I train him. I let nothing pass.
       'Look at each man', I say, 'as in a glass,
       See how they live, and draw reflections thence.'
       I point out good traits—
SYRUS: Clever!
DEMEA: And bad—
SYRUS: Sound sense.
DEMEA: Note things well done—
SYRUS: Quite right.
DEMEA: Find fault, nail crime.
SYRUS: Fine!
DEMEA: Furthermore—
SYRUS: Lord, sir, I haven't the time
       To listen to you now. I've got some fish
       As fine and fresh as anyone could wish,
       And I must see they're not spoiled in the cooking,
       Our cardinal sin, like *your* sort overlooking
       Those points of yours. And what I can I do do,
       To train my fellow-slaves the same way you do.
       I note what's too well done, find salt, nail grime,
       Or say, 'Just right! Remember that next time.'
       I point out the right ways, do all I can
       According to my lights. 'Look at each pan',
       I say, 'as in a glass.' I show what's needed.
       The way we act here's daft, sir, that's conceded;
       As a man's made he must be managed, though.
       Is there anything else you want? If not, I'll go.
DEMEA: A bit more sense round here would do no harm.
SYRUS: Yes, sir. Will you be going back to the farm?
DEMEA: At once.
SYRUS: Well, yes, with no one here obeying
       Your wise instructions, what's the good of staying?
       (Syrus goes indoors)
DEMEA: I'm off. The lad that was the why and wherefore
       Of my being here's down there. It's him I care for,
       Him solely I'm concerned with. Since my brother
       Wants it that way, let *him* look after the other . . .
       But now who's that I spy, away down there?
       Our tribesmate Hegio? I do declare,
       If I'm seeing straight it *is*. Well, what a joy!
       A man that was my friend right from a boy!

> God knows that nowadays there's a mighty dearth
> Of that type, men of old-time sterling worth
> And sense of honour. The city need have no fears
> Of harm from *their* sort, not in a million years.
> This is a pleasure! Seeing amongst us still
> The remnants of that race gives one the will
> To go on living even now. I'll stay
> And have a word with him, pass the time of day.
> *(Hegio enters with Geta. They do not at first notice Demea)*

HEGIO: Good God, a most outrageous way to act!
Geta, what tale is this?

GETA: This tale is fact.

HEGIO: What? That *that* house should do such wrong, should strike
Such low, foul blows! Young Aeschinus! How unlike
His father's son!

DEMEA: *(aside)*   He's heard—this speech reveals it—
About that lute-girl. He, a stranger, feels it.
To his adoptive father it's all fun.
Could he but hear what's said about his son!

HEGIO: They'll not get away with this, without they do
What's right.

GETA: Oh, sir, our whole hope lies in you.
We've only you to father and defend us.
The old man, dying, begged you to befriend us.
We're lost if you abandon us.

HEGIO: Never fear.
I won't. I can't, in conscience.

DEMEA: I'll go near.
Well, well! Good morning to you, Hegio.

HEGIO: *(shortly)*
Good morning. I was hoping to meet you.

DEMEA: Oh?
What is it?

HEGIO: Aeschinus, that elder son
You gave your brother to adopt, has done—
Well, things no decent, free-born boy should do.

DEMEA: What has he done, exactly?

HEGIO: I think you knew
Simulus, our contemporary?

DEMEA: Of course.

HEGIO: Your son has done his daughter wrong—by force.

DEMEA: Good God in heaven!

HEGIO: Let me finish first.

What you have heard so far is not the worst.

DEMEA: But is there worse?

HEGIO: There is, as you shall see.
That act one might condone, to some degree,
Say darkness, wine, desire worked on hot youth.
That's human nature. When he knew the truth,
Straight to her mother, of his own accord,
He came; he wept, he pleaded, he implored,
He pledged, he swore that he would marry her. They
Believed, forgave him, kept mum. Since that day
Nine months have passed, a child's expected; he's
Now left her—yes, our fine youth, if you please,
Has left her, and procured himself some other
House-mate.

DEMEA: Is this firm fact?

HEGIO: You can see the mother,
The girl herself, the whole case, every feature.
And Geta here—as slaves go, a good creature,
And certainly not lazy, since his labours
Feed and support them all—I mean your neighbours—
Well, you can take and bind him, find the 'fact'
You're after.

GETA: Yes, God help me, have me racked,
If this is not the truth; in any case
He'll not dare to deny it to my face.

DEMEA: *(aside)*
I'm so ashamed. What can I do or say?

PAMPHILA: *(within)*
Oh, I am torn with pains! Help, Juno, I pray!
Save me!

HEGIO: Oh heavens, is her time upon her?

GETA: It is.

HEGIO: *(to Demea)*
          See there, that call is to your honour.
Give with good will what else you'll give by force.
I pray God you may take the decent course;
But, if you're otherwise minded, I shall labour
With all my might for her and our dead neighbour.
His father, Demea, was my father's brother;
We were brought up from infancy with each other;
At home and in the wars we were together,
We faced with one heart poverty's foul weather.
So I shall shun no trial, action, strife,

Sooner, in fact, will I lay down my life
Than desert them. Well, what's your answer, then?

DEMEA: I'll go and find my brother.

HEGIO: Do. As men
In easy circumstances, I'd remind you
That wealth, power, standing, name are things which bind you
The more to show for others' rights right feelings—
That's if you want to be known for decent dealings.
(Turns away from Demea towards the house)

DEMEA: Come back. We'll do the right thing, fair and square.

HEGIO: You'd better. Geta, take me in to her.
(Hegio and Geta go into Sostrata's house)

DEMEA: I said as much! If this were only all!
But all these wild goings-on will surely call
Down on our heads some awful end or other.
Well, I'll go find, and face this with, my brother.
(Goes off towards the town. Hegio emerges from Sostrata's house, talking back to her inside)

HEGIO: Cheer up. Soothe her as best you can. I'll go
Meanwhile and see if I meet Micio
Down in the market. This whole tale I'll tell
Direct to him. If he'll do the right thing, well,
That's fine. But if he takes a different view,
Let him declare it—I'll know what to do.
(Goes off towards the town)

ACT IV

(Ctesipho comes out of Micio's house, talking to Syrus)

CTESIPHO: You say my father's left town?

SYRUS: Long ago.

CTESIPHO: Let me hear more, please.

SYRUS: Well, by what I know
He's busy at this moment on the farm.

CTESIPHO: I hope so. And I hope he'll—take no harm,
But tire himself till he can't leave his bed
For the next three days.

SYRUS: Amen to all you've said—
And more.

CTESIPHO: You see, I'm having such a jolly day,
And I'm mad keen to prolong my holiday
At least till tomorrow. And that country estate

Of ours for nothing do I so much hate
As its damned nearness. If it weren't so near,
Before my father could possibly get back here,
Night'd overtake him. Now he'll find I'm *not*
Down on the farm, and back to town he'll trot,
I know. He'll ask me where I've been—'All day
I've not set eyes on you.'—*Then* what do I say?

SYRUS: Does nothing suggest itself to your youthful wit, then?
CTESIPHO: Nothing at all.
SYRUS: So much the worse for it, then.
Could you have a tenant, foreign guest, family friend?
CTESIPHO: Yes, why?
SYRUS: To whose affairs you'd have to attend?
CTESIPHO: When I didn't? I can't say that!
SYRUS: You can.
CTESIPHO: I might,
Just for the day. But if I stay the night,
What alibi then?
SYRUS: I wish one could pretend
One gave one's nights, too, to that kind of friend
And those kind of affairs. Don't worry though. Look,
I know your father's feelings like a book;
I know the way when he is boiling hot,
To make him mild as an old sheep.
CTESIPHO: Oh, what?
What way?
SYRUS: He loves to hear your praises sung.
I make you out an angel. Oh, my tongue
Tells tales of virtue—
CTESIPHO: Mine?
SYRUS: Yes, yours, my boy?
And then his tears fall, like a child's, for joy.
But look!
CTESIPHO: Where?
SYRUS: Talk of the devil!
CTESIPHO: My dad?
SYRUS: He, he—
In person!
CTESIPHO: What's to be done?
SYRUS: Leave that to me.
You hop inside.
CTESIPHO: But if he asks, you never—
You know—I wasn't—

SYRUS: Can't you shut up—ever?
(He bundles Ctesipho inside. Demea enters, talking to himself, not seeing Syrus)

DEMEA: Oh, I've no luck at all, I do declare,
First, I can't find my brother anywhere;
Then, when I'm looking for him, what do I see
But one of the hired men from the farm, and he
Says *there* my son most certainly is not.
I don't know what to do.

CTESIPHO: *(peeping out, whispering)* Hi Syrus!

SYRUS: *(whispering)*   What?

CTESIPHO: Is he after me?

SYRUS: He is indeed.

CTESIPHO: Damnation!

SYRUS: Don't worry.

DEMEA: *(to himself)*   What can be the explanation?
Of my confounded ill-luck? I seem to be cursed
By destiny, doomed to bear crosses. I'm the first
To hear of our troubles, the first to know and tell
Bad news. Alone I've borne each blow that fell.

SYRUS: *(aside)*
He makes me laugh. The first to hear! What rot!
Alone in the dark, *he* is.

DEMEA: Now back I trot
To see if perhaps my brother's returned.

CTESIPHO: Oh, dear!
For heaven's sake don't let him burst in here!

SYRUS: Oh, shut up! I'll take care of that.

CTESIPHO: Your care
I'll never trust. I'll shut myself up with *her*
In some cubby-hole in the house.

SYRUS: Do, do, but go!
I'll shift the old man all the same.

DEMEA: *(as before)*   Hallo!
There's Syrus, the old rogue.

SYRUS: *(aloud, for Demea's benefit)* No man can bear it,
If things go on like this. That's fact. I'll swear it.
How many lords and masters have I got?
I'd like to know. God, what a life!

DEMEA: *(aside)*   Now what
Exactly *is* he mumbling? What does *this* mean?
(aloud)
Well, my good man. Is my brother to be seen?

SYRUS: You needn't 'good man' me. I'm through, dead, done.
DEMEA: How so?
SYRUS: How so? Why, Ctesipho, your son,
        Has bashed that lute-girl and poor little me
        Half-dead.
DEMEA: Eh, what?
SYRUS: He split my lip—there, see?
DEMEA: What for?
SYRUS: *I* was behind the girl's being bought,
        So *he* says.
DEMEA: But you'd taken him, I thought,
        Down to the farm?
SYRUS: I did, but back he came,
        Berserk—no mercy—think of it!—no shame—
        Beating an old man, the baby I once had
        Just *so* big in my arms!
DEMEA: Just like his dad!
        A real man! That's the spirit! Well done, my lad!
SYRUS: Well done? He'll keep his hands off when next we meet
        If he's any sense.
DEMEA: Brave boy!
SYRUS: Oh, yes, he beat
        A poor slip of a girl, and me a slave,
        Who daren't retaliate. Oh, very brave!
DEMEA: He couldn't have been more right. Like me, he knew
        Who's at the bottom of this business—*you.*
        But is my brother in?
SYRUS: *(sulky)*   No, he's not.
DEMEA: I see.
        So where would I find him?
SYRUS: *(muttering)*   I know where he ought to be—
        But I'm not telling you.
DEMEA: What's that you said?
SYRUS: You heard.
DEMEA: *(waving his stick)*
                    You're looking for a broken head.
SYRUS: I don't know the name of the party, only where.
DEMEA: Well, where?
SYRUS: Well, there's a colonnade down there—
        The cattle-market's right next to it, yonder—you know, sir?
DEMEA: Of course, of course.
SYRUS: Well, that's the way you go, sir,
        Straight up the street, that far; then right ahead there

You'll find a steep descent; well, drop down dead there—
Dead straight there, and you'll find, in a sort of valley,
A chapel on one side, next to that an alley.
DEMEA: Which—?
SYRUS: Where that big wild fig-tree is.
DEMEA: I know it.
SYRUS: Go down it.
DEMEA: But that alley's blind.
SYRUS: Why, blow it,
You're right. Aren't I a fool, sir? . . . Yes, I made
A slip there . . . Come back to the colonnade.
Of course! Much nearer—much less chance to wander.
You know Cratinus' house, the millionaire's—yonder?
DEMEA: Yes.
SYRUS: Well, go past it, then turn left, then straight—
Right at Diana's shrine—short of the gate,
Just by the pond, you'll find a little baker's,
And opposite that a workshop, a chair-maker's.
He's there.
DEMEA: What for?
SYRUS: Some seats they're fitting out
With legs of ilex-wood, you know, for sitting-out
In the sun with.
DEMEA: Getting sozzled. Oh, I know.
But why am I waiting? I *must* find him. *(Hurries off)*
SYRUS: Go!
Go, and this day I'll give you your fair due
Of exercise, you funeral baked meat, you!
Aeschinus is damned late, the dinner's spoiling,
Ctesipho's in love's toils—and how he's toiling!
So—I'll see to myself. I'll go and pluck
The pick of all those titbits, and then suck
And sip and soak, and so in lazy leisure
This livelong day link hour to hour of pleasure.
*(He goes into the house. After a minute or two Hegio and
Micio come in together from the town)*
MICIO: What I'm being so admired for, I don't know;
I'm only doing my duty, Hegio.
We've done you wrong, I'm putting it right again.
Or did you class me with the sort of men
Whose attitude, as soon as you protest
At their transgressions, is that you've transgressed,
It's all your fault? Because I didn't act

          Like that do I have to be thanked?

HEGIO: No, no. In fact
Your attitude's just what I thought I'd find.
But come along with me, if you don't mind,
To the girl's mother, and tell *her* the same
As you told me—that this suspicion came
Through the lad's brother and the lute-girl's *his*.

MICIO: By all means, if you really feel that is
The right thing. If it's got to be done, let's go.

HEGIO: That's kind of you. You'll ease her mind, you know;
She's sick with worry and grief, and you do owe it
To them in a way. But I can let her know it
If you'd rather not.

MICIO: No, no, I'll come along.

HEGIO: That's very kind. Folks who've found things going wrong
In every way, develop a disposition,
You know, to a sort of morbid over-suspicion,
Thinking, because of their defenceless plight,
People are playing tricks on them, left and right.
That's why they'll be better satisfied if you *do*
Explain all this in person.

MICIO: Very true.

HEGIO: So come with me inside here.

MICIO: After you.

(They go into Sostrata's house. Aeschinus rushes in very
agitated, and gives utterance first in a rhythmic recitative,
then calms down to couplets)

AESCHINUS: I'm riven, I'm racked!
           What a bolt from the blue!
    I can't think how to act,
           Where to turn, what to do—
    Limbs limp with terror,
           Brain numb with fear—
    A maze of error—
           How can I get clear
    Of these confusions
           Where everyone draws
    Such bad conclusions
           Of me—with good cause . . .
They think, so I was told by that old woman—
I bought that girl for myself. She'd gone to summon
The midwife, when I met her. Up I went—
'How is she? Is it near? Have you been sent',

Said I, 'to fetch the midwife?' 'No!' she cries.
'No, Aeschinus, we've had enough of lies,
Enough of falling for promises *you* make!
Get out of it!' 'Now, what, for heaven's sake,'
I asked, 'does all this mean? Just what's the game?'
'Good luck to you! You can keep your latest flame!'
She cries. I saw at once how they suspect me.
I didn't explain about Ctesipho. What checked me
Was fear that telling *that* gossip meant telling others.
What shall I do now? Say the girl's my brother's?
That must on no account leak out. And, even waiving
That question—for we *might* find means of saving
His secret—still my own worst doubt is whether
I'll be believed. So many facts added together
Seem to make truth. *I* got the girl, *I* paid,
We took her to *my* house. All can be laid
At my door, I admit. Had I but rather
Told all, however shameful, to my father!
I should have asked and got his leave for marrying . . .
Oh, what a tale of timid, two-faced tarrying!
Now, Aeschinus, wake up. Point one—a visit
To *them* to clear myself. Their door, where is it?
Oh, God! I can't stop trembling when I start
To knock at this of all doors. Oh, my heart! *(knocks)*
Hi, hi! It's Aeschinus. Open—quick, I say . . .
There's someone coming out. I'll move away.
*(Moves to one side. Micio comes out, talking back to
Sostrata, unheard by Aeschinus)*

MICIO: Do, madam, as I said. I'll see my son
And tell him what we've settled has got to be done.
But who knocked at the door?

AESCHINUS: *(aside)*   Oh, Lord! That's queer!
My father!

MICIO: Aeschinus?

AESCHINUS: *(aside)*   What brought *him* here?

MICIO: Did you knock at the door? *(aside)* No answer. Well,
Why shouldn't I, since he's too shy to tell,
Tease him a tiny bit? *(aloud)* What? No reply?

AESCHINUS: That door? . . . Not that I know of . . . Not me . . . Why?

MICIO: I see. I wondered what you could have to do there.
(aside)
He blushed. There's hope for him.

AESCHINUS: But what took *you* there?

          Do tell me, father.

MICIO: No business of my own.
          I was taken along to help a man I've known
          Some time, who met me in the market-place
          This morning.

AESCHINUS: Help him? How?

MICIO: In a legal case.
          Some women live there, not well off; you won't,
          I imagine, know them—in fact, I'm sure you don't.
          They moved in not so very long ago.

AESCHINUS: Well?

MICIO: It's a young girl and her mother.

AESCHINUS: So—?

MICIO: So, as she's fatherless, her next male relation,
          My friend, must marry her, by law.

AESCHINUS: *(aside)*   Damnation!

MICIO: What?

AESCHINUS: Nothing. Nothing. Good. Go on. Must marry her,
          You said?

MICIO: That's right. And now he's come to carry her
          Off to Miletus with him.

AESCHINUS: Did you say
          Carry her off?

MICIO: That's right.

AESCHINUS: What? All the way
          Back to Miletus?

MICIO: That's right.

AESCHINUS: *(aside)*   Oh, my heart!
          (aloud)
          But what about the women, for their part?
          What do they say?

MICIO: What *can* they say? The mother
          Says she's expecting a child from someone or other,
          First come, first served, so the cousin shouldn't marry her.

AESCHINUS: Don't you agree?

MICIO: No.

AESCHINUS: No? So off he'll carry her?
          Is that it?

MICIO: Why not?

AESCHINUS: Why not? It's unkind,
          Hard-hearted, father, and, to speak my mind
          Fairly and squarely, most high-handed dealing!

MICIO: How so?

AESCHINUS: How so? Why, what will *he* be feeling,

Poor wretch, who loved her first, do you suppose,
And madly loves her now—for all one knows—
Seeing her snatched away in front of his face,
Right under his eyes—oh, it's a damned disgrace.

MICIO: How can you say that? Who betrothed her, then?
Who gave the girl away? To whom, where, when?
What witnesses did he have? Who signed, sealed, saw?
Why did he take a bride debarred by law?

AESCHINUS: How could a girl of *her* age be expected
To sit at home and wait to be collected
By cousins from Miletus? That was rather
The case you ought to have urged and argued, father.

MICIO: Rubbish, my boy! You mean I should have made
A case against the man I'd come to aid?
But how are we concerned in all this fuss?
What are the women in that house to us?
Let's go . . . Hallo there! Why those tears?

AESCHINUS: One word,
Please, father, please.

MICIO: Oh, my dear boy, I've heard.
Yes, I know all. I'm fond of you, I care,
So all you do is my concern.

AESCHINUS: I swear,
I swear, as heartily as I hope you'll give
And I deserve that care as long as I live,
I do feel sorry for the wrong I've done.
I blush to face you.

MICIO: I believe you, son.
I see you have a natural sense of shame,
The free man's heritage. But all the same
Your recklessness gives reason for misgiving.
In what sort of a place do you think you're living?
You forced a girl that you'd no right to touch—
Bad, bad, but human; men have done as much
Without being vicious. But, when *this* came out,
Did you once look ahead or look about
To ends and ways and means? How, if you daredn't
For sheer shame tell, was I supposed to have learnt
Of your adventure? You let nine months pass
Dithering. Your own future, that poor lass
And the child you simply left in the safe keeping
Of Providence. Was *it* meant, while you were sleeping,
To settle the whole thing for you, bring your bride
Safe home and settle her nicely at your side?

        You won't be so outrageously remiss,
        I trust, in other matters as in this! . . .
        Cheer up. She's yours, lad.

AESCHINUS: What?

MICIO: Cheer up, my son.
        That's what I said.

AESCHINUS: Father, is this your fun?

MICIO: My fun? But why?

AESCHINUS: Oh, I don't know. It's just
        That wanting it to be true, I can scarcely trust
        It can be.

MICIO: It is. Now off with you inside.
        Ask heaven's blessing for bringing home the bride.

AESCHINUS: For bringing home—? Now?

MICIO: Now.

AESCHINUS: At once?

MICIO: Yes, straight.

AESCHINUS: Dad, I'll be damned, you've got me in such a state,
        I love you—more than these two eyes.

MICIO: Oh, do you?
        More than—? (Indicates Sostrata's house)

AESCHINUS: As much.

MICIO: I'm indebted to you.

AESCHINUS: But say—where's that Milesian?

MICIO: Dead, departed,
        Embarked, embalmed. But come, it's time we started.

AESCHINUS: You go and ask for heaven's blessing instead.
        I'm sure it's likely to listen to anything said
        By you far more than me, because you are
        A better fellow than your son, by far.

MICIO: Well, I'll go in and see to all that's needed.
        You, if you're wise, won't leave my words unheeded.
        (Exit into house)

AESCHINUS: What can I say? Is this like son and father?
        If he were a brother or a best friend rather,
        How could he more completely take my part?
        He makes me his, his with my whole, full heart!
        And yet I'm almost scared by so much kindness,
        Of falling short of his standards in sheer blindness.
        Forewarned's forearmed, though. But—no more delay!
        In, in! No dawdling on my wedding day!
        (He rushes into Micio's house. Demea enters from the town,
        exhausted)

DEMEA: I'm worn out with walking! All foul infections
Seize upon Syrus and his damned directions!
I've trudged the town. Gods, where have I not been?
Pond, gate—no workshop—not a soul who'd seen
My brother, it seems. So—back where I was before
I come, but now I'll lay siege to his door
Till he returns.
(Goes to sit down before Micio's house. Micio comes out, talking back to Aeschinus)

MICIO: I'll go across and say
As far as we're concerned there's no delay.

DEMEA: At last! Oh I've been hunting for you for hours.

MICIO: What's up?

DEMEA: I've found that fine young son of ours
Fouled with fresh scandal!

MICIO: Oh, indeed?

DEMEA: Yes, new,
Unheard-of, heinous—

MICIO: Oh, for God's sake!

DEMEA: You!
You don't know *him*!

MICIO: I think I do.

DEMEA: Dim-witted!!
I don't mean—her. This was a crime committed
Against a free-born girl.

MICIO: I know.

DEMEA: You—what?
You know, and take it just like that?

MICIO: Why not?

DEMEA: Doesn't it make you rave, man? Aren't you wild?

MICIO: No, though I might have chosen—

DEMEA: There's a child!

MICIO: God bless it!

DEMEA: She's a pauper.

MICIO: So I hear.

DEMEA: A portionless wife, then?

MICIO: So it would appear.

DEMEA: Steps must be taken. *What?*

MICIO: Oh, that's quite clear.
She'll have to take some steps—from there to here.

DEMEA: Almighty God! Is this a way to act?

MICIO: Well, what more can I do?

DEMEA: Do? If in fact

          You feel unmoved, to *seem* a bit excited
          Would be more human.
MICIO: No, they're pledged, they're plighted,
          They'll wed. All's fixed. All fears I thus remove—
          And that's more human.
DEMEA: But—do you approve
          The match, then, Micio?
MICIO: If I could unmake it,
          No, Demea. Seeing that I can't, I take it—
          Well—philosophically. For life, you know,
          Is like those games of chance where, if the throw
          You want's not fallen, then what fate has thrown
          You must amend with some art of your own.
DEMEA: Oh, you amender, you! You've made us part
          With twenty Attic minae by your art,
          For that lute-girl. I'll tell you what *her* fate is,
          The throw *she* wants—out, quick, cost price or gratis.
MICIO: Not she. That girl I'd never dream of selling.
DEMEA: What then?
MICIO: She stays.
DEMEA: Good God! You'd have her dwelling
          Under one roof with a young wife and mother?
MICIO: Why not?
DEMEA: Do you reckon you're sane?
MICIO: I think so, brother.
DEMEA: I see your crazy notion. Yes. You'll take her
          God help us, under your roof in order to make her
          Your partner, and she'll play fine tunes for you to sing to!
MICIO: Why not?
DEMEA: And teach his wife that sort of thing, too.
MICIO: Why not?
DEMEA: Of course! They'll have you on a string
          Between them, and make you dance, three in a ring.
          (Holds out his arms and trips in imitation)
MICIO: Bravo!
DEMEA: Bravo?!
MICIO: *(seizing his hand and tripping too)*
                         And you shall make another
          If we need more.
DEMEA: Aren't you ashamed?
MICIO: Now, brother,
          Relax, calm down at last. Be blithe and gay—
          It's only right—on your son's wedding day.

I'll see them and be back.
(Goes into Sostrata's house)

DEMEA: God, what a life!
What ways! Oh, Lord, what lunacy! One wife
Without a dowry, due; one wench, inside;
One house, with every source of waste supplied;
One young man ruined, and one old man raving:
God save us—but you can't, that lot's past saving.
*(Syrus, drunk, enters from Micio's house. He does not see
Demea at first)*

SYRUS: Syrus, you've done yourself well. You're a beauty.
You've most efficiently discharged your duty.
So, having here inside fed full and fat now
I thought I'd stroll outside.

DEMEA: Just look at that now!
There's discipline for you!

SYRUS: Ah, now, there's the boss.
How do, cock? Eh, what's made you look so cross?

DEMEA: Cross, you old crime-sheet!

SYRUS: Now, now, that's enough,
Old wisdom-tooth, you needn't cut up rough.

DEMEA: If you were mine—

SYRUS: You'd be in easy street.
You'd have your fortunes founded on firm feet.
(He lurches heavily)

DEMEA: I'd make you an example to the lot!

SYRUS: What for? What have I done?

DEMEA: You dare ask what?
You, in the middle of this mess, the height
Of scandals that are scarcely yet put right,
As if you'd something to crow about, you've been drinking,
You sot!

SYRUS: *(aside)*   I was wrong to come out here, I'm thinking.
(Dromo, another slave, peeps out and calls to Syrus)

DROMO: Hi, Syrus, Ctesipho says he wants you.

SYRUS: Oh,
Get out!

DEMEA: What did he say about Ctesipho?

SYRUS: Nothing.

DEMEA: You scoundrel, is he at my brother's?

SYRUS: No, no.

DEMEA: Then why his name?

SYRUS: Oh, that's another's—

        A weedy, scrounging type—you might be knowing
        The fellow—

DEMEA: I'll see.

SYRUS: Now, now, where are you going?

DEMEA: Hands off!

SYRUS: Now, don't, sir.

DEMEA: Take your hands off, will you?
        You rogue—or would you rather have me spill you
        Your brains out on the spot?
        *(He brandishes his stick. Syrus gives way and Demea rushes
        into the house)*

SYRUS: He's gone. Oh Pollux,
        There's an unfriendly partner for their frolics,
        For Ctesipho especially. Well, what now?
        What do I do? I know. Until the row
        Is settled, to some snug, dark nook I'll slink off—
        That's what I'll do—and sleep this little drink off.
        *(He goes off. Micio comes out of Sostrata's house, talking
        back to her. As he does so, there is a loud noise from inside
        his own house)*

MICIO: We're ready, madam, as I said before,
        When you are. Who's that banging down my door?

DEMEA: *(rushing out)*
        Oh, I'm bereft of utterance, action, motion!
        What's to match this, in Heaven or earth or ocean?

MICIO: *(aside)*
        Aha! All's out, all's up, and hence the row.
        The fight is on; forth to the rescue now!

DEMEA: You fount and source of all our sons' offences!
        You—!

MICIO: Steady. Keep cool. Don't lose control of your senses.

DEMEA: I'm cool, controlled. All cursing I'll let be.
        Let's look at simple fact. Did we agree—
        Did you yourself suggest, or not—that *you*
        Should leave my lad alone, and I should do
        The same by yours?

MICIO: We did, I don't deny.

DEMEA: Then why's he at your house now, boozing? Why
        Being harboured there? He's mine. Why do you pay
        For him to have this girl? Why should your say
        In my affairs be more than *you* grant *me*?
        I leave your lad alone so let mine be.

MICIO: You're wrong.

DEMEA: Oh, am I?

MICIO: Remember the old saying, now—
'Friends share all.'

DEMEA: A fine tune for you to be playing now!

MICIO: Listen to me for one short minute. If
It's the money the lads are spending worries you stiff,
Look at it this way. At first you reared the two
According to your means, means meant to do
For both. For I, you thought, would take a wife.
Well, then, you stick to that old way of life.
Make, keep, save—if you're set, for their sakes, on leaving
The most you can. To that ambition cleaving,
What comes from me as windfalls let them use.
The capital's intact—count what accrues
From me as interest. This, marked and measured duly,
Will take a weight off yourself, the boys, and yours truly.

DEMEA: Oh, Micio, I'd let the money go,
But the lads' morals, brother!

MICIO: Yes, I know.
I was coming to that. Men's moral constitutions
Show symptoms which enable certain conclusions
To be inferred. Two persons may, in fact,
Do the same thing, and yet one finds the act
Harmless in one case, not so in the other.
It's not the thing done, it's the doer, brother,
That makes the difference. And I have no doubt
From such signs that our youngsters *will* turn out
All that we'd wish for. Oh, yes. I detect
Sense there, and sensibility, and due respect
And mutual affection. You may see
In them the natural bent of boys born free.
Let them run loose, you can always rein them in.
If recklessness about money is the sin
That worries you, well, with time we may grow wiser
In other ways, but it's age that makes the miser.
We're all too keen on cash. They'll soon be seasoned
To that same sharpness.

DEMEA: I hope your fine, well-reasoned
Philosophy doesn't wreck us all.

MICIO: Now, now,
No more of that. It won't. Just smooth your brow.
Your face for one day's revelling let me borrow.

DEMEA: Needs must when the revel drives, eh? But tomorrow

I'll take my son and get down to the farm
At first light.

MICIO: Or before—it'd do no harm.
I only ask you just for today to make
A little bit merry.

DEMEA: And that wench I'll take
Along as well.

MICIO: One up for you! That way
You'll tie him down there. Yes, you make her stay,

DEMEA: I'll see she stays. I'll see she has her fill
Of ash and dust and meal from hearth and mill;
She shall glean stubble in the glare of noon;
I'll have her burned and black as cinders soon.

MICIO: Good! That's the way! Then make him, willy-nilly,
Love her, and her alone.

DEMEA: You think I'm silly.
I envy you. I feel—

MICIO: Still, still?

DEMEA: I'm dumb.

MICIO: Let's make this day what it was meant for. Come!
(They go indoors)

ACT V

*(Demea comes out again some time later, having changed
into more festive attire)*

DEMEA: His life's account books no man ever drew up
So well, but time, chance, change brings something new up,
Some lesson. Your known laws become unknown;
Things prized, when put to fresh proof, you disown.
This is my fate. The hard life that I've led
Till now I leave, my span of life nigh sped.
And why? Because I've found, on fact's own showing,
The best thing's to be soft and easy-going.
Which truth by us two brothers you may measure.
He gave his days to ease and social pleasure,
Calm, gracious, always smiling, never offending,
While on himself his time and money spending.
And I, the boor, harsh, sour, grim, grasping, mean,
Married—and in that state what troubles I've seen!
Sons came—more cares. *Now* look at me. Intent
On making what I could for them, I've spent

My best years money-grubbing. Now, life past,
This harvest of my pains I have at last—
Their hate. My brother with no pain has won
A father's fruits. They love him, me they shun;
To him their confidence they freely give,
Of him they're fond, with him they both now live,
And I—am left. For his long life they pray,
And wait, I'm well aware, for my last day.
He's made his own, at little cost, the boys
Brought up with my brow's sweat; he takes the joys,
I all the pain ... But, come, let's turn the table,
Take up this challenge, see who's better able
To speak sweet and act large. I also claim
My sons' esteem and love, and if the game
Is 'give and give way', well, I'll not be hindmost.
If funds run short, why should the eldest mind most?
(Syrus appears at Micio's door and calls to Demea)

SYRUS: Hi, sir! Your brother says don't stray too far.
DEMEA: *(heartily)*
Who's that? Old Syrus! Let's hear how you are.
What ho! How's life?
SYRUS: *(surprised)*　　　All right, sir.
DEMEA: 　　　　　　　　　　　Well, that's fine.
(aside)
Three bits already clean out of my line—
'Old', 'what ho' and 'how's life'. *(aloud)* You seem to me, man,
The sort of slave who is by nature a free man.
I'll gladly help you.
SYRUS: *(incredulously)*　　　Thanks.
DEMEA: 　　　　　　　　　　　Oh, but I mean it,
And before the day's much older you'll have seen it.
(Geta comes out of Sostrata's house, talking back to her)
GETA: Madam, I'll go across to the other side
And find how soon they mean to fetch the bride.
But there's old Demea. Sir, God bless you.
DEMEA: *(heartily)*　　　　　　　　　　　Oh,
How do they call *you*?
GETA: 　　　　　　　Geta.
DEMEA: 　　　　　　　　　　　Well, you know,
Geta, I've come to the conclusion today
That you're a man in a million. For I say
A servant's proved his worth if he's devoted
To those he serves, and that in you I've noted.

Should need arise, I'll help you, Geta, gladly.
(aside)
I'm learning bonhomie, and not doing badly!

GETA: Thank you for your kind opinion.

DEMEA: *(aside)*   A good beginning!
The working masses, one by one, I'm winning!
(Aeschinus comes out of Micio's house, not seeing Demea at first)

AESCHINUS: They want too posh a wedding. A bit wearing
I find it. Why, they'll waste the day preparing.

DEMEA: Well, Aeschinus, how's things?

AESCHINUS: Oh, dad, it's you.

DEMEA: Yes, lad, your dad, in name and nature too,
Who loves you more than these two eyes. But, hey!
Why don't you bring the bride?

AESCHINUS: That's what I say!
But all these extras seem to take so long,
Flute-girls, a choir to sing the wedding-song—

DEMEA: Bah! Take an old man's tip.

AESCHINUS: What?

DEMEA: Skip it all—
Songs, flutes, flares, flap. Get down this garden-wall
Quick. Fetch her *that* way. Make one house of two
And bring her mother and the whole lot through.

AESCHINUS: Done! Dad, you're sweet, you're swell!

DEMEA: *(aside)*   Bravo! Swell, sweet!
My brother's house will be a public street,
He'll be plus a horde of inmates, minus a lot
Of money entertaining them—so what?
I'm sweet. I win all hearts. Let Midas pay
His twenty minae every time, I say.
(aloud)
Go, Syrus, jump to it.

SYRUS: What am I to do?

DEMEA: Pull down the wall. *(Exit Syrus)* Geta, go, bring them through.

GETA: God bless you. You're so kind. *(Exit Geta)*

DEMEA: I know true worth,
What?

AESCHINUS: Sure thing.

DEMEA: For your wife, weak from the birth,
It's better than bringing her along the highway.

AESCHINUS: It's much the best way, father.

DEMEA: Well, it's *my* way.

But here comes Micio.
(Micio enters, showing for the first time some perturbation)

MICIO: My brother bid you
Pull down the wall? Where is he? Demea, did you?

DEMEA: *(calmly)*
I did, and do, this way and every other,
Bid us make one big happy family, brother,
In love and help and harmony.

AESCHINUS: *(to Micio)*   Do, father.

MICIO: *(taken aback)*
I don't gainsay *that*.

DEMEA: Say it's our duty, rather.
First, there's the mother of this young man's wife.

MICIO: There is. So what?

DEMEA: Of sober, godly life.

MICIO: *(off-handedly)*
They say so.

DEMEA: Not young.

MICIO: No!

DEMEA: In fact, past bearing
More children, all alone, with no one caring—

MICIO: What is he after?

DEMEA: *(suddenly, firmly)* You must marry her!
(to Aeschinus)
And you must see he does. It's only fair.

MICIO: Me marry!

DEMEA: You.

MICIO: Me?!

DEMEA: You, I say.

MICIO: You're mad!

DEMEA: *(to Aeschinus)*
If you're a man, you'll make him.

AESCHINUS: *(coaxingly)*   Come on, dad.

MICIO: Don't listen to *him*, donkey!

DEMEA: That won't aid you.
There's no way out.

MICIO: You're daft!

AESCHINUS: Can't I persuade you,
Dear dad? *(Lays his hand on Micio's shoulder)*

MICIO: Get off! You've water on the brain.

DEMEA: Come, do your son a favour.

MICIO: Are you sane?
Me a newly-wed at sixty-five,

                        And take an old hag less than half-alive!
                        Is that it?
AESCHINUS: Please! They've had my word.
    MICIO: They've had
                        Your what?! Be lavish with yourself, my lad.
    DEMEA: Come, what if he begged something bigger?
    MICIO: What?
                        As if that weren't the biggest thing I've got!
    DEMEA: *(taking one shoulder)*
                        Come on.
AESCHINUS: *(taking the other)*
                        Don't grudge it.
    DEMEA: Promise, now.
    MICIO: Let go!
AESCHINUS: Not till I've won you over.
    MICIO: This, you know
                        Is downright force.
    DEMEA: Now, Micio, don't be mean.
    MICIO: Well, though I think it's bad, mad, clownish, clean
                        At variance with all my views of life,
                        If it's your will, I will—take her for wife.
AESCHINUS: You're great—as great as my feelings for you!
    DEMEA: Still—
    MICIO: Well? What?
    DEMEA: Well, since in this you grant my will—
    MICIO: What's coming next?
    DEMEA: Well, now, there's Hegio,
                        Their next relation, our in-law, you know—
                        He's not well-off. We ought to help him.
    MICIO: How?
    DEMEA: There's that small farm near town—we could allow
                        Our friend free use of that—the one you let.
    MICIO: *Small* farm, you said?
    DEMEA: If it's a large one, yet
                        Noblesse oblige. He's been a father to her.
                        We couldn't gain a nobler, kinder, truer
                        Connexion. It's a fair deal. And, you know,
                        I'm only taking to heart, dear Micio,
                        What you so well said—nothing could be wiser—
                        What was it now?—about age making the miser,
                        Too keen on cash. That shame we ought to shun.
                        Being truly said, this should be duly done.
AESCHINUS: Dear father, please!

MICIO: Oh, all right, if the lad
          Would like it, he shall have it.
AESCHINUS: I'm so glad.
DEMEA: Now soul and body, brother, you're my twin!
          (aside)
          I'm stealing his own juice to stew him in!
          (Syrus enters from the house)
SYRUS: I've done, sir, as you said.
DEMEA: Fine! Now I'd plead
          That Syrus should immediately be freed.
MICIO: *That* freed? For what?
DEMEA: For many things.
SYRUS: *(wheedling)*   Oh, sir,
          You're really kind. I've taken constant care
          Of both these boys for you from babyhood,
          And taught and told and counselled all I could.
DEMEA: The case is clear. His various employment—
          Procuring food and females for enjoyment
          So faithfully, organising all night drinking—
          Takes lots of talent, to my way of thinking.
SYRUS: Sweet soul!
DEMEA: And then today, his help, his care
          Got us that girl. Reward is right and fair
          And will encourage others, and—*the lad
          Would like it.*
MICIO: *(to Aeschinus)*
                          Would you like it?
AESCHINUS: Yes, like mad.
MICIO: Well, if you'd like it—Syrus, here—to me.
          *(He gives Syrus the symbolical blow for manumission—
          rather hard)*
          I hereby with this blow set Syrus free.
SYRUS: Most kind. I thank you all, especially you, sir.
DEMEA: I share your pleasure.
AESCHINUS: Me too.
SYRUS: I'm sure you do, sir.
          It would complete my happiness to see
          My dear wife, Phrygia, freed as well as me.
DEMEA: An excellent woman!
SYRUS: And today she's given *(pointing to
                                                         Aeschinus)*
          His son, your grandchild, his first suck.
DEMEA: By heaven,

His first suck did you say? Why that indeed
Leaves no more room for doubt. She *must* be freed.
MICIO: For that?
DEMEA: For that. I'll pay you what she's worth.
SYRUS: Oh, sir, God send you all you seek on earth!
MICIO: *(to Syrus)*
So! You've done well today.
DEMEA: But if you will,
Dear Micio, doing your duty by him still,
Lend Syrus for immediate needs a little,
He'll soon repay.
MICIO: Not one tenth of a tittle!
AESCHINUS: He's a good chap.
SYRUS: I'll pay you back, don't doubt it.
Do trust me.
AESCHINUS: Come on, dad.
MICIO: I'll think about it.
DEMEA: *(to Syrus)*
He will.
SYRUS: You're marvellous.
AESCHINUS: Dear, delightful dad!
MICIO: What's this—this lightning change? What whim? What fad?
Why suddenly so free? One wouldn't know you.
DEMEA: I'll tell you, Micio. It was to show you
These boys have based their verdicts—'dear, delightful'
On no true form, on nothing fair or rightful
In conduct, but complying, pleasing, giving.
Now, lads, if you dislike my way of living
Because I don't indulge each time each taste,
Good, bad—I wash my hands of you. Spend, waste,
Do as you will. But if you want, in truth,
On those occasions when hot-blooded youth
Is rash and blind, and takes too little thought,
Some guide to curb, correct, or, where he ought,
Indulge your wish—if that is what you'd rather,
I'm here to do it.
AESCHINUS: You *shall* do it, father.
You *do* know better . . . What about my brother?
DEMEA: Oh, he can keep the girl—but not another.
MICIO: Agreed!
PRODUCER: Clap, please!

Frederick William Clayton 1913–1999
The Man and His Work

Born in 1913 to relatively modest parents—his father was headmaster of a village school near Liverpool—the second of three exceptional boys, Frederick William Clayton was soon recognized as intellectually gifted. Consequently 'trained like a racehorse', as he put it, at the Liverpool Collegiate School, he took the fences easily to win one of only four open scholarships which were not reserved for Etonians and went up to King's College Cambridge to read Classics before his eighteenth birthday in 1931. His undergraduate career at King's was spectacular: he swept up prizes including prizes for original verse in English as well as in Latin and Greek. His exceptional talent communicated itself to others destined to achieve wider and more permanent recognition: Alan Turing, for instance, would describe him as 'the most learned man I ever met'. On the social front too he enjoyed success, despite or perhaps partly because of his origins. 'Did I conquer the place by being so novel—so naive but potentially promising?' he was later to wonder. In particular he was taken up by Maynard Keynes, who made sure that he met such prominent cultural figures as Maurice Bowra, T.S. Eliot, E.M. Forster and George 'Dadie' Rylands, who was later to describe him as one of the most brilliant scholars of his generation. Under Dadie's direction he also excelled in theatrical productions of the Marlowe Society, notably as the fool in *King Lear* and as one of the gravediggers in *Hamlet*, roles in which he made the most of a Liverpool accent for which he was otherwise mocked by fellow public school students. Never attempting to deny his origins he developed a good-humoured critical awareness of English class snobbery: chuckling at the naivety of the elite classes as much as his own, he would, for instance, tell how, at a dinner party given by Keynes, he was faced with a plate of oysters for the first time in his life and asked by his host: 'Well, Clayton, which are you, a swallower or a chewer?'

His academic success was rewarded in 1937 by a prize fellowship for a dissertation on Edward Gibbon. Prior to taking this up he went to Vienna to learn German and spent a year teaching at the Kreuzschule in Dresden. This defining experience provided the raw material for the one book he was to publish, a novel called *The Cloven Pine*, which was published in 1942 under the pseudonym Frank Clare.[1] The book, he wrote later, was intended 'to depict

---

1 This has recently been translated into German: Frank Clare, *Zwei Welten. Eine Jugend im nationalsozialistischen Deutschland*, Bibliothek Rosa Winkel (Hamburg: Männerschwarm-Skript Verlag, 2003).

German boys as creatures to be loved and pitied,. . . as one might feel for any young creature trapped and condemned'. But it was more than that, as E. M. Forster recognized in a letter of encouraging praise. For interwoven with the more personal narrative is a trenchant analysis of the character and origins of Nazism, including its relation to romantic aesthetics, and the limits of rationality in dealing with it. As Forster also remarked, it was not a book likely to go down well in Britain in 1942. At least one copy was sent back to the publisher by an indignant public librarian. But there were more positive responses including a sympathetic review by Elizabeth Bowen.

This was, however, in 1942. During his stay in Germany Fred Clayton had become increasingly concerned by the failure of most Western politicans to understand the threat posed by Nazism and Fascism. Unlike many observers of the German political scene he had actually read *Mein Kampf* and found it very disturbing as well as stupid. Convinced that war was inevitable he felt compelled on his return to write to politicians imploring them to reject appeasement. And yet he belonged to the generation that had grown up with fathers no longer silent about the horrors of war and 'never again' had been the common chorus. With the turbulence of the 1930s—the outbreak of the Spanish civil war and Italy's annexation of Abyssinia in 1936—student opinion had become increasingly polarized. While the Oxford Union voted never again to fight for King and Country, a substantial number in Cambridge turned to Communism as the only safeguard of peace. As a grammar school boy of modest origins it was assumed that Fred Clayton would be naturally sympathetic to the cause. But impatient with Old Etonians like Guy Burgess trading on their style and charm and pontificating about the working class, he resisted attempts to recruit him: 'I didn't like their tactics. I didn't like being encircled.'

Meanwhile his compassion for young creatures trapped and condemned expressed itself in practical action: in 1938, with Alan Turing, he was instrumental in getting two Viennese boys to England, although he could not save their Jewish mother, who in 1942 wrote to thank him from Poland where she disappeared. Later he would look back on this as the redeeming act of his life. And his compassionate sympathy for the victims of war and its attendant abuse of power stayed with him, as the epilogue which he added to his translation of *The Mother-in-Law*, and which is quoted by Matthew Leigh, powerfully attests.

Though it is difficult to imagine anyone less fitted for the military life, Fred Clayton joined the Royal Signal Corps in the summer of 1940 only to find himself whisked away to Bletchley Park where he immediately made his mark by successfully decoding Luftwaffe material. Yet, though he was fluent in German, and without any knowledge of Japanese, the military authorities talked him into a posting as a breaker of Japanese codes in India and Burma. He agreed, partly, as he later confessed to his brother George, because he felt that until then he had had a 'rather soft war'. He soon found himself shuttled between Delhi and Barrackpore, his services as code-breaker fought over by two rival colonels. 'The war', he wrote later when reflecting on how his mind came to work as it did, 'made guessing my game, if you can call it guessing, and not the imagination and logic of a verbal mind pushed to its limits.' But it was not only his mind that was pushed to its limits. Although it was generally accepted that exposure to the hardships of the Indian and Burmese theatre of war for more than two years constituted a health risk, he stayed for three and a half years, to return six months after VJ day in 1946. By this time he had been pushed beyond his psychological as well as physical limits and had suffered a severe breakdown. Though he recovered remarkably quickly, thanks largely to the care of his brother, his psychic health had been irreversibly damaged. He was as much a casualty of the war as if he had lost a leg or an arm. The tragic irony is that British Intelligence subsequently admitted that this man, who had been so insistent in his warnings about Nazism, had been posted far from Europe, because he was regarded as too pro-German. It was difficult, if not impossible, for the authorities to imagine that a man could be wholly committed to war with a regime while still remaining attached to those trapped by it. And attached he still was: in India in 1942 he would wake from prophetic nightmares of 'Dresden being bombed, of all those boys being slaughtered'.

Once the war was over he sought to re-establish contact with the family that had welcomed him in 1936. The youngest daughter—Friederike—wrote back. She too had had a devastating war: her brother Götz (one of the trapped young creatures Fred was thinking of) had been shot by snipers on the march into Poland at the age of 18 and the deaths of her parents had soon followed. Only days after the bombing in February 1945 she had walked through a still smoking Dresden, oppressed by the stench of the slaughter, to face the Russians. They began to correspond and in 1948 Frederick and Friederike were married. Theirs is indeed an extraordinary love story which it is hard to resist reading symbolically, like the marriages of three of their four children, to Italian, Irish and French partners respectively. The 'united nations' he would fondly and proudly call his family. Here at last was stability, love and a kind of success.

There was success and stability in the professional sphere too. In 1948, after two years at the University of Edinburgh, he was appointed Professor of Classics at the University College of the South West, which, in 1955, became the University of Exeter. From 1962 to 1965 he was dean of the arts faculty and from 1965 to 1973 public orator, long remembered for the wit, elegance and erudition of his speeches. His skill in handling the English language is evident too in his translations of the plays of Terence, which are published here for the first time and which were produced during the early years at Exeter. Amongst his papers is a letter dated 1962, from E. V. Rieu, editor of the Penguin Classics series, who, evidently appreciative of what he has read, expresses regret that a translation in prose had already been commissioned for the series. With his extraordinary range of vocabulary and his acute sense of rhythm Fred Clayton had risen to the challenge of a verse translation, opting specifically for rhyming couplets which, far from having the stilted effect one might expect, carry the reader with them. The plays indeed acquire an immediacy and a startling contemporaneity in these translations, a contemporaneity which is foregrounded in the epilogue which Clayton added to *The Mother-in-Law*.

Here then was the young man who had won prizes at King's for English verse. But where was the brilliant scholar? Why, once settled, did he not produce a stream of learned books and articles? Certainly, he continued to have ideas. With a memory full of the Latin and English literature he had read to stave off boredom in India and a mind habituated through his work as code-breaker to lateral connections, he began 'in about 1950' to notice 'in both Latin and English. . . curious apparent echoes of quotations, conscious or unconscious, inside a single author or between authors, based on associated ideas or words.' Two areas came to fascinate him: astrology in Horace and the echoes of Latin writers in Shakespeare. But he was on his own, unlike those colleagues who had stayed at Bletchley Park and who had continued their academic work in their spare time. When one of these dismissed his ideas about Horace at a seminar in Cambridge, he was shattered. It was the final blow to an already damaged self-confidence and he never risked airing these ideas in public again. He worked obsessively with concordances trying to prove in those pre-computer days that the collocations of words and phrases that leapt out at him were not simply random. 'If ever I publish a book', he said, 'I shall give it as a subtitle, "A Consideration of Coincidences".'

But no book would be published, only a lecture on the echoes of Latin texts in Shakespeare's *A Midsummer Night's Dream*.[2] Mixing personal memoir with virtuoso leaps from text to text and from one set of verbal associations to another, the piece is at once brilliant and impenetrable. Yet it has its admirers, notably the current editor of the third Arden edition of the play, who commented to one of his daughters just before his death, 'your father was before his time'. Undoubtedly, in his intellectual endeavours, he was before his time and it is to be hoped that, thanks to posthumous publications, he will at last receive some of the recognition he deserved.[3] Yet he was also *of* his time— trapped and condemned to severe, lifelong mental distress by the hideous twentieth century through which he lived—like Ariel imprisoned by the witch Sycorax in the cloven pine.

M.T-C

---

2   Frederick W. Clayton, 'The Hole in the Wall: A New Look at Shakespeare's Latin Base for *A Midsummer Night's Dream*' (Exeter: Exeter University, 1979).
3   As well as the German translation of *The Cloven Pine* mentioned above, there is an article on his work on *Love's Labour's Lost* in *Shakespeare Survey*: Frederick W. Clayton and Margaret Tudeau-Clayton, 'Mercury, Boy yet and the "harsh words" of *Love's Labour's Lost*', *Shakespeare Survey* 57 (2004): 209–224.

Epilogue to The Mother-in-Law

by Frederick W. Clayton

My modern audience wants my modern moral?
Man rules, okay? With that no man can quarrel.
Though some might murmur at my seeming to draw
Two over-kind, non-comic mothers-in-law
While making two omnipotent paterfamiliases
A pair of male chauvinist mules or silly asses,
Each tracing Truth's First Cause of trouble and strife
And firmly fixing fault on his own wife—
Inside the family. Outside it, heavy father
May lean on light—soft, henpecked, *he* says—rather.
But it's the female characters, one after another,
Who get found guilty. First it's the young man's mother,
And then his mother-in-law who gets well chidden
By her lord and master, first for having hidden
Her daughter's pregnancy, then for being near the truth
In mistrusting her son-in-law, that lovely youth,
Who, well-off, with a good mistress, just for a lark,
Raped a strange girl and pinched her ring in the dark.
But youth's a stuff one cannot be too hard on,
If male, freeborn and handsome. A man must pardon—
As Micio remarks in my play *The Brothers*
(Why not, discussing this play, plug some of the others?)
What man needs must with that devil's drive—physical urge—
And even more when Bacchus and Venus merge,
Drink, so to speak, *and* drive. Oh, I don't say it's right,
But what was the girl doing out late at night
Leading *us* into temptation? I'm not making suggestions,
But men, very naturally, knowing men, ask such questions.
Well, this girl's lucky. In any play of mine
Their luck, I can assure you, is something divine,
Gods—masculine, of course—out of machines
Shaping playwrights' mechanical ends, recognition scenes,
Sex-urge or romance, if that's the word, reconciled
With social realities. A girl kidnapped as a child,

Sold into slavery, yet may marry a lover,
Who had appeared several social spheres above her,
By unearthing buried treasure, kept from the cradle,
Proofs she was born with, big as a silver ladle,
Providing a clean bill of wealth and worldly position.
Each age has its own means of recognition,
For long-lost child or criminal. Playwrights use
What fate or fashion give, warts, moles, tattoos,
Good or bad tokens. Charm necklace, identity disk
In wartime, might increase the rapist's risk
With girls who had the wit to see and act
In unenlightened days—or nights. Attic dark, out-blacked
By black-out, could be on *his* side, however,
That '*omne animal*' feeling '*post coitum*' clever,
Finding it funny that he and she might meet
Tomorrow morning in the village street,
Unknowing, unknown. After all, in the air-raid shelter,
The spice of the experience was, not seeing, he felt her
More sensuously, so he said, and the cream of the joke was
The girl would never know who the blacked-out bloke was.
Yes, Pamphilus *was* blind-drunk not to know a neighbour,
In case that's a point some critic would want to labour,
My own point's that by facts within the range
Of our experience fiction's made less strange
Than others may suppose. In fact we all
By our own lights or blessed blindness call
Probable or improbable, on the stage,
Acts, attitudes, of our own or another age.
To Venus, Youth and Bacchus my males add Night
As male excuses or temptations. *Your* light
May leave you suddenly, leaving you less inclined
In the light of your streets or moral giant strides to find
My plots improbable. Of course your good Roman or Briton
May refuse to put funny caps that don't fit on,
You all have alibis. It's not happening here!
Great fun to watch Greeks—or Frogs—being quaint or queer!
More seriously, since 'barbaric' means 'non-Greek',
What height of barbarism beats that lonely peak
Where Oedipus was left? *We* expose a baby
Like that? Well, no, not really. Little Ormond maybe,
Found in a public phone box, fruit of sin,
Named from the kindly place that took him in,
Is rarity, not routine, not taken so lightly,

So casually, you might remind me rightly,
Though obviously Effie Deanses and Hetty Sorrels
Do still exist. And how your modern morals
May expose children, to what, in war or peace,
As measured against ancient Rome or Greece—
Not my business. Back to identity disks. One thing
Unusual in this play is—*he* grabs *her* ring,
Not the other way round. He was lucky to escape
A charge of robbery aggravated by rape,
You may think. *But*, if charges could have been pressed,
Would anyone be happier? God—and I—did all for the best.
That ring was a godsend. Yes, God—and I—were sending
'What men, our masters, call a happy ending',
As Julia's going to say in Shaw's *Philanderer*.
But Claudio finds it fun being called 'foul slanderer'
By toothless old men. And the bitter truth
As Laches sees it is—all's fair in youth.
That hero's anti-Hero lies? Shrugged off. Much ado
About nothing. All's well that ends well. Just what two
Young gentlemen of Verona might any day do.
Gentlemen? Yes, I know. Don't tell me the bard's reckoned one
Too many as you simply can't see the second one.
Our variance of vision from youth to age
Makes the main stuff and matter of my stage,
Where age might seem, I admit, unfairly dopier,
A prey to obsessive mental presbyopia,
Far-sighted, but missing, through some *idée fixe*,
Home-truths at hand, which its far focus seeks
In vain. This trait four of my old men show
In other plays, in various forms. Apropos,
However, of far-sighted fathers, *you*
May feel—a small point—that a child nearly due
Could scarcely in this play have escaped Phidippus.
But after all, we men find such points slip us,
And even women have been known to state
To the papers they just thought they were putting on weight,
While *The Heart of Midlothian* informs us there are men
Like Saddletree, who, his wife says, 'woudna ken
In a lying-in hospital what the women came *there* for'.
Improbable? P'raps. But with our two, the why and wherefore
Of trouble meaning in *their eyes* 'Cherchez la femme',
Bitch-hunting, finding what devil to damn,
They turn to Bacchis. We know that sort like a book,

A hooker not likely to let any lad off the hook.
She, as perceptive Parmeno shrewdly said,
As soon as the boy was well and truly wed,
Went sour on him, repelling but possessive—
The Graces, good custom lost, might grow aggressive.
Or did she, as she claims, with better reason,
Ban once-fair game, now bad taste, out of season?
Did she, the worldly wiser, warm but older,
Put on a dry cold front, a high cold shoulder,
To show, with no hard feelings but undiminished
Soft ones, deep down, yet firm, the game was finished?
So—a pre-Hollywood 'whore with a heart of gold'?
We actors know that every tale can be told
Two ways. Whose shapes we've put on and whose skin
We for the moment merely may be in,
Makes us, like barristers, advocates for the devil,
Or even the opposite sex. Make life's odds level,
Reform, redress? Those words I never uttered,
I know, after all, which side my bread is buttered.
And I've no tendency to be tendentious;
But, while I owe Rome much—my name, Terentius,
My bread and boards to tread; plots the Greeks gave—
Regard my roots. I *am* a freed black slave.

(The speaker removes his mask)